Collins School **Atlas** for Trinidad and Tob...

T0364571

Published by Collins
An imprint of HarperCollins Publishers
Westerhill Road
Bishopbriggs
Glasgow G64 2QT
www.harpercollins.co.uk

First edition 2020

© HarperCollins Publishers 2020
Maps © Collins Bartholomew Ltd 2020

Collins ® is a registered trademark of HarperCollins Publishers Ltd

ISBN 978-0-00-836190-7

10 9 8 7 6 5 4 3 2 1

MIX
Paper from responsible sources
FSC
www.fsc.org
FSC™ C007454

This book is produced from independently certified FSC™ paper to ensure responsible forest management.

For more information visit: www.harpercollins.co.uk/green

Printed by Bell & Bain, Glasgow, Scotland

All mapping in this atlas is generated from Collins Bartholomew digital databases. Collins Bartholomew, the UK's leading independent geographical information supplier, can provide a digital, custom, and premium mapping service to a variety of markets.
For further information:
Tel: +44 (0) 208 307 4515
e-mail: collinsbartholomew@harpercollins.co.uk

Visit our websites at:
www.collins.co.uk
www.collinsbartholomew.com

If you would like to comment on any aspect of this book, please contact us at the above address or online.
e-mail: collinsmaps@harpercollins.co.uk

Dates in this publication are based on the Christian Era and the designations BC and AD are used throughout. These designations are directly interchangeable with those referring to the Common Era, BCE and CE respectively.

This is a photograph of a classroom. You can see most of the room but not all of it. It shows how the desks and chairs are arranged in rows with the teacher and the whiteboard at the front of the classroom. Look at the plan view below to see what you can't see in the photograph.

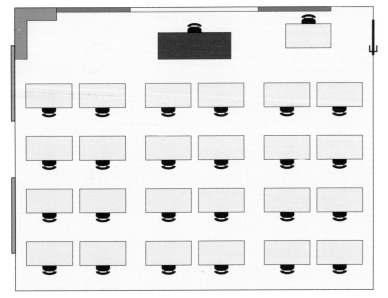

This is a plan of the same classroom. It shows the layout of the room and shows the shapes of the furniture. It is drawn as if you were looking down on it. On a plan we need to use the key to understand what each block of colour means.

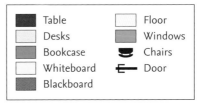

■	Table	☐	Floor
■	Desks	■	Windows
■	Bookcase	🪑	Chairs
☐	Whiteboard	⟵	Door
■	Blackboard		

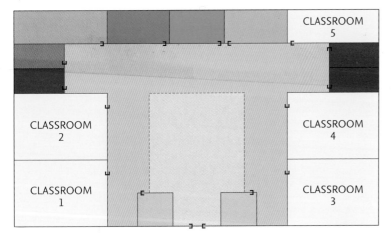

CLASSROOM 5

CLASSROOM 2

CLASSROOM 4

CLASSROOM 1

CLASSROOM 3

This is a plan of the whole school. It shows all the rooms in the school. Like the plan of the classroom, the key tells you what each block of colour means.

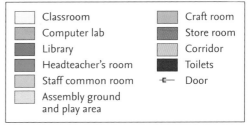

☐	Classroom	■	Craft room
■	Computer lab	■	Store room
■	Library	■	Corridor
■	Headteacher's room	■	Toilets
■	Staff common room	⟵	Door
■	Assembly ground and play area		

This is a map of the area around the school. It includes a larger area than the plan above and shows houses, a church and shops. The individual buildings here are smaller and less detail is given for each.

☐	School	■	Shop
■	Play area	■	Public building
☐	Grass	▾	Bushes
■	Shed	●	Trees
■	House	┈	Path
■	Church	──	Road

Map types

Many types of map are included in the atlas to show different information. The type of map, its symbols and colours are carefully selected to show the theme of each map and to make them easy to understand. The main types of map used are explained below.

Political maps provide an overview of the size and location of countries in a specific area, such as a continent. Coloured squares indicate national capitals. Coloured circles represent other cities or towns.

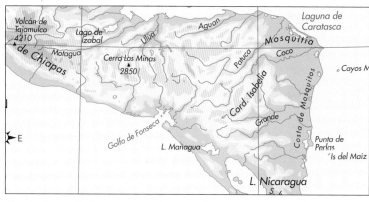

Physical or **relief maps** use colour to show oceans, seas, rivers, lakes, and the height of the land. The names and heights of major landforms are also indicated.

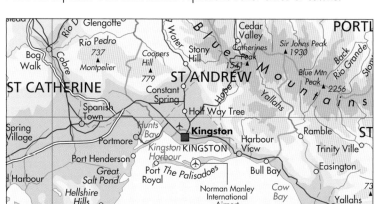

Physical/political maps bring together the information provided in the two types of map described above. They show relief and physical features as well as boundaries, major cities and towns, roads, railways and airports.

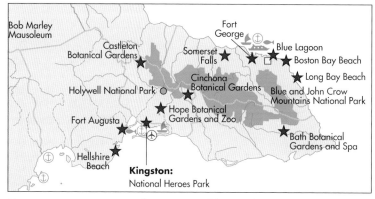

Features maps are given for most Caribbean islands in this atlas. They show points of interest, national parks, main resorts, marinas and important ports for fishing, commerce and cruise ships.

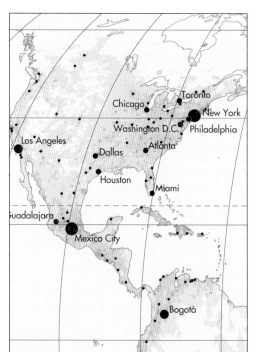

Distribution maps use different colours, symbols, or shading to show the location and distribution of natural or man-made features. In this map, symbols indicate the distribution of the world's largest cities.

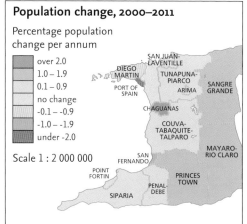

Population change, 2000–2011

Percentage population change per annum

- over 2.0
- 1.0 – 1.9
- 0.1 – 0.9
- no change
- -0.1 – -0.9
- -1.0 – -1.9
- under -2.0

Scale 1 : 2 000 000

Graduated colour maps use colours or shading to show a topic or theme and a measure of its intensity. Generally, the highest values are shaded with the darkest colours. In this map, colours are used to show the percentage change of the population per year in the different areas of local government in Trinidad. It can be seen from this map that the population is increasing in the east of the island, while it is declining in the northwest.

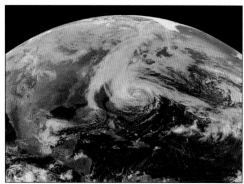

Satellite images are recorded by sensors similar to television cameras which are carried aboard satellites. These satellites orbit 500 km above our planet and beam images back to Earth. This is a natural-colour image of Hurricane Sandy, taken on 28 October 2012.

Maps use **symbols** to show the location of a feature and to give information about it. The symbols used on each map in this atlas are explained in the **key** to each map.

Symbols used on maps can be dots, diagrams, lines or area colours. They vary in colour, size and shape. The numbered captions to the map below help explain some of the symbols used on the maps in this atlas.

Different styles of type are also used to show differences between features, for example, country names are shown in large bold capital letters, small water features, rivers and lakes in small italics.

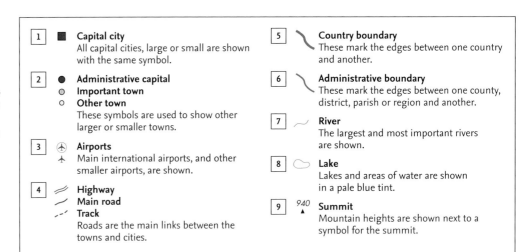

1. **Capital city**
All capital cities, large or small are shown with the same symbol.

2. **Administrative capital**
Important town
Other town
These symbols are used to show other larger or smaller towns.

3. **Airports**
Main international airports, and other smaller airports, are shown.

4. **Highway**
Main road
Track
Roads are the main links between the towns and cities.

5. **Country boundary**
These mark the edges between one country and another.

6. **Administrative boundary**
These mark the edges between one county, district, parish or region and another.

7. **River**
The largest and most important rivers are shown.

8. **Lake**
Lakes and areas of water are shown in a pale blue tint.

9. *940* **Summit**
Mountain heights are shown next to a symbol for the summit.

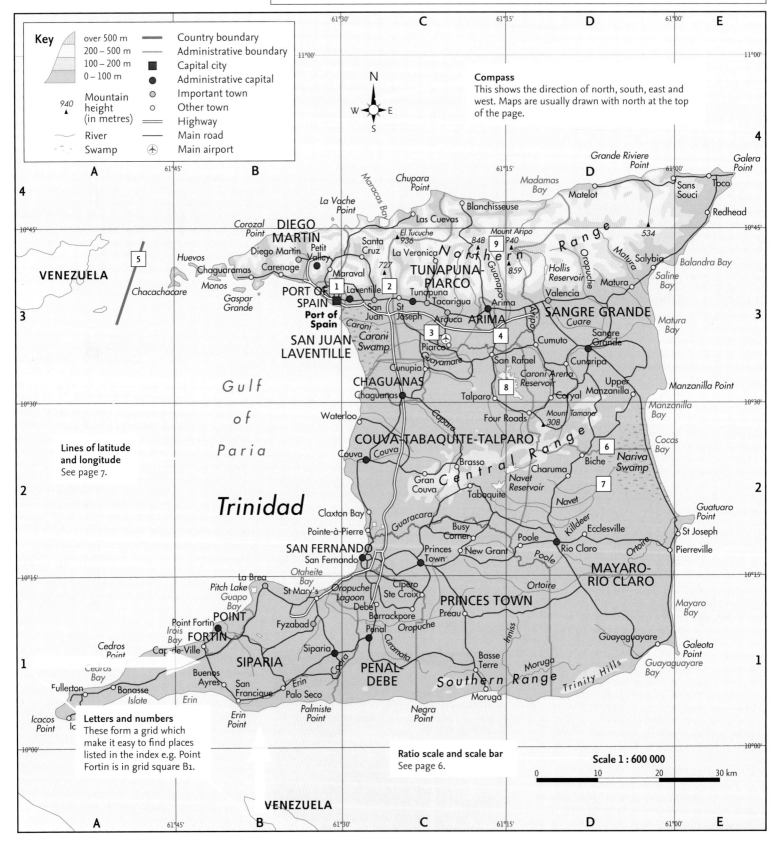

Key

over 500 m
200 – 500 m
100 – 200 m
0 – 100 m

940 Mountain height (in metres)

River
Swamp

Country boundary
Administrative boundary
■ Capital city
● Administrative capital
◉ Important town
○ Other town
Highway
Main road
Main airport

Compass
This shows the direction of north, south, east and west. Maps are usually drawn with north at the top of the page.

Lines of latitude and longitude
See page 7.

Letters and numbers
These form a grid which make it easy to find places listed in the index e.g. Point Fortin is in grid square B1.

Ratio scale and scale bar
See page 6.

Scale 1 : 600 000

0   10   20   30 km

Location maps

These appear on most pages of the atlas. The little map shows you where the area mapped on that page is located in the world.

Photographs

There are many photographs in the atlas. Photos show you what places look like. Some photos show cities and relate to people. Other photos may relate to nature and the landscape.

Map keys

All maps have a key. A map key is a little box next to the map. The key explains all the symbols and colours that are on the map.

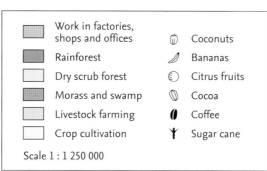

Work in factories, shops and offices	🥥 Coconuts
Rainforest	🍌 Bananas
Dry scrub forest	🍊 Citrus fruits
Morass and swamp	Cocoa
Livestock farming	Coffee
Crop cultivation	Y Sugar cane

Scale 1 : 1 250 000

Features
- National park
- ★ Point of interest
- □ Major resort
- Port
- Cruise ships
- Major marina
- Fishing port
- Lighthouse

Fact boxes

Fact boxes give you extra information about the map or region mapped on the page.

Caribbean islands facts

Population
39 871 635

Largest country
Cuba 110 860 sq km

Country with most people
Cuba 11 167 325

Largest city
Santo Domingo 3 317 800

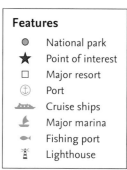

THE BAHAMAS

Population *(2010)*	353 658
Capital city	Nassau
Area	13 939 sq km
Languages	English
National flower	Yellow Elder
National bird	West Indian Flamingo
National animal	Blue Marlin

Graphs and tables

Statistical information is shown through a variety of different kinds of graphs (histograms, line graphs and pie charts) and tables.

Average rainfall

Georgetown

mm
300
250
200
150
100
50
0
J F M A M J J A S O N D

Population increase, 1960–2011

Population in thousands
3000
2500
2000
1500
1000
500
0
1960 1965 1970 1975 1980 1985 1990 1995 2000 2005 2010
Year

Urban/rural population, 2011

48% 52%

▶ Urban
▶ Rural

Text

Bulleted text and tables give more detailed information on particular topics of interest for the area featured.

Brian Lara (born 1969)
- Nicknamed the 'Prince of the Port of Spain', Brian Lara is one of Trinidad and Tobago's most famous sportspeople.
- Until 2008, he held the record as the leading run-scorer in test cricket.
- He holds many records as a batsman, including the highest individual score in first class cricket in 1994 (501 not out) and, in 2004, the highest individual score in test cricket (400 not out).

Island	Area (sq km)	Population (2011)	Pop. density (per sq km)
Trinidad	4827	1 267 145	263
Tobago	300	60 874	203

Using scale

The **scale** of each map in this atlas is shown in two ways:

1. The ratio scale is written, for example, as 1 : 1 000 000. This means that one unit of measurement on the map represents 1 000 000 of the same unit on the ground.

e.g. **Scale 1 : 1 000 000**

2. The line or **bar scale** shows the scale as a line with the distance on the ground marked at intervals along the line.

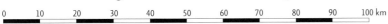

Different scales

The three maps below cover the same area of the page but are at different scales. Map A is a large scale map which shows a small area in detail. Map C is a small scale map which means it shows a larger area in the same space as Map A, however in much less detail. The area of Map A is highlighted on maps B and C. As the scale ratio increases the map becomes smaller.

Scale 1 : 3 500 000

Map A

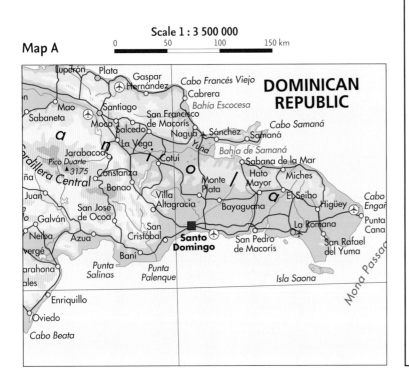

Measuring distance

The scale of a map can also be used to work out how far it is between two places. In the example below, the straight line distance between Caracas and St George's on the map is 6 cm. The scale of the map is 1 : 10 000 000. Therefore 6 cm on the map represents 6 x 10 000 000 cm or 60 000 000 cm on the ground. Converted to kilometres this is 600 km. The real distance between Caracas and St George's is therefore 600 km on the ground.

Scale 1 : 10 000 000

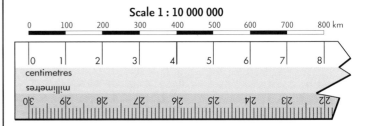

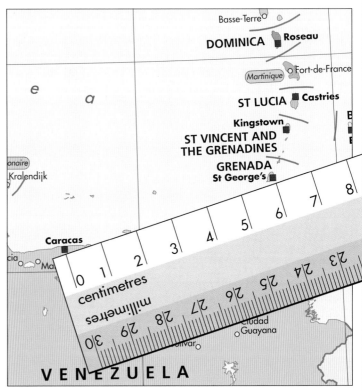

Scale 1 : 10 000 000

Map B

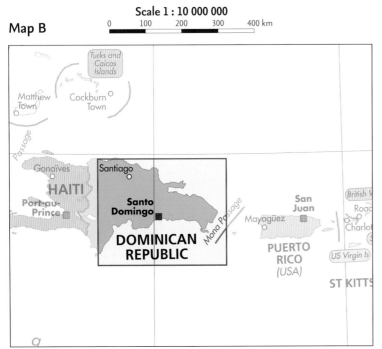

Scale 1 : 80 000 000

Map C

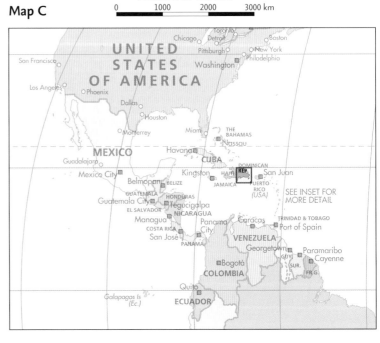

Latitude and longitude

Lines of latitude are imaginary lines which run in an east-west direction around the globe. They run parallel to each other and are measured in degrees, written as °. The most important line of latitude is the Equator, 0°. All other lines of latitude have a value between 0° and 90° north or south of the Equator. 90° north is the North Pole and, 90° south, the South Pole.

Lines of longitude are imaginary lines which run in a north-south direction between the North Pole and the South Pole. The most important line of longitude is 0°, the Greenwich Meridian, which runs through the Greenwich Observatory in London. Exactly opposite the Greenwich Meridian on the other side of the world, is the 180° line of longitude. All other lines of longitude are measured in degrees east or west of 0°.

When both lines of latitude and longitude are drawn on a map they form a grid. It is easy to find a place on the map if the latitude and longitude values are known. The point of intersection of the line of latitude and the line of longitude locates the place exactly.

The Equator can be used to divide the globe into two halves. Land north of the Equator is the Northern Hemisphere. Land south of the Equator is the Southern Hemisphere. The 0° and 180° lines of longitude can also be used to divide the globe into two halves, the Western and Eastern Hemispheres. Together, the Equator and 0° and 180°, divide the world into four areas, for example, North America is in the Northern Hemisphere and the Western Hemisphere.

1 The globe

2 Lines of latitude

3 Lines of longitude

4 Lines of latitude and longitude

Time zones

Time varies around the world due to the earth's rotation. This causes different parts of the world to be in light or darkness at any one time.

To account for this, the world is divided into 24 Standard Time Zones based on 15° intervals of longitude (1 hour of time). All places in a time zone have the same time of day. The shapes of some zones have been adjusted so that all of the country or region lies in the same zone.

There is one hour difference between each zone – one hour in the day earlier to the west, one hour later to the east. The local time in another city can be found by counting the number of hours earlier or later than the local time in your own country.

The time at 0° is known as Greenwich Mean Time (GMT) because the line passes through Greenwich in London. Most countries of the Caribbean are either 4 or 5 hours behind GMT.

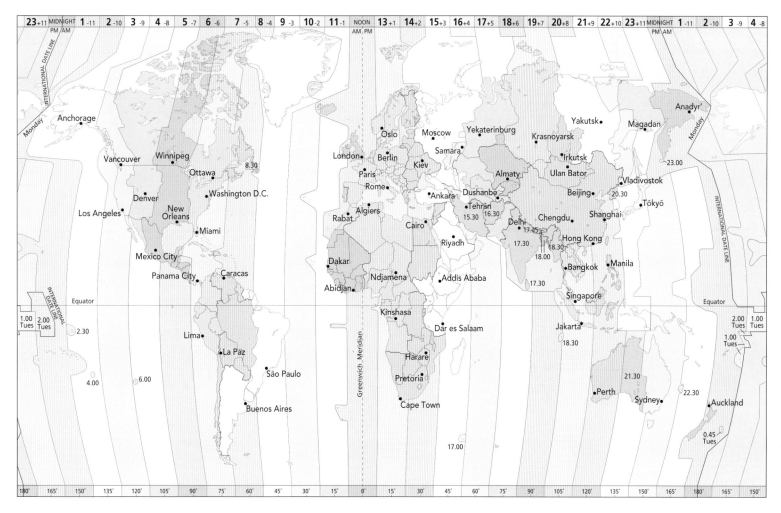

The Solar System

The Solar System is the Sun and the many objects that orbit it. These objects include eight planets, at least five dwarf planets and countless asteroids, meteoroids and comets. Orbiting some of the planets and dwarf planets are over 160 moons. The Sun keeps its surrounding objects in its orbit by its pull of gravity which has an influence for many millions of kilometres.

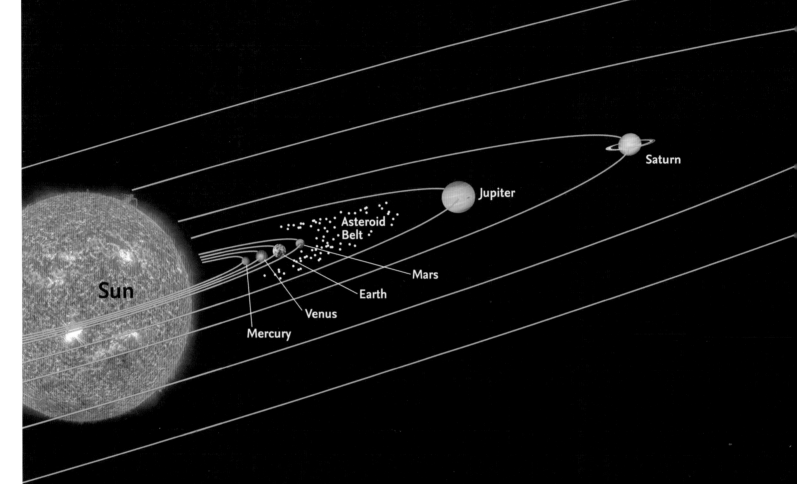

Sun

Saturn

Jupiter

Asteroid Belt

Mars

Earth

Venus

Mercury

The Sun

Diameter
1 391 016 km
Circumference
4 370 000 km
Average temperature
5504 °C
Rotation about axis
(measured at its equator)
25 Earth days 9 hours

The Planets

	Mercury	Venus	Earth	Mars
	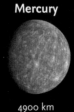			
Diameter	4900 km	12 100 km	12 700 km	6779 km
Circumference	15 300 km	38 000 km	40 000 km	21 300 km
Distance from Sun	58 million km	108 million km	150 million km	228 million km
Length of year	88 Earth days	244 Earth days 17 hours	365 days 6 hours	687 Earth days
Length of day	59 Earth days	243 Earth days	23 hours 56 minutes	24 hours 37 minutes

	Jupiter	Saturn	Uranus	Neptune
Diameter	143 000 km	116 500 km	50 700 km	49 200 km
Circumference	450 000 km	366 000 km	159 000 km	154 700 km
Distance from Sun	778 million km	1427 million km	2871 million km	4498 million km
Length of year	11 Earth years 314 days	29 Earth years	84 Earth years	165 Earth years
Length of day	9 hours 55 minutes	10 hours 39 minutes	17 hours 14 minutes	16 hours 7 minutes

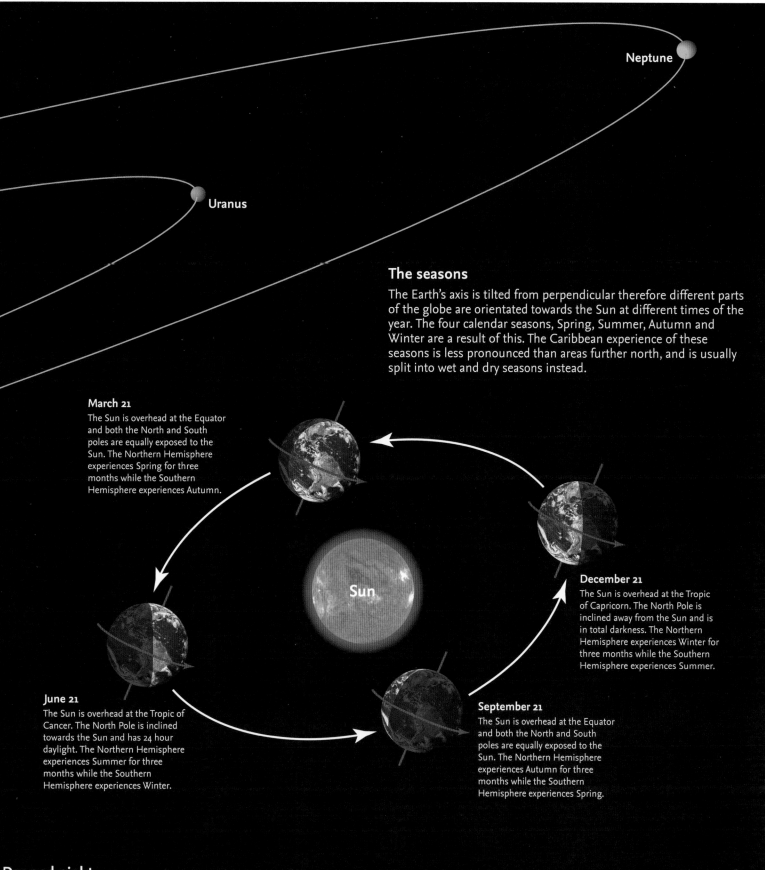

Neptune

Uranus

The seasons

The Earth's axis is tilted from perpendicular therefore different parts of the globe are orientated towards the Sun at different times of the year. The four calendar seasons, Spring, Summer, Autumn and Winter are a result of this. The Caribbean experience of these seasons is less pronounced than areas further north, and is usually split into wet and dry seasons instead.

March 21
The Sun is overhead at the Equator and both the North and South poles are equally exposed to the Sun. The Northern Hemisphere experiences Spring for three months while the Southern Hemisphere experiences Autumn.

Sun

December 21
The Sun is overhead at the Tropic of Capricorn. The North Pole is inclined away from the Sun and is in total darkness. The Northern Hemisphere experiences Winter for three months while the Southern Hemisphere experiences Summer.

June 21
The Sun is overhead at the Tropic of Cancer. The North Pole is inclined towards the Sun and has 24 hour daylight. The Northern Hemisphere experiences Summer for three months while the Southern Hemisphere experiences Winter.

September 21
The Sun is overhead at the Equator and both the North and South poles are equally exposed to the Sun. The Northern Hemisphere experiences Autumn for three months while the Southern Hemisphere experiences Spring.

Day and night

The Earth turns round on its axis every 23 hours 56 minutes and it is this rotation that is responsible for the daily cycles of day and night. At any one moment in time, one half of the Earth is in sunlight, while the other half, facing away from the Sun, is in darkness. As the Earth rotates it also creates the apparent movement of the Sun from east to west across the sky.

Direction of rotation

| North Pole | North Pole | North Pole | North Pole |

Dawn in the UK   **Midday in the UK**   **Dusk in the UK**   **Midnight in the UK**

(The Caribbean will be 4 or 5 hours earlier in the day than the UK at this point.)

Caribbean islands facts

Population
39 871 635

Largest country
Cuba 110 860 sq km

Country with most people
Cuba 11 167 325

Largest city
Santo Domingo 3 317 800

N
W E
S

Gulf of Mexico

U.S.A.

Freeport City

Nassau

Andros Town

T H E   B A H A M A

Straits of Florida

Tropic of Cancer

Havana

Cienfuegos

C U B A

Bayamo

Guantánamo

Yucatán Channel

Bahía de Campeche

20°N

M E X I C O

Cayman Is

George Town

C a r i b b

Montego Bay

Jamaica Channel

JAMAICA

Kingston

Wind

Belize City

Belmopan

BELIZE

Flores

Gulf of Honduras

GUATEMALA

15°N

San Pedro Sula

Guatemala City

H O N D U R A S

Santa Ana

Tegucigalpa

PACIFIC OCEAN

San Salvador

EL SALVADOR

NICARAGUA

Puerto Cabezas

Scale 1 : 10 000 000

0   100   200   300 km

International organisations

● CARICOM member
○ CARIFTA member
◑ CARICOM and CARIFTA member
○ OECS member

Scale 1 : 20 000 000

U.S.A.

THE BAHAMAS

Turks and Caicos Islands (UK)

CUBA

Cayman Is (UK)

HAITI

DOMINICAN REPUBLIC

PUERTO RICO (USA)

British Virgin Is (UK)

Anguilla (UK)

St-Martin (France)

St-Barthélemy (France)

Saba (Neth.)

St Eustatius (Neth.)

MEXICO

BELIZE

GUATEMALA

HONDURAS

EL SALVADOR

NICARAGUA

JAMAICA

US Virgin Is (USA)

Sint Maarten (Neth.)

ST KITTS AND NEVIS

Montserrat (UK)

ANTIGUA AND BARBUDA

Guadeloupe (France)

DOMINICA

Martinique (France)

ST LUCIA

ST VINCENT AND THE GRENADINES

BARBADOS

Aruba (Neth.)

Curaçao (Neth.)

Bonaire (Neth.)

GRENADA

TRINIDAD AND TOBAGO

VENEZUELA

COLOMBIA

GUYANA

Bog

SURINAME

The Caribbean Community (CARICOM) was established in 1973 and has a membership of 15 Caribbean countries and dependencies. It aims to improve living standards, promote economic integration and cooperation, and coordinate foreign policy.

The Caribbean Free Trade Association (CARIFTA) was founded in 1965 to encourage balanced development in the region by increasing and diversifying trade, removing tariffs and quotas, and ensuring fair competition within the area.

The Organisation of Eastern Caribbean States (OECS) was created in 1981 with the purpose of promoting economic integration, protecting human and legal rights, and encouraging cooperation, unity and solidarity between member states.

Country/territory	Last coloniser	Independence/ Current status	Country/territory	Last coloniser	Independence/ Current status
Anguilla	UK	British Overseas Territory	Haiti	USA	1934
Antigua and Barbuda	UK	1981	Jamaica	UK	1962
Aruba	Netherlands	Self-governing Territory	Martinique	France	Department of France
The Bahamas	UK	1973	Montserrat	UK	British Overseas Territory
Barbados	UK	1966	Puerto Rico	USA	US Commonwealth
Belize	UK	1981	Saba	Netherlands	Special Municipality
Bonaire	Netherlands	Special Municipality	St-Barthélemy	France	Overseas Collectivity
British Virgin Islands	UK	British Overseas Territory	St Eustatius	Netherlands	Special Municipality
Cayman Islands	UK/Jamaica	British Overseas Territory	St Kitts and Nevis	UK	1983
Cuba	USA	1902	St Lucia	UK	1979
Curaçao	Netherlands	Self-governing Territory	St-Martin	France	Overseas Collectivity
Dominica	UK	1978	Sint Maarten	Netherlands	Self-governing Territory
Dominican Republic	Haiti/Spain	1844/1865	St Vincent and the Grenadines	UK	1979
Grenada	UK	1974	Suriname	Netherlands	1975
Guadeloupe	France	Department of France	Trinidad and Tobago	UK	1962
Guyana	UK	1966	Turks and Caicos Islands	UK	British Overseas Territory
			US Virgin Islands	USA	Unincorporated Territory

Key

— Country boundary
-- Disputed boundary
■ Capital city
○ Important city / town

Territories
France
Netherlands
United Kingdom
United States

Lambert Conformal Conic projection

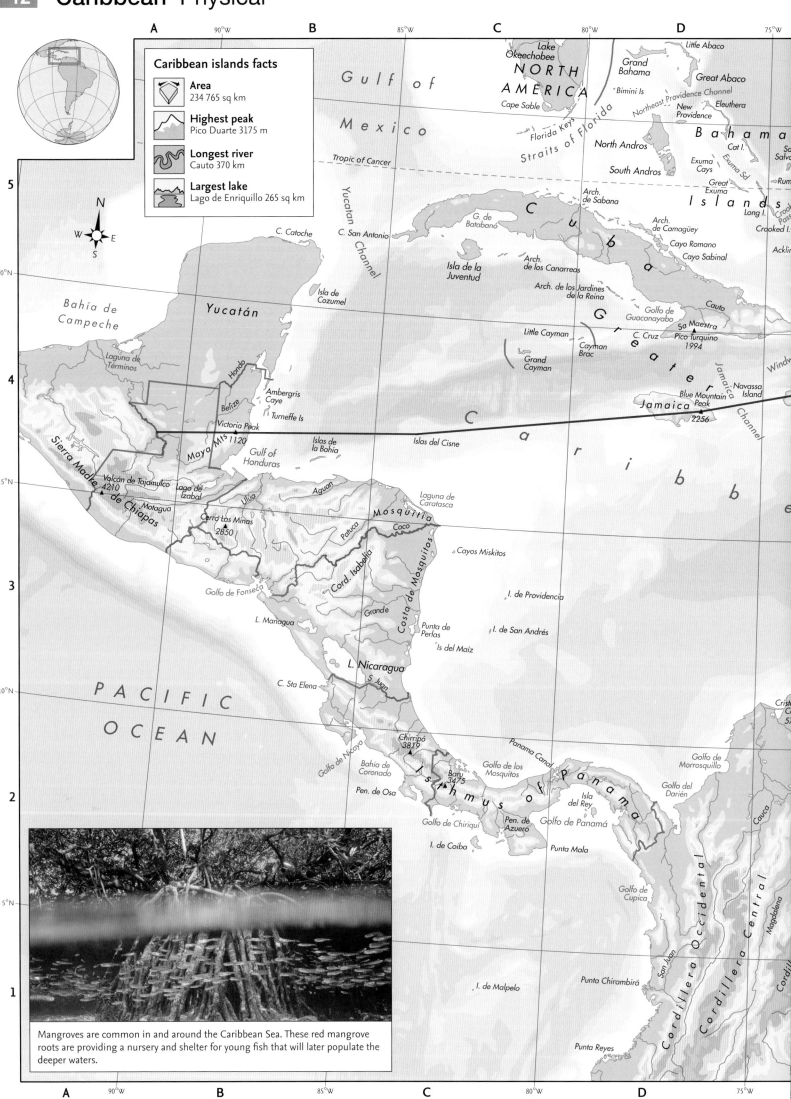

Caribbean islands facts

Area
234 765 sq km

Highest peak
Pico Duarte 3175 m

Longest river
Cauto 370 km

Largest lake
Lago de Enriquillo 265 sq km

Mangroves are common in and around the Caribbean Sea. These red mangrove roots are providing a nursery and shelter for young fish that will later populate the deeper waters.

Cross-section

metres
4000
2000
sea level 0
2000
4000
6000
8000
10 000

Maya Mountains · Islas del Cisne · Caribbean Sea · Jamaica · Hispaniola · Pico Duarte · Atlantic · Milwaukee Deep · Ocean

90°W · 85°W · 80°W · 75°W · 70°W · 65°W

ATLANTIC OCEAN

Mayaguana

Caicos Is
Turks I. Passage
Turks Is
Great Inagua

Milwaukee Deep
8605

Pico Duarte
3175
Hispaniola

Mona Passage
Puerto Rico
Cerro de Punta
1338
I. Mona
Vieques

Pic la Selle
2680
Lago de Enriquillo
I. Beata
C. Beata

Leeward Islands

Anegada
Anguilla
St-Martin
Tortola
Sint Maarten
St-Barthélémy
St Thomas
Saba
St Kitts
St Croix
St Eustatius
Nevis
Antigua
Montserrat
Basse-Terre
Grande-Terre
Marie-Galante
Dominica

Barbuda

Antilles

Lesser Antilles

Sea

Windward Islands

Martinique
St Lucia
St Vincent
The Grenadines
Carriacou
Grenada

Barbados

Punta Gallinas
Península de la Guajira
Aruba
Curaçao
Bonaire
Islas Los Roques
Isla Orchila
Isla Blanquilla
Isla de Margarita
Los Testigos
Tobago

Isla La Tortuga
Pen. de Paria
C. Codera
Trinidad

Golfo de Venezuela
Lake Maracaibo
de Perija
Cord. de Mérida
Pico Bolívar
5007

SOUTH AMERICA

Guanipa
Tigre
Orinoco Delta
Orinoco
Waini Point
Serranía de Imataca
Embalse de Guri
Cuyuni
Mazaruni
Caroni
Demerara
Berbice

La Gran Sabana
Cerro Curutú
1800
Mt Roraima
2810
Ayanganna
2040
Pakaraima Mountains
Cotingo
Ireng
Essequibo
Corentyne
Courantyne
Corantijn
Prof. van Blommestein Meer
Juliana Top
1230
Guiana Highlands

Uraricoera
Mucajaí
Serra Grande
1150
Takutu
Kamoa Mts
Maroni
Tapanahoni
Coeroeni
Hoan Gebergte
Eilerts de Haan Gebergte
Oranje Gebergte
Serra Tumucumaque

Island / Area (sq km)

Island	Area (sq km)	Island	Area (sq km)
Cuba	105 806	Great Abaco	1144
Hispaniola	75 449	Martinique	1079
Jamaica	10 991	Isla de Margarita	1020
Puerto Rico	8896	Basse-Terre	848
Trinidad	4827	Cayo Romano	777
North Andros	3439	Dominica	750
Isla de la Juventud	2237	Île de la Gonâve	743
Great Inagua	1543	Isla de Cozumel	647
South Andros	1447	St Lucia	617
Grand Bahama	1373	Grande-Terre	587

Key

over 5000 m
3000 – 5000 m
2000 – 3000 m
1000 – 2000 m
500 – 1000 m
200 – 500 m
0 – 200 m

0 – 200 m
200 – 500 m
500 – 1000 m
1000 – 2000 m
2000 – 3000 m
3000 – 4000 m
4000 – 5000 m
5000 – 6000 m
6000 – 7000 m
7000 – 8000 m
over 8000 m

▲ 5775 Mountain height (in metres)
▼ 8605 Ocean depth (in metres)
—— Country boundary
- - - Disputed boundary
—— Path of cross-section

Scale 1 : 10 000 000
0   100   200   300 km

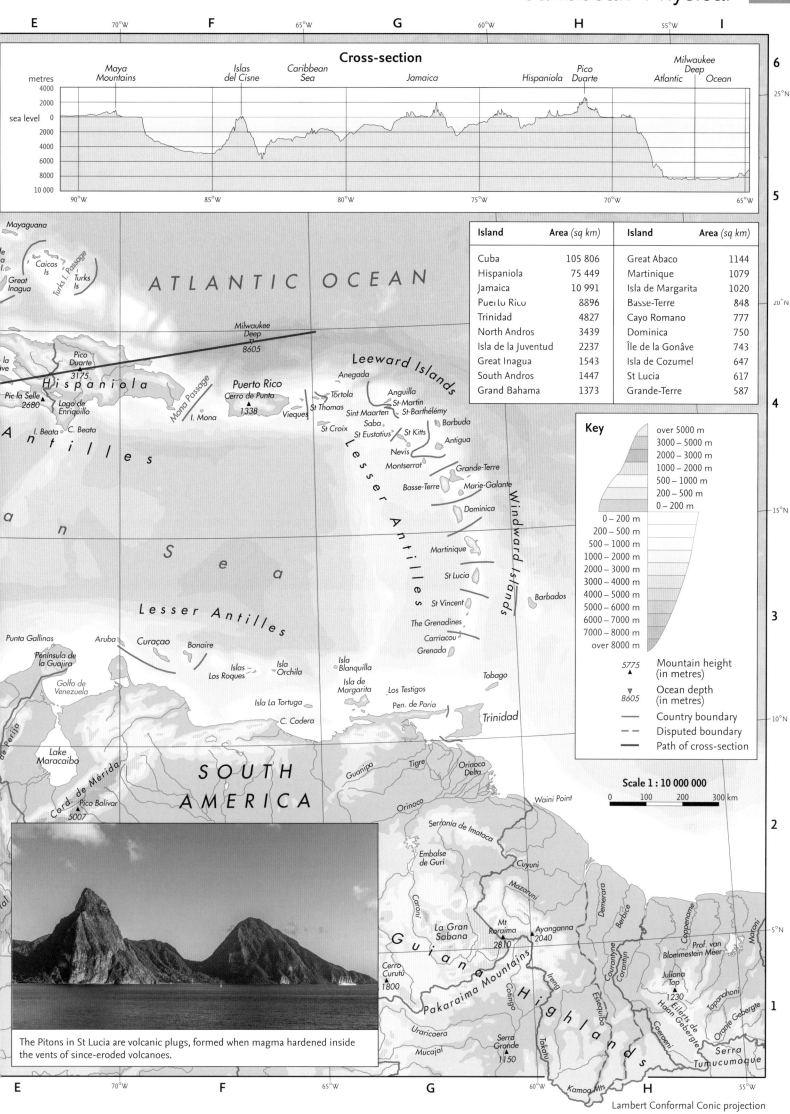

The Pitons in St Lucia are volcanic plugs, formed when magma hardened inside the vents of since-eroded volcanoes.

Lambert Conformal Conic projection

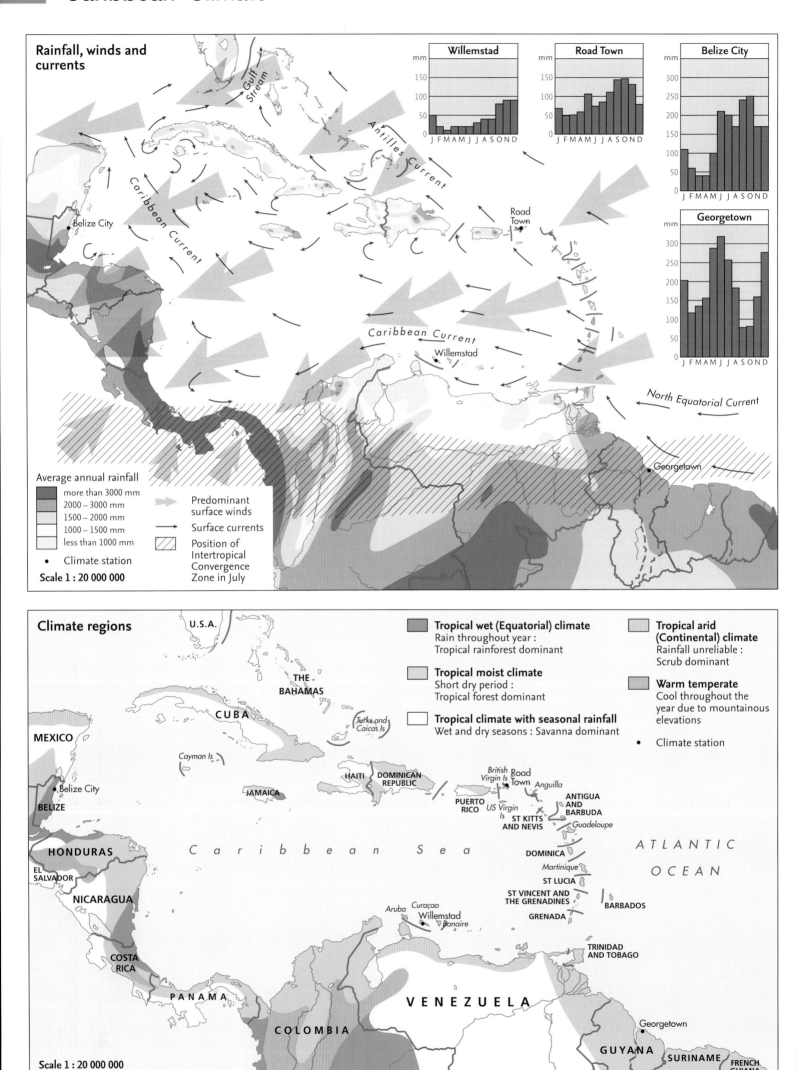

Rainfall, winds and currents

Willemstad

mm
150
100
50
0
J F M A M J J A S O N D

Road Town

mm
150
100
50
0
J F M A M J J A S O N D

Belize City

mm
300
250
200
150
100
50
0
J F M A M J J A S O N D

Georgetown

mm
300
250
200
150
100
50
0
J F M A M J J A S O N D

Gulf Stream

Antilles Current

Caribbean Current

Caribbean Current

North Equatorial Current

Belize City

Road Town

Willemstad

Georgetown

Average annual rainfall

- more than 3000 mm
- 2000 – 3000 mm
- 1500 – 2000 mm
- 1000 – 1500 mm
- less than 1000 mm
- • Climate station

Scale 1 : 20 000 000

→ Predominant surface winds

→ Surface currents

⫽ Position of Intertropical Convergence Zone in July

Climate regions

Tropical wet (Equatorial) climate
Rain throughout year :
Tropical rainforest dominant

Tropical moist climate
Short dry period :
Tropical forest dominant

Tropical climate with seasonal rainfall
Wet and dry seasons : Savanna dominant

Tropical arid (Continental) climate
Rainfall unreliable :
Scrub dominant

Warm temperate
Cool throughout the year due to mountainous elevations

• Climate station

U.S.A.

THE BAHAMAS

CUBA

Turks and Caicos Is

MEXICO

Cayman Is

HAITI

DOMINICAN REPUBLIC

JAMAICA

British Virgin Is

Road Town

Anguilla

PUERTO RICO

US Virgin Is

ST KITTS AND NEVIS

ANTIGUA AND BARBUDA

Guadeloupe

BELIZE

Belize City

HONDURAS

EL SALVADOR

NICARAGUA

C a r i b b e a n   S e a

DOMINICA

Martinique

ST LUCIA

ST VINCENT AND THE GRENADINES

GRENADA

BARBADOS

ATLANTIC OCEAN

Aruba

Curaçao

Willemstad

Bonaire

COSTA RICA

PANAMA

V E N E Z U E L A

TRINIDAD AND TOBAGO

COLOMBIA

GUYANA

Georgetown

SURINAME

FRENCH GUIANA

Scale 1 : 20 000 000

Hurricanes affecting the Caribbean originate over the warm waters of the Atlantic Ocean or Caribbean Sea. They rotate anticlockwise and always try to move north, but are often forced to travel west or northwest before they can turn. The tracks on the map below show how they do this. Their wind strength declines rapidly once they reach land, but they may still be very wet and cause extensive flooding.

- The most deaths usually occur in the poorest communities
- Heavy rainfall during a hurricane may be more damaging than the wind or storm surge
- Mountainous islands are vulnerable to severe flooding, mudslides and landslides
- Flatter islands suffer much damage from storm surges and coastal flooding
- Many islands are hit by major hurricanes, but those with good preparations and a sound building code rarely have any deaths
- The extent and cost of damage can be excessive even if there are no deaths

Outer bands
Eye of storm

As the hurricane passes, wind speeds and rainfall decrease and the outer bands bring sunny intervals

After the eye has passed, hurricane-force winds begin immediately from the opposite direction, often accompanied by heavy rain

In the eye of the storm, winds are light and the sky is clear with little rain

Closer to the centre, wind speeds increase to over 100 km/hr, and there may be torrential rain (more than 200 mm/day)

As the hurricane approaches, clouds form and the wind speed increases. The outer bands bring alternate rain showers and sunny intervals

Hurricane tracks

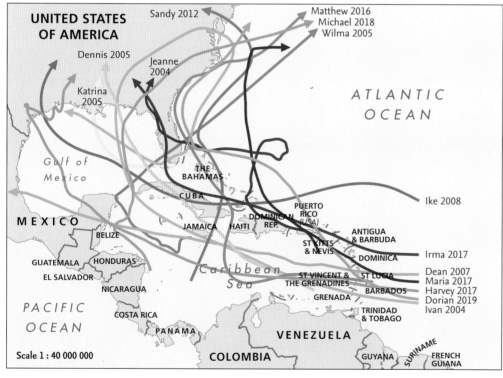

Hurricane risk

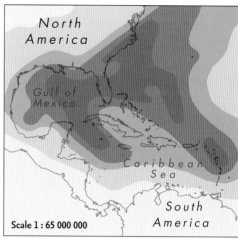

Scale 1 : 65 000 000

Chance of a hurricane during one year

| less than 5% | 5 – 35% | 35 – 55% | 55 – 65% | 65 – 90% |

Total number of recorded storms for each month over a century

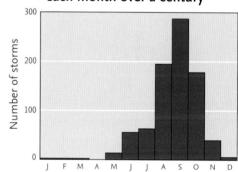

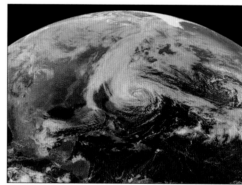

Hurricane Sandy extended over 1000 km and moved very slowly, staying over Cuba, Haiti and The Bahamas for many days and causing much damage.

Recent hurricanes

Year	Name	Category	Main countries/territories affected (number of deaths)
2004	Ivan	5	Grenada (39), Dom. Rep. (4), Jamaica (17), Cayman Is (1), Cuba, USA (54)
2004	Jeanne	3	Puerto Rico (8), Dom. Rep. (18), Haiti (>3000), The Bahamas, USA (5)
2005	Dennis	4	Haiti (56), Jamaica (1), Cuba (16), USA (15)
2005	Katrina	5	USA (>1200)
2005	Wilma	4	Haiti (12), Jamaica (1), Cuba (4), Mexico (8), USA (61)
2007	Dean	5	Martinique (3), Dominica (2), Haiti (14), Jamaica (3), Belize, Mexico (13)
2008	Ike	4	Turks & Caicos Is, The Bahamas, Dom. Rep. (2), Haiti (74), Cuba (7), USA (113)
2012	Sandy	3	Jamaica (2), Cuba (11), Haiti (54), Dom. Rep. (2), The Bahamas (2), USA (157)
2016	Matthew	5	Haiti (>500), Dom. Rep. (4), Cuba (4), The Bahamas, USA (47)
2017	Harvey	4	Suriname, Guyana (1), Barbados, St Vincent & Grenadines, USA (76)
2017	Irma	5	Antigua & Barbuda (3), St-Martin/St-Barthélemy (11), Sint Maarten (4), British Virgin Is (4), US Virgin Is (4), Puerto Rico (3), Cuba (10), USA (88)
2017	Maria	5	Dominica (65), Guadeloupe (2), Puerto Rico (2975), Dom. Rep. (5), USA (4)
2018	Michael	4	Honduras (8), Nicaragua (4), El Salvador (3), USA (45)
2019	Dorian	5	The Bahamas (≥61), USA (10)

The Red Cross distributes supplies in Port-au-Prince, Haiti, in the aftermath of Hurricane Sandy.

The world's major earthquakes occur most frequently at the boundaries of the crustal plates. As all the Caribbean islands are located around the edge of the Caribbean plate they are vulnerable to earthquakes as this plate moves relative to its neighbours. The greatest movement is in the west in Central America, which has the worst earthquakes. Next in severity is the northern boundary, which includes Jamaica and Hispaniola, and the least pressure is exerted in the Eastern Caribbean, which has smaller earthquakes.

The Caribbean islands have around 20 – 30 minor earthquakes a year; they are more common than hurricanes.

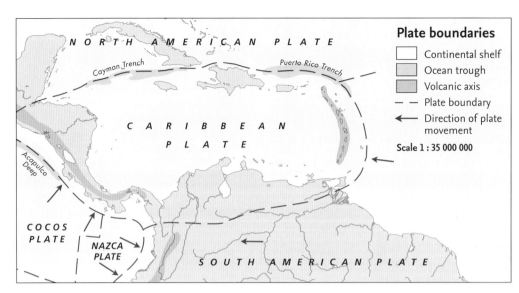

Plate boundaries

☐	Continental shelf
▨	Ocean trough
▨	Volcanic axis
– – –	Plate boundary
←	Direction of plate movement

Scale 1 : 35 000 000

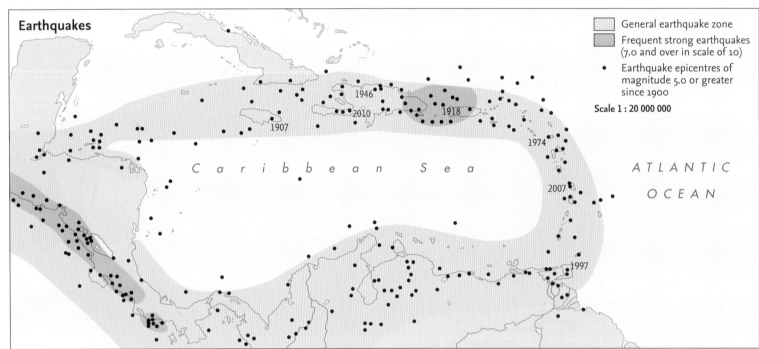

Earthquakes

☐	General earthquake zone
▨	Frequent strong earthquakes (7.0 and over in scale of 10)
•	Earthquake epicentres of magnitude 5.0 or greater since 1900

Scale 1 : 20 000 000

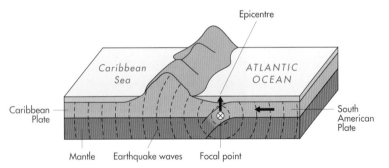

Major earthquakes

Year	Location	Magnitude (Richter scale)	
1692	Port Royal, Jamaica	7.5	2000 dead; also minor earthquakes in 1907 and 1993
1842	Cap-Haïtien, Haiti	8.1	5000 dead
1843	near Guadeloupe	8.0 – 8.5	2000 – 3000 dead on Guadeloupe; English Harbour on Antigua submerged
1907	Kingston, Jamaica	6.5	800 – 1000 dead
1918	western Puerto Rico	7.5	118 dead
1946	El Cibao, Dom. Rep.	8.1	75 dead
1974	near Antigua	7.5	many islands affected; epicentre in Venezuela
1997	Trinidad and Tobago	6.5	81 dead in Venezuela
2007	Martinique	7.4	6 dead
2010	Port-au-Prince, Haiti	7.0	230 000 dead

Transitional shelter homes being built in large numbers near Port-au-Prince, Haiti, in the aftermath of the devastating earthquake of 2010.

Like earthquakes, volcanoes occur mainly along plate boundaries and the Caribbean is no exception. One difference is that they do not occur along the northern edge of the plate as this is not a collision zone, but they do occur in the west and east. For the same reason that Central America has the largest earthquakes it also has the largest number of volcanoes, and the most active ones. The Eastern Caribbean is a less active plate margin, but the few active volcanoes it does have are extremely dangerous and these, and older dormant volcanoes, are what formed many of the islands.

- Most Caribbean volcanoes are dormant but may erupt in the future
- Volcanic activity, such as sulphur springs and fumaroles, is common on many islands (e.g. Dominica, St Lucia, St Kitts, Montserrat)

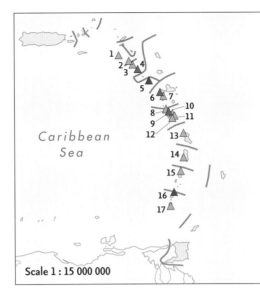

Volcanoes

▲ Currently active   ▲ Dormant   ▲ Extinct

1   Saba, 1640
2   The Quill, St Eustatius, 250 AD ± 150 years
3   Mount Liamuiga, St Kitts and Nevis, 160 AD ± 200 years
4   Nevis Peak, St Kitts and Nevis
5   Soufrière Hills, Montserrat, 1995 – 2011, 2012
6   Bouillante Chain, Guadeloupe
7   La Soufrière, Guadeloupe, 1977
8   Morne Aux Diables, Dominica
9   Morne Diablotins, Dominica
10   Morne Trois Pitons, Dominica, 920 AD ± 50 years
11   Morne Watt, Dominica, 1997
12   Morne Plat Pays, Dominica, 1270 ± 50 years
13   Montagne Pelée, Martinique, 1932
14   Qualibou, St Lucia, 1766
15   Soufrière, St Vincent and the Grenadines, 1979
16   Kick 'em Jenny, Grenada, 2001
17   Mount St Catherine, Grenada

Scale 1 : 15 000 000

List gives year of last eruption

Volcanic eruptions

Year	Volcano	Location	
1902 (and 1979, minor)	Soufrière	St Vincent	2000 dead
1902 (and 1932, minor)	Montagne Pelée	Martinique	30 000 dead
1939 – present	Kick 'em Jenny	off the coast of Grenada	
1977	La Soufrière	Basse-Terre, Guadeloupe	evacuated, no deaths
1995 – present	Soufrière Hills	Montserrat	southern two-thirds of the island abandoned

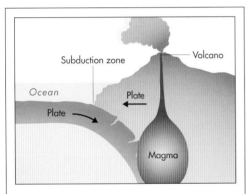

Formation of Caribbean volcanoes

Wherever two tectonic plates collide a destructive margin is formed. One of these plates will be forced under the other in an area called the subduction zone. Friction (and the increase in temperature as the crust moves downwards) causes the crust to melt and some of the newly formed magma may be forced to the surface to form volcanoes.

The structure of a typical volcano formed in this way is shown below. The increase in pressure as the plate is forced downwards can also trigger severe earthquakes.

Montserrat

- In 1995 there were minor eruptions at the summit of Soufrière Hills, and then later in the year more severe eruptions covered parts of Plymouth in ash
- It was decided to evacuate Plymouth at the end of 1995 and although there were attempts to resettle the town, a major eruption in September 1996 destroyed much of the southern half of the island
- In 1997 a further eruption destroyed the rest of Plymouth and the airport, killing 26 people who had not left the area. Ash and sediment covered much of Plymouth
- As volcanic activity has continued to this day, the southern two-thirds of the island has been abandoned and new settlements, and an airport, set up in the northern sector
- The larger part of Montserrat will remain uninhabitable for the foreseeable future. A permanent volcanic observatory monitors the situation around the clock
- The population has declined from about 10 000 in 1995 to about 5000 today

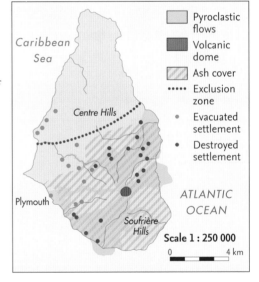

Pyroclastic flows
Volcanic dome
Ash cover
••••• Exclusion zone
• Evacuated settlement
• Destroyed settlement

Scale 1 : 250 000

0   4 km

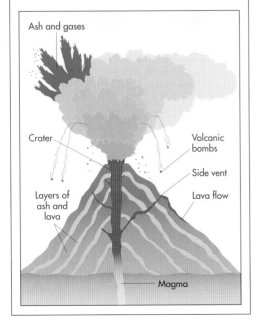

A view of the buried town of Plymouth from the sea. In the foreground the ash and sediment has reached the sea. The Soufrière Hills are in the centre background, and the highest point, Chances Peak, is on the right covered in cloud. The South Soufrière Hills are on the far right.

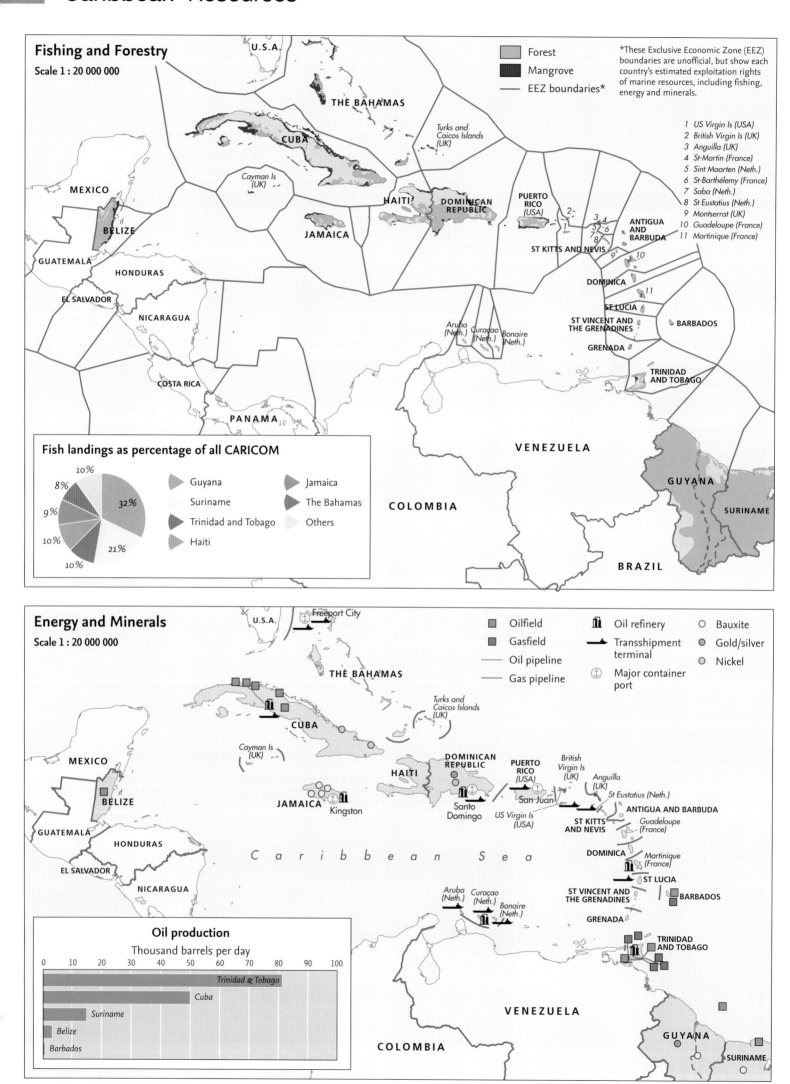

Fishing and Forestry

Scale 1 : 20 000 000

Forest
Mangrove
EEZ boundaries*

*These Exclusive Economic Zone (EEZ) boundaries are unofficial, but show each country's estimated exploitation rights of marine resources, including fishing, energy and minerals.

1 US Virgin Is (USA)
2 British Virgin Is (UK)
3 Anguilla (UK)
4 St-Martin (France)
5 Sint Maarten (Neth.)
6 St-Barthélemy (France)
7 Saba (Neth.)
8 St Eustatius (Neth.)
9 Montserrat (UK)
10 Guadeloupe (France)
11 Martinique (France)

U.S.A.
THE BAHAMAS
Turks and Caicos Islands (UK)
CUBA
MEXICO
Cayman Is (UK)
BELIZE
GUATEMALA
HONDURAS
EL SALVADOR
NICARAGUA
HAITI
JAMAICA
DOMINICAN REPUBLIC
PUERTO RICO (USA)
ANTIGUA AND BARBUDA
ST KITTS AND NEVIS
DOMINICA
ST LUCIA
ST VINCENT AND THE GRENADINES
BARBADOS
GRENADA
Aruba (Neth.)
Curaçao (Neth.)
Bonaire (Neth.)
TRINIDAD AND TOBAGO
COSTA RICA
PANAMA
VENEZUELA
COLOMBIA
GUYANA
SURINAME
BRAZIL

Fish landings as percentage of all CARICOM

10%
8%
9%
10%
10%
21%
32%

Guyana
Suriname
Trinidad and Tobago
Haiti
Jamaica
The Bahamas
Others

Energy and Minerals

Scale 1 : 20 000 000

Oilfield
Gasfield
Oil pipeline
Gas pipeline
Oil refinery
Transshipment terminal
Major container port
Bauxite
Gold/silver
Nickel

Freeport City
U.S.A.
THE BAHAMAS
Turks and Caicos Islands (UK)
CUBA
Cayman Is (UK)
MEXICO
BELIZE
GUATEMALA
HONDURAS
EL SALVADOR
NICARAGUA
HAITI
JAMAICA
Kingston
DOMINICAN REPUBLIC
Santo Domingo
PUERTO RICO (USA)
San Juan
British Virgin Is (UK)
Anguilla (UK)
St Eustatius (Neth.)
ANTIGUA AND BARBUDA
ST KITTS AND NEVIS
Guadeloupe (France)
DOMINICA
Martinique (France)
ST LUCIA
ST VINCENT AND THE GRENADINES
BARBADOS
GRENADA
US Virgin Is (USA)
Caribbean Sea
Aruba (Neth.)
Curaçao (Neth.)
Bonaire (Neth.)
TRINIDAD AND TOBAGO
VENEZUELA
COLOMBIA
GUYANA
SURINAME

Oil production

Thousand barrels per day

0   10   20   30   40   50   60   70   80   90   100

Trinidad & Tobago
Cuba
Suriname
Belize
Barbados

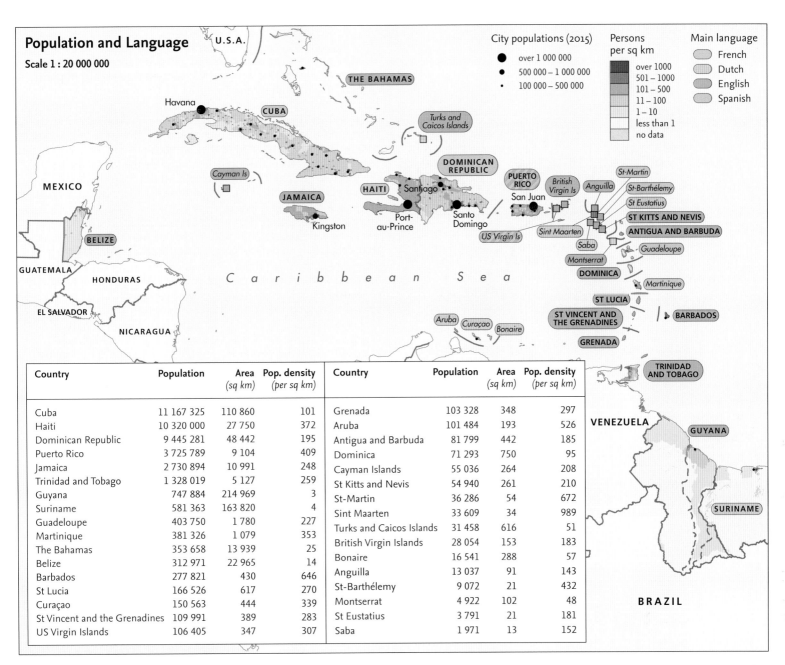

Population and Language

Scale 1 : 20 000 000

City populations (2015)
- ● over 1 000 000
- ● 500 000 – 1 000 000
- · 100 000 – 500 000

Persons per sq km
- over 1000
- 501 – 1000
- 101 – 500
- 11 – 100
- 1 – 10
- less than 1
- no data

Main language
- French
- Dutch
- English
- Spanish

Country	Population	Area (sq km)	Pop. density (per sq km)
Cuba	11 167 325	110 860	101
Haiti	10 320 000	27 750	372
Dominican Republic	9 445 281	48 442	195
Puerto Rico	3 725 789	9 104	409
Jamaica	2 730 894	10 991	248
Trinidad and Tobago	1 328 019	5 127	259
Guyana	747 884	214 969	3
Suriname	581 363	163 820	4
Guadeloupe	403 750	1 780	227
Martinique	381 326	1 079	353
The Bahamas	353 658	13 939	25
Belize	312 971	22 965	14
Barbados	277 821	430	646
St Lucia	166 526	617	270
Curaçao	150 563	444	339
St Vincent and the Grenadines	109 991	389	283
US Virgin Islands	106 405	347	307

Country	Population	Area (sq km)	Pop. density (per sq km)
Grenada	103 328	348	297
Aruba	101 484	193	526
Antigua and Barbuda	81 799	442	185
Dominica	71 293	750	95
Cayman Islands	55 036	264	208
St Kitts and Nevis	54 940	261	210
St-Martin	36 286	54	672
Sint Maarten	33 609	34	989
Turks and Caicos Islands	31 458	616	51
British Virgin Islands	28 054	153	183
Bonaire	16 541	288	57
Anguilla	13 037	91	143
St-Barthélemy	9 072	21	432
Montserrat	4 922	102	48
St Eustatius	3 791	21	181
Saba	1 971	13	152

Tourism

Scale 1 : 22 500 000

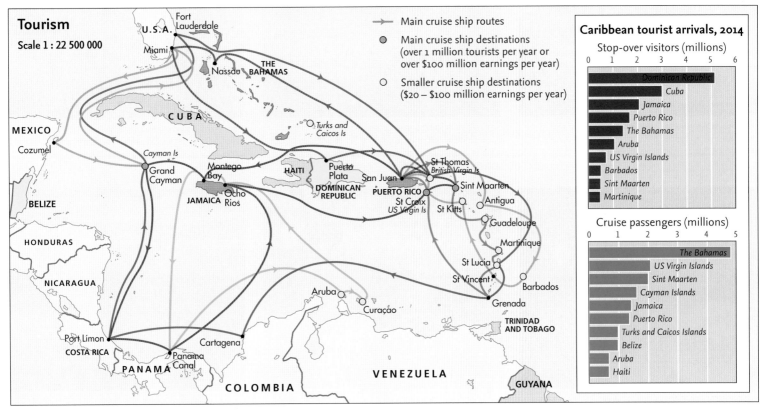

- → Main cruise ship routes
- ● Main cruise ship destinations (over 1 million tourists per year or over $100 million earnings per year)
- ○ Smaller cruise ship destinations ($20 – $100 million earnings per year)

Caribbean tourist arrivals, 2014

Stop-over visitors (millions)
0 1 2 3 4 5 6
- Dominican Republic
- Cuba
- Jamaica
- Puerto Rico
- The Bahamas
- Aruba
- US Virgin Islands
- Barbados
- Sint Maarten
- Martinique

Cruise passengers (millions)
0 1 2 3 4 5
- The Bahamas
- US Virgin Islands
- Sint Maarten
- Cayman Islands
- Jamaica
- Puerto Rico
- Turks and Caicos Islands
- Belize
- Aruba
- Haiti

Amerindian civilisations, 1000 BC – AD 1500

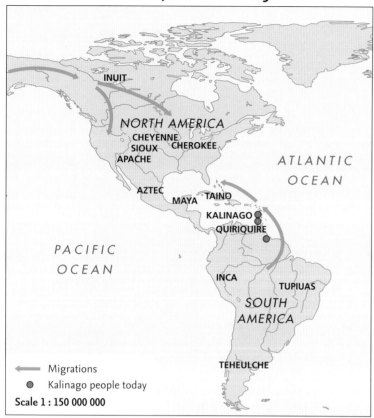

Migrations
Kalinago people today
Scale 1 : 150 000 000

The migration of people from Asia to America across the Bering Strait began about 13 000 years ago. These people, today known as Amerindians, moved southwards from Alaska establishing great civilisations throughout the Americas.

Kalinago and Taino peoples migrated northwards towards Jamaica, Cuba and The Bahamas, and the Lesser Antilles. The Taino mostly settled in Cuba, Hispaniola, Jamaica and The Bahamas. It is generally believed that they migrated to the Caribbean from Venezuela around AD 600-700, because the population outgrew the food supply and other resources; and competition with other groups for land. They settled along the coastal regions of these islands, close to fresh water. They grew cassava and fished.

The Kalinago mostly settled in the Lesser Antilles. The rocky mountains of these islands did not provide much land for agriculture so the Kalinago raided the Taino islands for food. Trinidad and Puerto Rico were shared by both the Kalinago and Taino.

Kalinago who survived the European invasions are now mainly concentrated in Dominica where some 3000 live, with a few hundred spread throughout the other Eastern Caribbean islands. Many Amerindian tribes, including Kalinago, survive today in parts of Guyana, Suriname and French Guiana. Belize's present day population includes people descended from the Maya civilisation.

The Amerindian peoples of the Caribbean are often referred to as 'Arawaks' and 'Caribs'. It is better to use the term 'Taino' instead of 'Arawak' in the Caribbean as 'Taino' distinguishes people in the Caribbean from the Arawakian groups living in South America. Today, we prefer to use the term 'Kalinago' to 'Carib'.

	Social life	Economic life	Political life
Tainos	Played a game called batos. Held religious beliefs; believed in multiple gods and kept idols called zemis.	Did hunting, farming, fishing and often traded with other Tainos. Hunted birds, iguanas, conies and other small animals. Planted cassava, sweet potato, pepper and peanuts.	Villages were headed by a cacique whose position was hereditary. All laws and judgements were passed by the cacique who had many privileges.
Kalinagoes	Also had idols called moyabas.	Also did farming, hunting and fishing.	Chief was called the oboutou. This position was earned through the demonstration of military skills.

The El Castillo ruin in the ancient Mayan city of Xunantunich in Belize. El Castillo was probably built around AD 800.

The Caguana Indigenous Ceremonial Park in Puerto Rico is one of the most important Taino archaeological sites in the Antilles. Archaeologists believe that the site was considered sacred by the Taino.

Historians and archaeologists have studied how Amerindians in the Caribbean lived, and a team in Cuba have reconstructed a Taino village.

Mayan artefacts discovered by archaeologists in Actun Tunichil Muknal Cave, Belize.

We can find traces of Amerindian culture in everyday activities around the Caribbean, such as basket weaving...

...and cassava cultivation.

European exploration westwards, up to AD 1500

Early Norse explorers
First voyage of Columbus
1492 – 1493
Scale 1 : 150 000 000

The ancient Silk Road

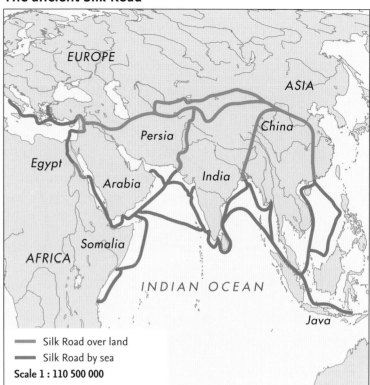

Silk Road over land
Silk Road by sea
Scale 1 : 110 500 000

There is evidence to suggest that there was European exploration of North America before Christopher Columbus. According to the Icelandic Sagas, Vikings first settled in Greenland in the 980s. The only known site of a Viking village in North America outside Greenland is L'Anse aux Meadows in Newfoundland, which may be connected with an attempt by the explorer Leif Ericson to establish the colony of Vinland around 1003. In 1492 Christopher Columbus set sail westwards from Spain. The main aim of his voyage was to try to find a new route to Asia.

The Silk Road to India and China was becoming dangerous and affecting the trade in valuable goods such as spices and silks. People believed that sailing westwards would lead to China, Japan and Indonesia (then called Java). Columbus needed funding for a voyage westwards to try to reach Asia and he approached King Henry VII of England and King John II of Portugal for money before the Spanish monarchs – Ferdinand II of Aragon and Isabella I of Castile – agreed to fund his voyage. Columbus was to claim all new lands for Spain, and in return would be given 10 per cent of all revenues from these new lands.

Columbus timeline

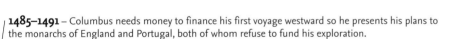

1451 – Columbus is born in the Republic of Genoa (now part of modern-day Italy).

1485–1491 – Columbus needs money to finance his first voyage westward so he presents his plans to the monarchs of England and Portugal, both of whom refuse to fund his exploration.

1492 – In January Ferdinand and Isabella, the rulers of Spain, agree to fund his voyage. After his preparations are complete Columbus finally sets sail on 3 August 1492.

1492 – In October Columbus sights one of the islands in The Bahamas. He calls the island San Salvador (which means 'Holy saviour' in Spanish) but the local name was Guanahani. On this voyage Columbus also lands in Cuba and Hispaniola.

1493 – Columbus arrives back in Europe, landing in Portugal in March.

1493 – Columbus sets off on his second voyage on 24 September. During this voyage, he lands on Marie-Galante and Guadeloupe before travelling northwards and sighting Montserrat, Dominica, Antigua, Redonda, Nevis, St Kitts, St Eustatius, Saba, St-Martin, St Croix, and the chain of the Virgin Islands. He then goes on to land in Puerto Rico and Jamaica.

1496 – Columbus arrives back in Europe, landing at Cadiz in southern Spain in June.

1498–1500 – Columbus embarks on his third voyage on 30 May 1498. The aim of this voyage is to try to find a continent that King John II of Portugal believed existed to the southwest of the Cape Verde Islands. We know this continent as South America. On this voyage, Columbus lands on Trinidad, explores the gulf that separates Trinidad and Venezuela, sights Tobago, Grenada and St Vincent, and visits Hispaniola.

1502–1503 – Columbus leaves Europe for his fourth and final voyage on 11 May 1502. He lands first at Martinique, then sights St Lucia and explores the coasts of Honduras, Nicaragua and Costa Rica, arriving in Panama in October. He sights the Cayman Islands in May 1503, but is then stranded on Jamaica for nearly a year.

1504 – Columbus arrives back in Spain.

1506 – Columbus dies.

Christopher Columbus (1451–1506) was Italian, but his great voyages were undertaken for the king and queen of Spain, which ensured the long-term influence of Spain in the Caribbean.

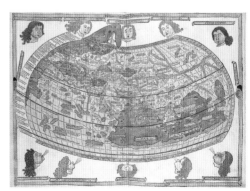

This map is from 1482, before Columbus landed in the Caribbean, and shows the western 'known world' at that time. It illustrates that Europeans didn't know that the Americas and Caribbean existed.

Triangular Trade route

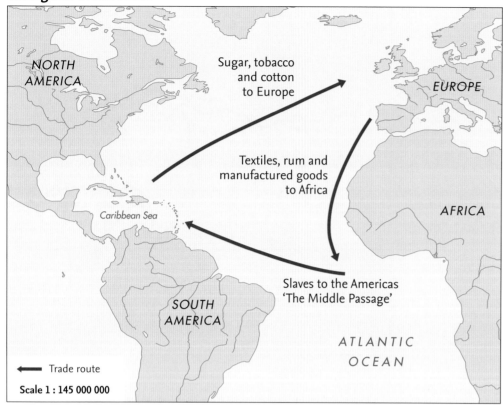

Sugar, tobacco and cotton to Europe

Textiles, rum and manufactured goods to Africa

Slaves to the Americas 'The Middle Passage'

Trade route

Scale 1 : 145 000 000

West Africa, showing Senegal and the location of Goree, the largest slave-trading centre between the fifteenth and nineteenth centuries.

The circular fort on the island of Goree off the coast of Senegal.

The **Triangular Trade** was the name given to the trade that operated between Europe and Africa, Africa and the Caribbean and from the Caribbean back to Europe. In Europe, ships were loaded with items such as copper, glass beads, trinkets, cloth, rum, guns and ammunition. The ships then sailed to the west coast of Africa. In Africa, these goods were exchanged for slaves, who were then transported in the same ships to the Caribbean: this was called the **Middle Passage**. On reaching the Caribbean, the enslaved Africans were sold on to plantation owners, and the ships were loaded with cash crops – tobacco, cotton and in particular sugar, often in the form of molasses – to be sent to Europe.

Enslavement of Africans, 1500 – 1870

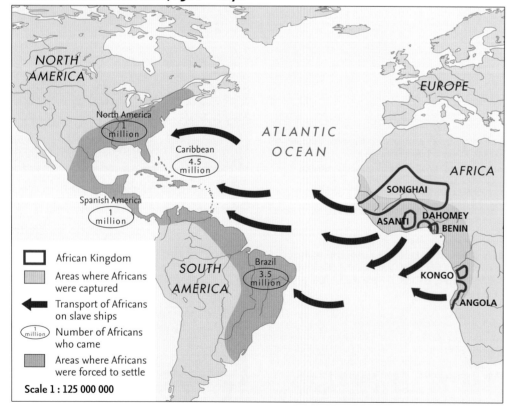

North America
1 million

Caribbean
4.5 million

Spanish America
1 million

Brazil
3.5 million

SONGHAI

ASANTI   DAHOMEY
BENIN

KONGO

ANGOLA

☐ African Kingdom

▨ Areas where Africans were captured

◄ Transport of Africans on slave ships

(million) Number of Africans who came

▨ Areas where Africans were forced to settle

Scale 1 : 125 000 000

This image of a sugar plantation (1852) shows the slave quarters to the left of the plantation-owner's house (centre), with the sugar mill on the right.

One of the most devastating effects of the arrival of Europeans in the Caribbean was on the Amerindian population. Millions of Amerindians were killed in wars and by diseases brought by the Europeans. As a result, there was a need for cheap and reliable enslaved labour to work on the growing sugar, tobacco and cotton plantations.

From the beginning of the sixteenth century Africans were captured and transported across the Atlantic in ships to be sold as slaves in the Americas. Many died on the three-month voyage but 10 million Africans did arrive, with 4.5 million forced to settle in the Caribbean. The majority of African enslaved people were captured in the interior of West African states and then transported on foot to the coastal regions by African slave traders.

Migration of peoples to the Caribbean, 1830s – 1920s

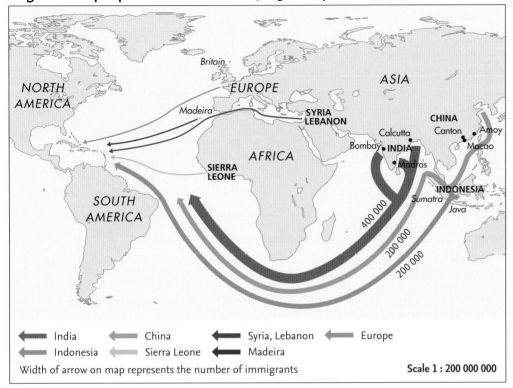

India	China	Syria, Lebanon	Europe
Indonesia	Sierra Leone	Madeira	

Width of arrow on map represents the number of immigrants

Scale 1 : 200 000 000

Colonies that recruited immigrants

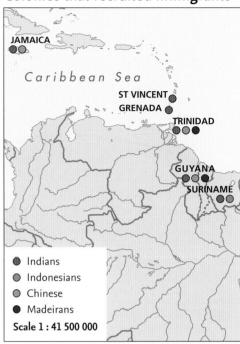

● Indians
● Indonesians
● Chinese
● Madeirans
Scale 1 : 41 500 000

The larger British colonies of Jamaica, Guyana and Trinidad received the largest number of Asian immigrants, and their legacy and influence are still felt today. More than 400 000 East Indian immigrants entered the Caribbean between 1838 and 1917, and approximately 20 000 Chinese immigrants came between 1852 and 1893.

The abolition of slavery in British territory in 1834 led to a frantic search by plantation owners for another source of cheap labour. Labour recruiters started to approach heavily populated and poverty stricken regions in Asia, in particular China, India and Indonesia. People migrated to the Caribbean of their own free will, often as indentured labourers. Under the indentureship scheme, people were given free passage to the Caribbean in return for a set period of work.

The people who migrated to the Caribbean brought with them new religions as well as their languages, cultural practices, industries and food.

Doubles – a popular street food in Trinidad of Indian origin – are made with two pieces of fried flatbread filled with curried chickpeas.

The Syrian community in Martinique is about 1 000-strong and has become fully integrated.

Greek migrants from the Aegean Islands introduced sponge-diving to The Bahamas in the late nineteenth century. This was a thriving industry – estimated as the third-largest sponging industry in the world in the mid 1930s – until a fungal infection wiped out most of the sponge beds in around 1938.

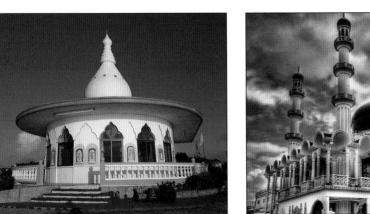

The Hindu Temple in the Sea in Trinidad.

The Keizerstraat mosque in Paramaribo, Suriname.

Cultural dance performance during the East Indian festival of Divali in Chaguanas, Trinidad.

Emigration from the English-speaking Caribbean

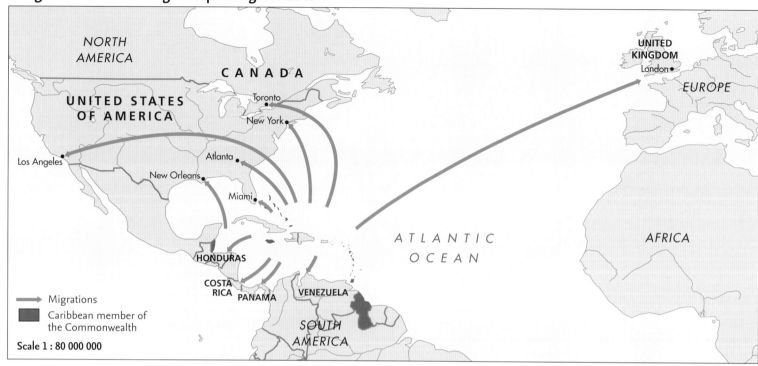

As well as people migrating to the Caribbean, large numbers of Caribbean people have emigrated from the region. From the 1850s to the 1930s migrants from the former British Caribbean colonies moved to Latin America where developments such as the opening of the oilfields in Venezuela and the building of the Panama Canal created new employment opportunities.

From the end of the nineteenth century onwards, Caribbean people started to migrate northwards to the USA and Canada in search of a better life. For example, many Bahamians – struggling under the poor economic climate of the time – made the short trip to Florida to work in agriculture, fishing, turtle-fishing and sponging. Caribbean migration transformed cities in the USA. By around 1896, 40 per cent of people living in Miami were foreign-born blacks, and early twentieth century Caribbean immigration to New York transformed the Harlem area of the city. Many people also travelled during the Second World War to serve in the military and work in countries like the UK and USA. Serious labour shortages in Britain after the Second World War resulted in government recruitment schemes aimed at encouraging Colonial workers to fill this gap. Nearly a million people crossed the Atlantic from the West Indies to take up employment in Britain, with the main migration taking place between 1945 and 1962. The most noticeable impact of the migration of Caribbean peoples the world over is the formation of diaspora communities. These are communities where people from the West Indies converge and form communities reminiscent of their Caribbean homelands. Diaspora communities can be very influential.

One of the first large groups arrived in Britain on board the *Empire Windrush* from Jamaica in 1948.

Looking west along an unpaved Flagler Street, Miami, Florida, circa 1900.

Patricia Scotland was born in Dominica in 1955 but her family migrated to the UK. She studied law and became the first black woman to be made Queens Counsel, the most senior form of barrister. Scotland was made a Baroness in 1997. She is the first woman to become Secretary-General of the Commonwealth of Nations.

The Notting Hill Carnival, held in London at the end of August each year, is an opportunity for the West Indian communities of Britain to celebrate Caribbean carnival music, dancing and food.

The Cuban people of Florida are said to have had a major influence in determining the outcome of every United States presidential election since 2000. Marco Rubio, who is of Cuban origin, is a Republican senator for Florida.

Impact of colonisation in the Caribbean

Labour systems

Encomienda – a labour system introduced by the Spanish in 1523 to help manage and control the indigenous people. Under this system Taino families were assigned to Spanish settlers called encomenderos. The Taino were required to work for the encomenderos on projects like farming and mining. The encomenderos ensured that the Taino were converted to Christianity. Many Taino families were abused under the system.

Slavery – the system of slavery started with the Spanish when their labour force became depleted as the number of Tainos declined. Slavery in the Caribbean was referred to as chattel slavery. This meant that the enslaved had no rights; physical, economic, political or social. Slaves were taken from West and Central Africa.

Indentureship – this system involved the use of contracted immigrant labourers after Emancipation. Some migrants came from European countries while others came from places such as Sierra Leone in Africa, and India and China in Asia.

Social structure

Prior to Emancipation, race was the most significant factor influencing how Caribbean societies were structured. Whites controlled all political and economic power even though they were smallest in numbers. Blacks were the largest in number but remained at the bottom of the social pyramid. They had very few rights and no power.

Following Emancipation, class became the most significant factor by which persons were ranked. Class is determined mainly by wealth but education has played an important role in this.

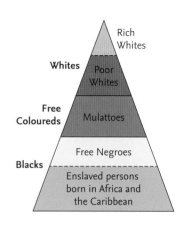

An example of social structure in the islands controlled by the British before Emancipation.

Movement towards independence

Timeline

- **1930**
- **1935–1938** – Labour riots develop out of the demand for better wages and working conditions; cries for political independence are also stirred.
- **1940**
- **1945** – Labour leaders meet in Barbados to discuss both labour and political matters; demands made for minimum wage laws and a British West Indian Federation.
- **1947** – Conference held in Montego Bay, Jamaica, to determine how a federation would be achieved.
- **1950**
- **1956** – Constitution of the Federation formally agreed; British Caribbean Federation Act passed by the British Parliament.
- **1958** – West Indian Federation established; English speaking territories become one political unit. Members include Antigua and Barbuda, Barbados, Dominica, Grenada, Jamaica, Montserrat, St Kitts, Nevis and Anguilla, St Lucia, St Vincent, and Trinidad and Tobago. The capital city is located in Trinidad; Sir Grantley Adams of Barbados installed as prime minister of the Federation.
- **1960**
- **1961** – Jamaica withdraws from the Federation; the other countries follow suit. The Federation collapses.
- **1962** – Jamaica and Trinidad and Tobago become independent.
- **1966** – Barbados and Guyana become independent.
- **1968** – The Caribbean Free Trade Association (CARIFTA) is established – Trinidad and Tobago, Guyana, Antigua and Barbados are the first to join.
- **1970**
- **1973** – The Bahamas becomes independent.
- **1974** – The Caribbean Common Market (CARICOM) is established by the signing of the Treaty of Chaguaramas by the CARIFTA Heads of Government; Grenada becomes independent.
- **1978** – Dominica becomes independent.
- **1979** – The Grenada Revolution – on 13 March, the People's Revolutionary Army overthrow the Grenada United Labour Party government and install Maurice Bishop as prime minister; St Lucia, and St Vincent and the Grenadines become independent.
- **1980**
- **1981** – Antigua and Barbuda, and Belize become independent.
- **1983** – St Kitts and Nevis independence; Maurice Bishop, prime minister of Grenada, is assassinated; the United States and other Caribbean forces invade Grenada.

Some key figures in independence movements

Sir Grantley Adams is one of the National Heroes of Barbados. He was a labour leader and one of the founders of the Barbados Labour Party. He was the first Premier for the island and later became the Prime Minister of the West Indian Federation.

Dr Eric Williams founded the People's National Movement in Trinidad. He was Trinidad's first Premier and helped to secure the country's independence in 1962. Thereafter, he served as Prime Minister until his death in 1981.

Sir Eric Matthew Gairy, national hero and Premier of Grenada from 1967–1974. Sir Gairy became the first Prime Minister when the country became independent in 1974. He was overthrown in a coup in 1979.

George Cadle Price played a key role in Belizean independence and is honoured as the 'Father of the Nation'. He worked tirelessly for independence, serving as the country's first Premier from 1964 when the country gained self-government, and as Prime Minister from independence in 1981 until 1984, and again from 1989–1993.

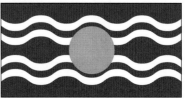

Flag of the West Indian Federation, designed by Edna Manley of Jamaica. The blue represented the Caribbean Sea and the yellow the sun.

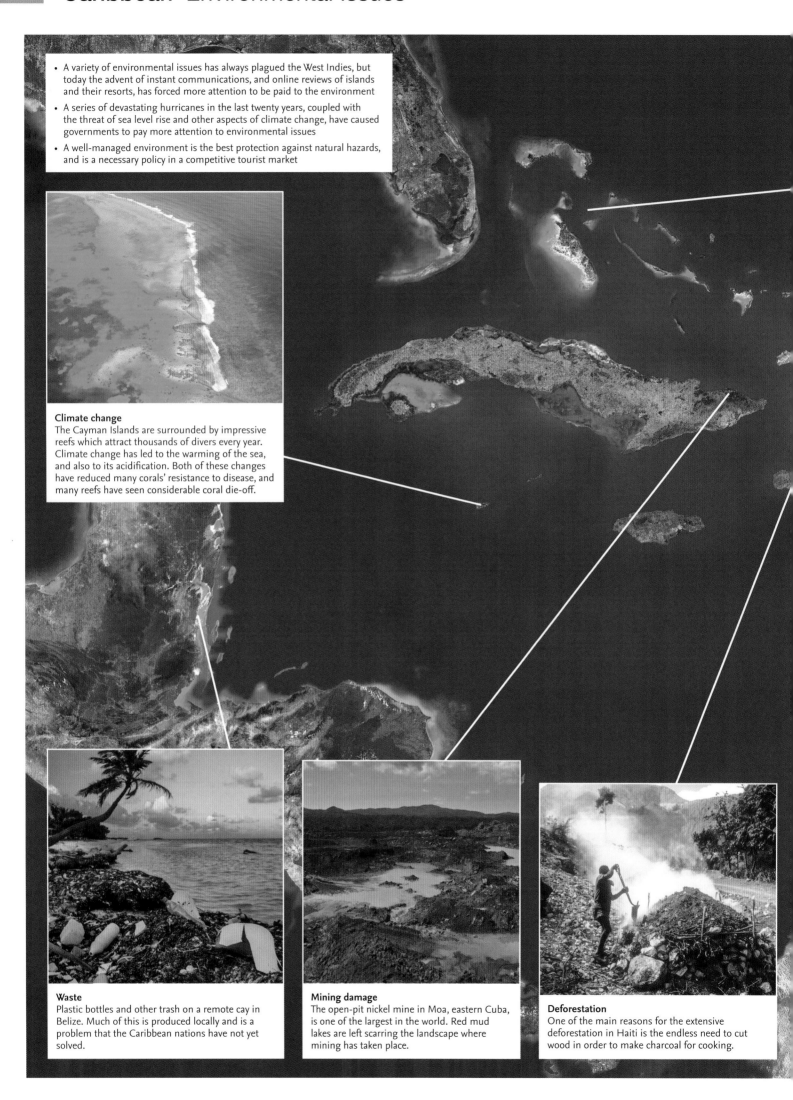

- A variety of environmental issues has always plagued the West Indies, but today the advent of instant communications, and online reviews of islands and their resorts, has forced more attention to be paid to the environment
- A series of devastating hurricanes in the last twenty years, coupled with the threat of sea level rise and other aspects of climate change, have caused governments to pay more attention to environmental issues
- A well-managed environment is the best protection against natural hazards, and is a necessary policy in a competitive tourist market

Climate change
The Cayman Islands are surrounded by impressive reefs which attract thousands of divers every year. Climate change has led to the warming of the sea, and also to its acidification. Both of these changes have reduced many corals' resistance to disease, and many reefs have seen considerable coral die-off.

Waste
Plastic bottles and other trash on a remote cay in Belize. Much of this is produced locally and is a problem that the Caribbean nations have not yet solved.

Mining damage
The open-pit nickel mine in Moa, eastern Cuba, is one of the largest in the world. Red mud lakes are left scarring the landscape where mining has taken place.

Deforestation
One of the main reasons for the extensive deforestation in Haiti is the endless need to cut wood in order to make charcoal for cooking.

Invasive species

The **cane toad** is a native of South America, but was introduced into the Eastern Caribbean as long ago as the 19th century. It is an omnivore and will eat small animals, as well as being poisonous (including its tadpoles). As recently as 2013 it had invaded The Bahamas.

The **casuarina** (commonly called the Australian pine) is widespread in the Caribbean, where it suppresses the native vegetation and can cause beach erosion. This stand on Paradise Island in The Bahamas has since been removed.

The **lionfish** is an Indo-Pacific species that is a voracious carnivore with poisonous spines. It has invaded the entire Caribbean, probably starting from the US coast, where some are believed to have escaped from an aquarium, then spreading south through The Bahamas. It can be eaten and this is one way of reducing its numbers.

Endangered species
Whale-watching is a popular tourist attraction on many Caribbean islands from the Turks and Caicos to Dominica and St Lucia. Unfortunately many whales, like this humpback, are endangered.

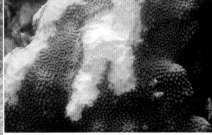

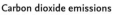

Wind power
Aruba is blessed with strong winds throughout the year. Power from wind turbines has reduced its energy costs and dependence on oil.

Coral reef damage
Coral bleaching is the effect of any disease causing the coral to die and leave a white patch on its skeleton, as seen by this example from Curaçao. This has seriously affected all the Caribbean reefs and the dive tourist industry.

Carbon dioxide emissions
Trinidad and Tobago has one of the highest amounts of CO_2 emissions per person in the Caribbean – 25 tonnes per person in 2014, compared to the global average of 5. The former Netherlands Antilles is another high emitter; both areas have large oil refineries.

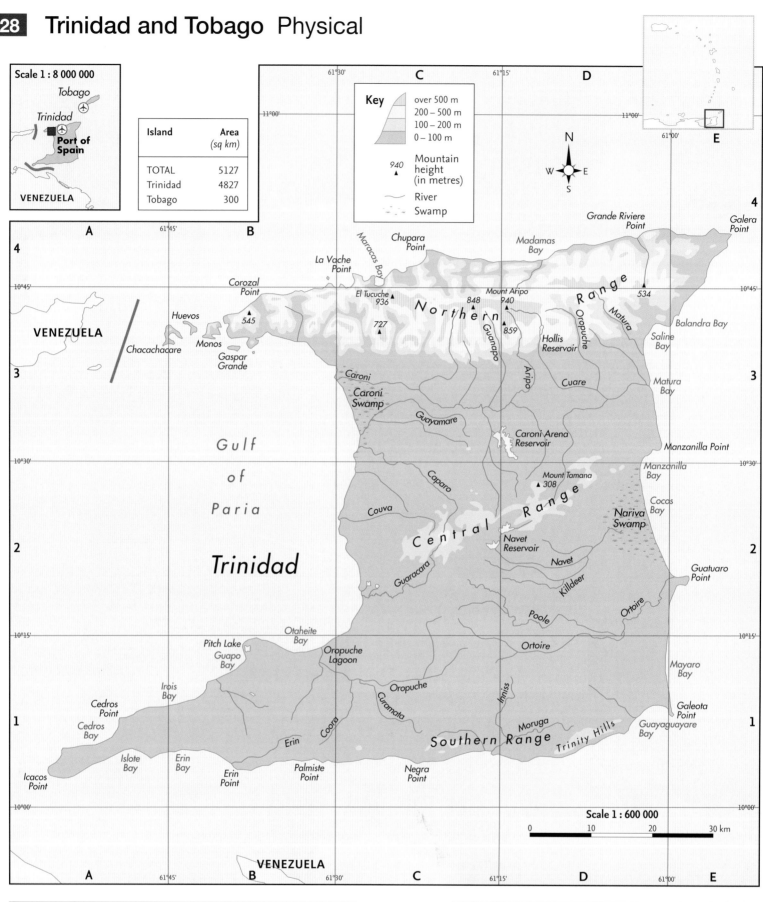

Scale 1 : 8 000 000

Tobago

Trinidad

Port of Spain

VENEZUELA

Island	Area (sq km)
TOTAL	5127
Trinidad	4827
Tobago	300

Key

over 500 m
200 – 500 m
100 – 200 m
0 – 100 m

940 ▲ Mountain height (in metres)

River

Swamp

Chupara Point

Madamas Bay

Grande Riviere Point

Galera Point

La Vache Point

Maracas Bay

Corozal Point

El Tucuche 936 ▲

Northern

Range

534 ▲

VENEZUELA

Huevos

Mount Aripo 940 ▲

848 ▲

859 ▲

Balandra Bay

Chacachacare

Monos

Gaspar Grande

727 ▲

545 ▲

Guanapo

Aripo

Hollis Reservoir

Oropuche

Matura

Saline Bay

Caroni

Caroni Swamp

Guayamare

Cuare

Matura Bay

Gulf

Caroni Arena Reservoir

Manzanilla Point

of

Caparo

Mount Tamana ▲ 308

C e n t r a l

Manzanilla Bay

Paria

Couva

R a n g e

Cocas Bay

Navet Reservoir

Nariva Swamp

Trinidad

Guaracara

Navet

Killdeer

Guatuaro Point

Poole

Ortoire

Otaheite Bay

Ortoire

Pitch Lake

Guapo Bay

Oropuche Lagoon

Ortoire

Mayaro Bay

Irois Bay

Oropuche

Inniss

Galeota Point

Cedros Point

Curamata

Moruga

Guayaguayare Bay

Cedros Bay

Erin

Coora

Southern Range

Trinity Hills

Islote Bay

Erin Bay

Erin Point

Palmiste Point

Negra Point

Icacos Point

VENEZUELA

Scale 1 : 600 000

0   10   20   30 km

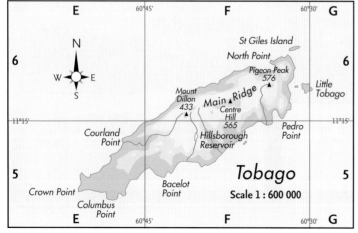

St Giles Island

North Point

Pigeon Peak 576 ▲

Little Tobago

Mount Dillon 433 ▲

Main Ridge

Centre Hill 565 ▲

Pedro Point

Courland Point

Hillsborough Reservoir

Crown Point

Bacolet Point

Tobago

Scale 1 : 600 000

Columbus Point

A satellite image of the islands of Trinidad and Tobago. The areas of land which can be seen in the west and southwest are Venezuela.

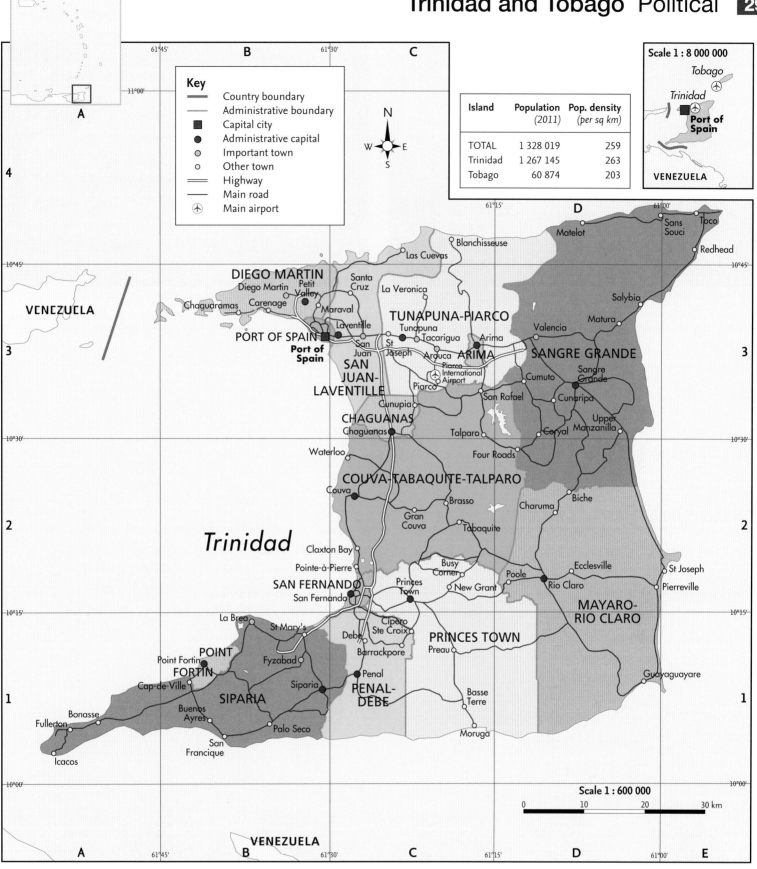

Key
- Country boundary
- Administrative boundary
- ■ Capital city
- ● Administrative capital
- ◔ Important town
- ○ Other town
- Highway
- Main road
- ✈ Main airport

Scale 1 : 8 000 000

Island	Population (2011)	Pop. density (per sq km)
TOTAL	1 328 019	259
Trinidad	1 267 145	263
Tobago	60 874	203

VENEZUELA

Trinidad

Scale 1 : 600 000
0   10   20   30 km

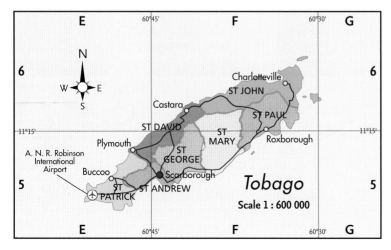

Tobago
Scale 1 : 600 000

Trinidad Counties

Trinidad has a surviving historical legacy of administrative divisions – eight counties – which were replaced in the early 1990s with fourteen regional corporations and municipalities. These are often still referred to, and still play a role in government activities.

Scale 1 : 1 000 000

Maracas Bay, on the north coast of Trinidad, is about an hour's drive through the mountains from Port of Spain.

Port of Spain is the capital city of Trinidad and Tobago.

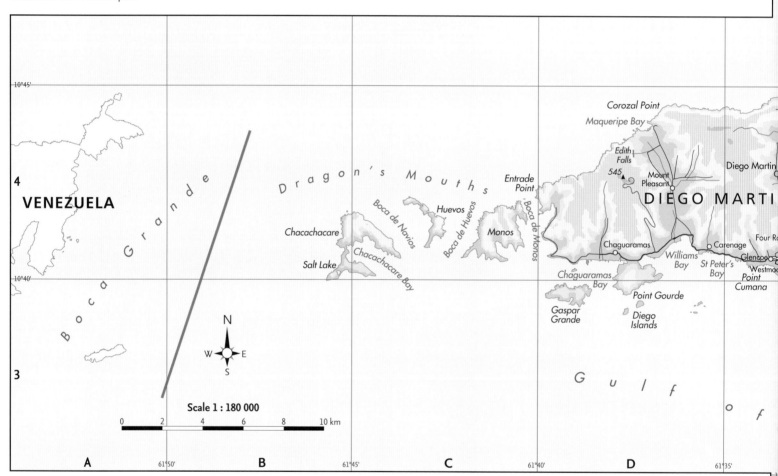

Average rainfall

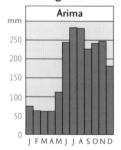
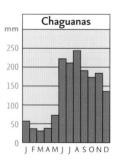
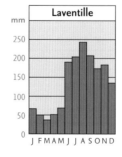
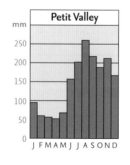
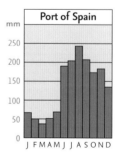
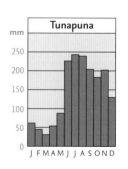

Average temperature

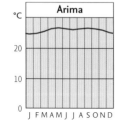
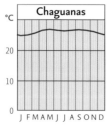
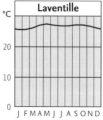
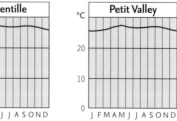
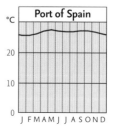
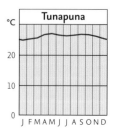

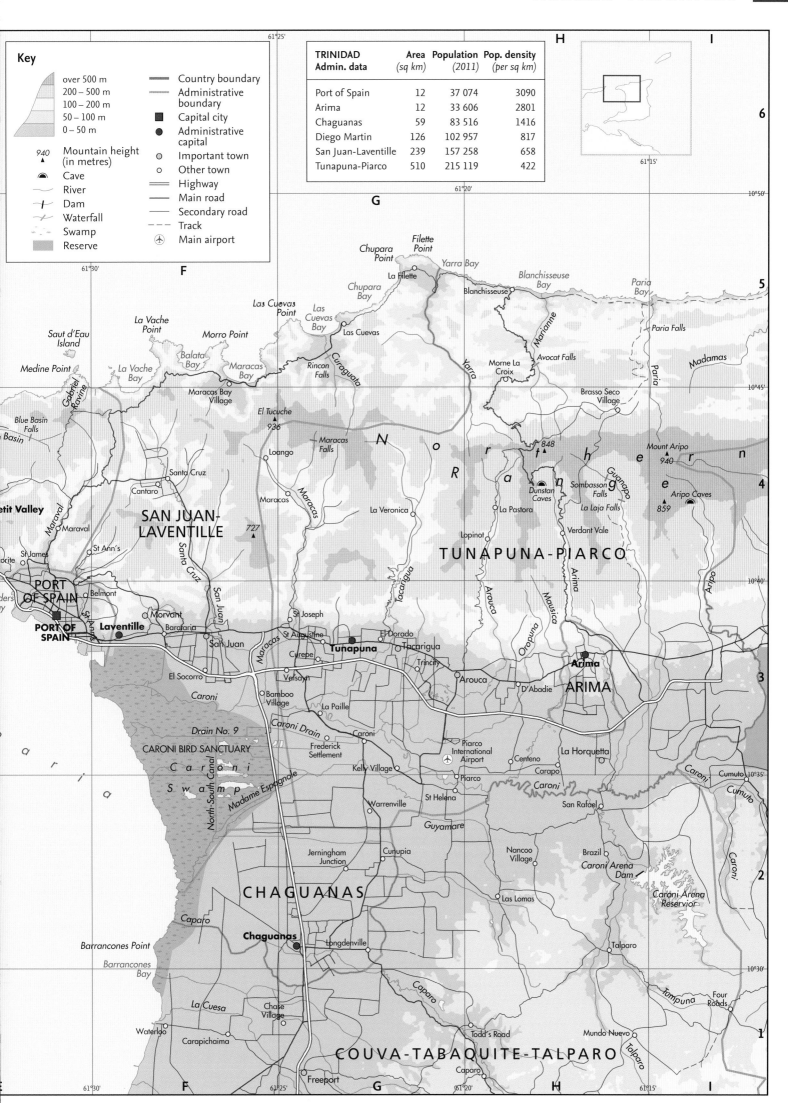

Key

| over 500 m |
| 200 – 500 m |
| 100 – 200 m |
| 50 – 100 m |
| 0 – 50 m |

940 ▲ Mountain height (in metres)

◓ Cave

◞ River

↦ Dam

↦ Waterfall

Swamp

Reserve

═══ Country boundary

┈┈┈ Administrative boundary

■ Capital city

● Administrative capital

◉ Important town

○ Other town

═══ Highway

─── Main road

─── Secondary road

╌╌╌ Track

✈ Main airport

TRINIDAD Admin. data	Area (sq km)	Population (2011)	Pop. density (per sq km)
Port of Spain	12	37 074	3090
Arima	12	33 606	2801
Chaguanas	59	83 516	1416
Diego Martin	126	102 957	817
San Juan-Laventille	239	157 258	658
Tunapuna-Piarco	510	215 119	422

Average rainfall

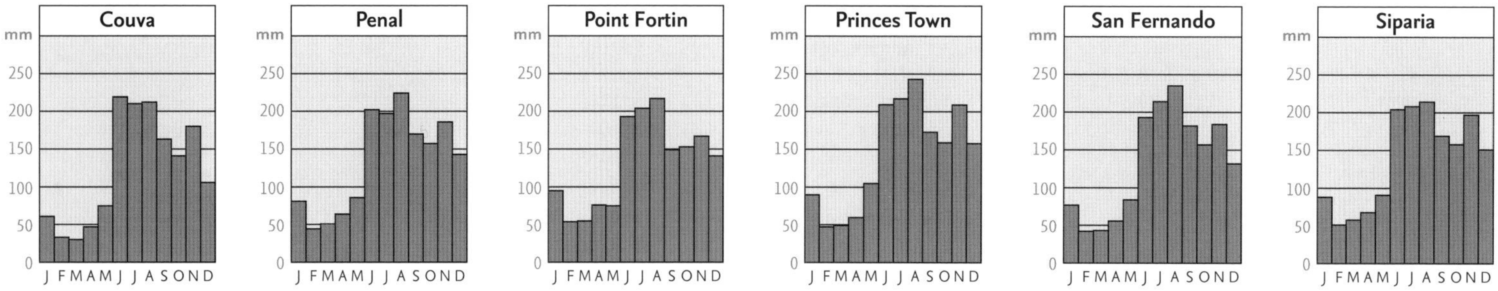

Couva	Penal	Point Fortin	Princes Town	San Fernando	Siparia

Average temperature

Couva	Penal	Point Fortin	Princes Town	San Fernando	Siparia

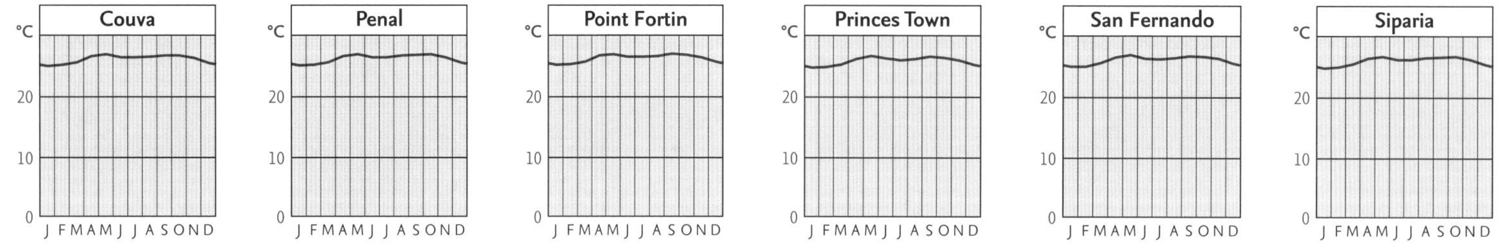

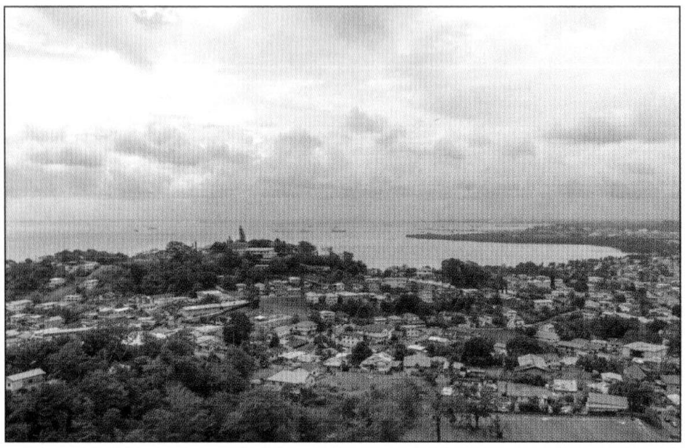

San Fernando, on the southwest coast, is known as the industrial capital.

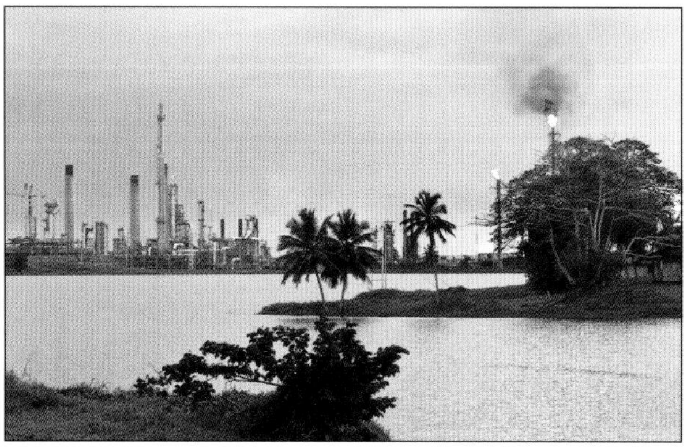

A methanol plant at Point Lisas, near San Fernando.

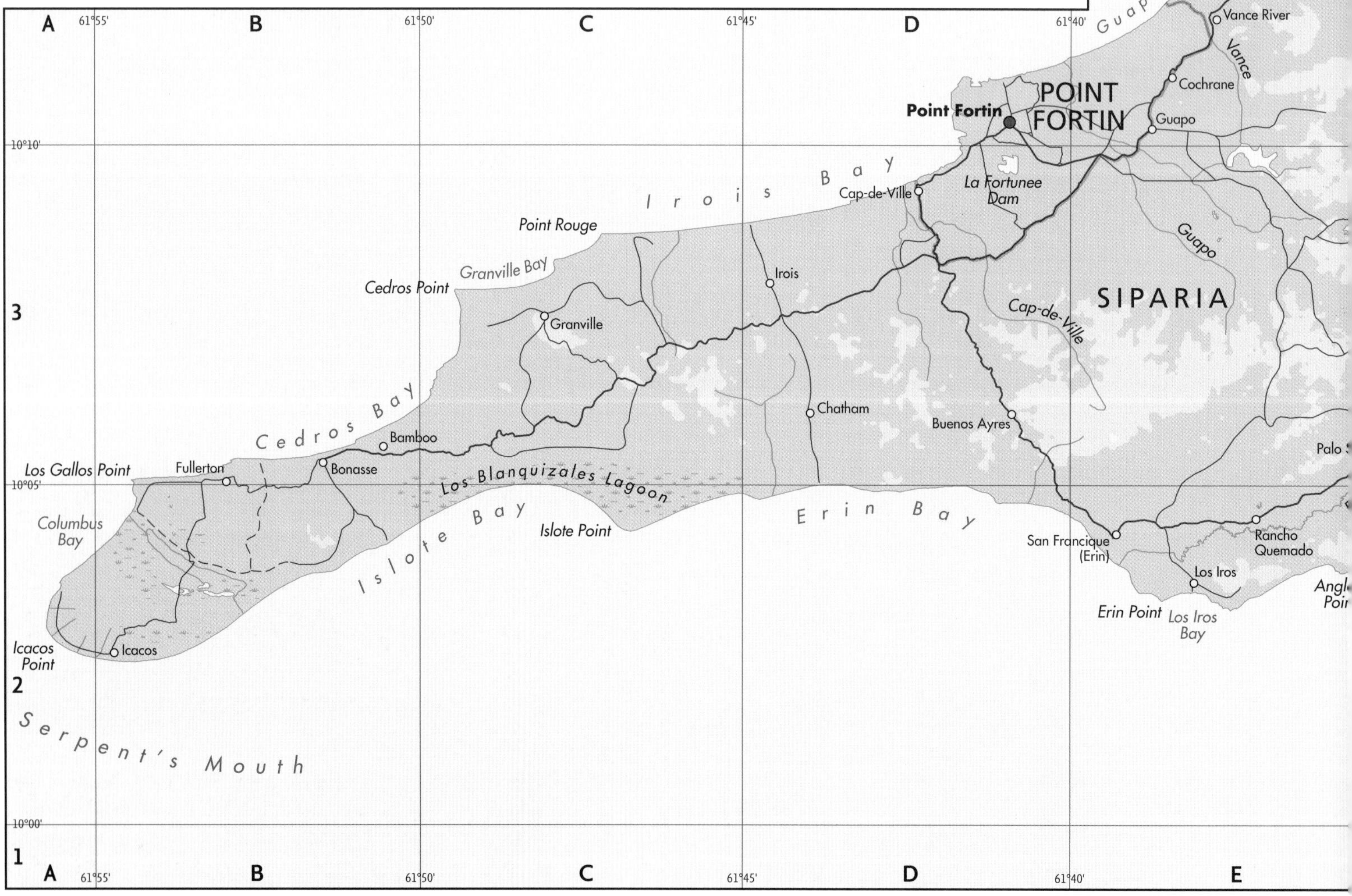

Pitch Point

Pitch Lake   La Brea   Rou Sw

Vessigny

Vance River

Cochrane

POINT FORTIN

Point Fortin   Guapo

Cap-de-Ville   La Fortunee Dam   Guapo

Irois Bay

Irois

SIPARIA

Cap-de-Ville

Point Rouge

Granville Bay

Cedros Point

Granville

Chatham   Buenos Ayres   Palo S

Cedros Bay

Bamboo

Los Gallos Point   Fullerton   Bonasse

Los Blanquizales Lagoon

Islote Bay   Islote Point   Erin Bay

Columbus Bay

San Francique (Erin)   Rancho Quemado

Angl Poir

Los Iros

Icacos Point   Icacos

Erin Point   Los Iros Bay

Serpent's Mouth

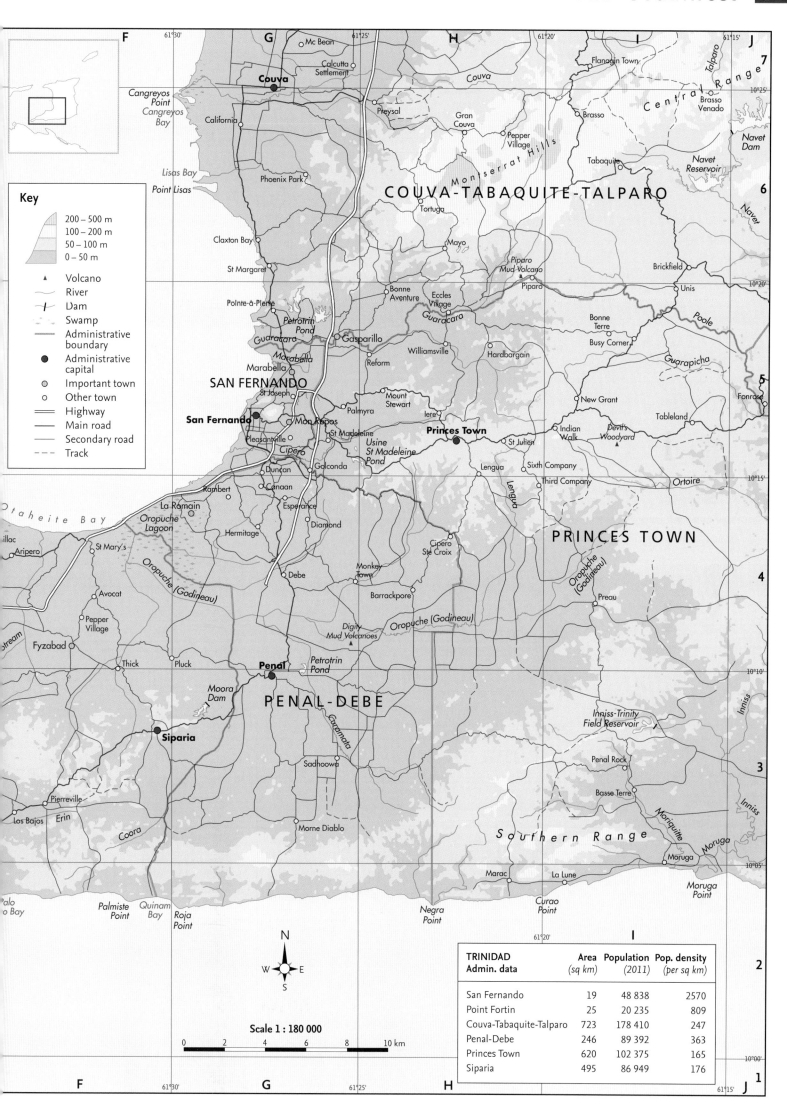

Key

200 – 500 m
100 – 200 m
50 – 100 m
0 – 50 m

▲ Volcano
River
Dam
Swamp
Administrative boundary
● Administrative capital
◉ Important town
○ Other town
Highway
Main road
Secondary road
Track

Scale 1 : 180 000

0   2   4   6   8   10 km

TRINIDAD Admin. data	Area (sq km)	Population (2011)	Pop. density (per sq km)
San Fernando	19	48 838	2570
Point Fortin	25	20 235	809
Couva-Tabaquite-Talparo	723	178 410	247
Penal-Debe	246	89 392	363
Princes Town	620	102 375	165
Siparia	495	86 949	176

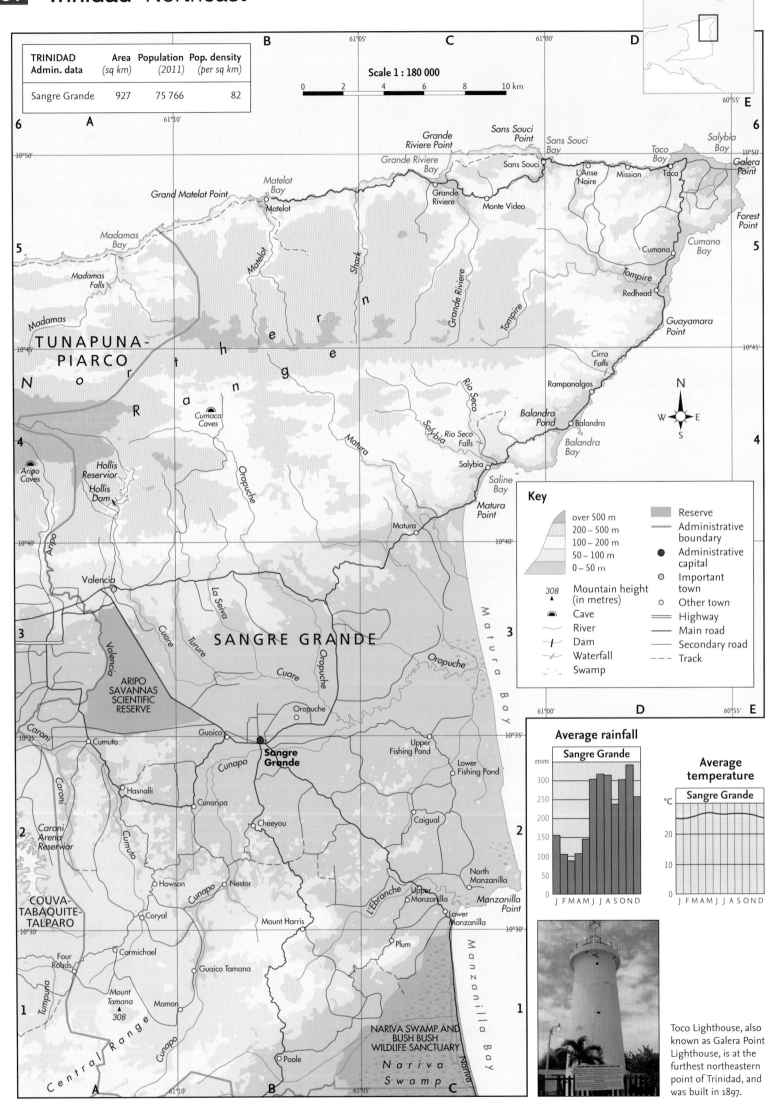

TRINIDAD Admin. data	Area (sq km)	Population (2011)	Pop. density (per sq km)
Sangre Grande	927	75 766	82

Scale 1 : 180 000

0 2 4 6 8 10 km

Key

over 500 m
200 – 500 m
100 – 200 m
50 – 100 m
0 – 50 m

308 ▲ Mountain height (in metres)

Cave

River

Dam

Waterfall

Swamp

Reserve

Administrative boundary

● Administrative capital

◉ Important town

○ Other town

Highway

Main road

Secondary road

Track

Average rainfall

Sangre Grande

mm
300
250
200
150
100
50
0
J F M A M J J A S O N D

Average temperature

Sangre Grande

°C
20
10
0
J F M A M J J A S O N D

Toco Lighthouse, also known as Galera Point Lighthouse, is at the furthest northeastern point of Trinidad, and was built in 1897.

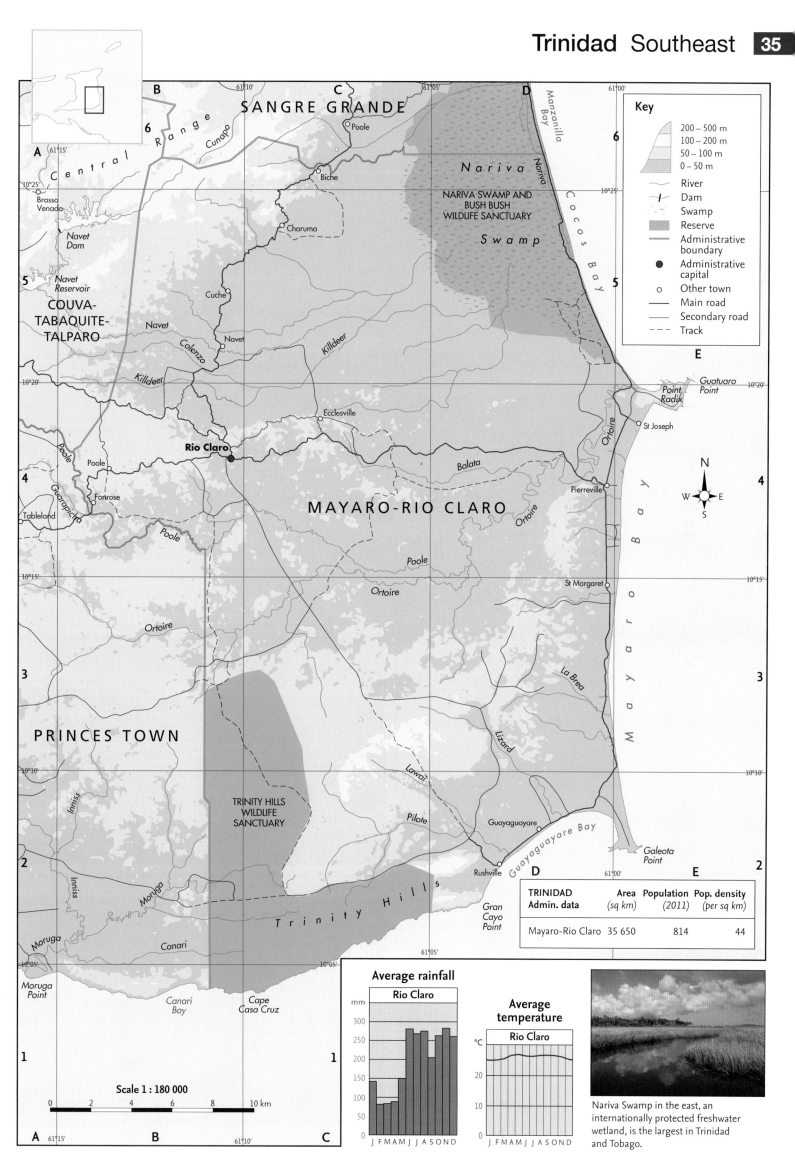

Key

	200 – 500 m
	100 – 200 m
	50 – 100 m
	0 – 50 m
	River
	Dam
	Swamp
	Reserve
	Administrative boundary
●	Administrative capital
○	Other town
	Main road
	Secondary road
	Track

SANGRE GRANDE

Central Range

Cunapo

Poole

Biche

Charuma

Navet Dam

Navet Reservoir

COUVA-TABAQUITE-TALPARO

Brasso Venado

Navet

Colenzo

Cuche

Killdeer

Navet

Killdeer

Nariva

NARIVA SWAMP AND BUSH BUSH WILDLIFE SANCTUARY

Nariva Swamp

Manzanilla Bay

Cocos Bay

Ecclesville

Rio Claro

Poole

Poole

Fonrose

Tableland

Guaracicha

Poole

Balata

Ortoire

MAYARO-RIO CLARO

Poole

Ortoire

Ortoire

Point Radix

Guatuaro Point

St Joseph

Pierreville

St Margaret

Mayaro Bay

PRINCES TOWN

Ortoire

Inniss

La Brea

Lizard

Lawai

Pilote

TRINITY HILLS WILDLIFE SANCTUARY

Moruga

Inniss

Canari

Trinity Hills

Guayaguayare

Rushville

Guayaguayare Bay

Gran Cayo Point

Galeota Point

Moruga

Moruga Point

Canari Bay

Cape Casa Cruz

N
W E
S

TRINIDAD Admin. data	Area (sq km)	Population (2011)	Pop. density (per sq km)
Mayaro-Rio Claro	35 650	814	44

Scale 1 : 180 000

0   2   4   6   8   10 km

Average rainfall
Rio Claro

mm
300
250
200
150
100
50
0
J F M A M J J A S O N D

Average temperature
Rio Claro

°C
20
10
J F M A M J J A S O N D

Nariva Swamp in the east, an internationally protected freshwater wetland, is the largest in Trinidad and Tobago.

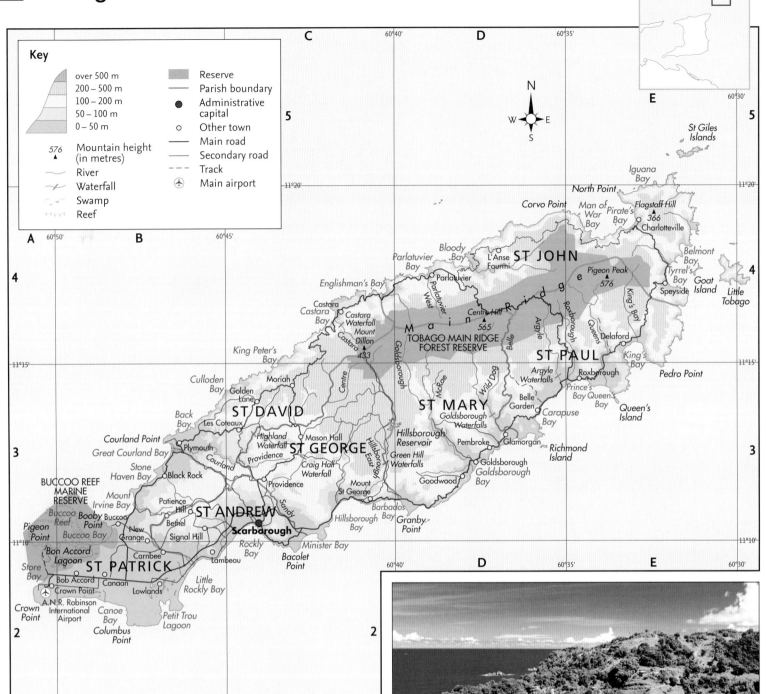

Key

over 500 m	
200 – 500 m	
100 – 200 m	
50 – 100 m	
0 – 50 m	

576 ▲ Mountain height (in metres)

~~~ River

Waterfall

Swamp

Reef

Reserve
Parish boundary
● Administrative capital
○ Other town
—— Main road
—— Secondary road
--- Track
✈ Main airport

Scale 1 : 165 000

0 2 4 6 8 10 km

Average rainfall

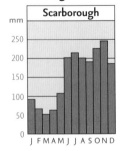

Scarborough

mm
250
200
150
100
50
J F M A M J J A S O N D

Average temperature

°C

Scarborough

20

10

0
J F M A M J J A S O N D

TOBAGO Parish data	Area (sq km)	Population (2011)	Pop. density (per sq km)
St Andrew	21	17 536	835
St David	38	8733	230
St George	43	6875	160
St John	55	2825	51
St Mary	56	3297	59
St Patrick	38	15 560	409
St Paul	49	6048	123

The natural enclosure of Parlatuvier Bay on the north coast of Tobago is popular with visitors.

Fort King George, Scarborough, was in military use on the island from 1777 to 1854, and has recently been refurbished.

National symbols

National emblems are a reminder of a country's goals, values and history. They are reminders to citizens to respect the heritage of their country and ongoing development.

Trinidad and Tobago has five national emblems:
- the **coat of arms**, which represents the country
- the **national flag**, which represents the philosophy and principles of the country
- the **national flower**, the double Chaconia, which represents the last and most progressive Spanish governor of Trinidad, Don José María Chacón (1784–97)
- the **national birds**, the Scarlet Ibis (which represents Trinidad) and the Cocrico (which represents Tobago)
- the **steelpan drum**.

Flag

The flag of Trinidad and Tobago uses **red** to represent the vitality of the land and its people, the warmth and energy of the sun, and the courage and friendliness of the people; **white** to represent the sea, the purity of the country's aspirations, and the equality of all people; and **black** to represent the dedication of the people joined together; strength, unity and the wealth of the land.

Coat of arms

The top of the coat of arms has a ship's steering wheel with a **palm tree** above it. On the shield, the colours of the national flag – **black, white and red** – are arranged in an upward-pointing chevron shape and contain images of hummingbirds at the top and the Santa Maria, Nina and Pinta below. The national birds – the **Scarlet Ibis** on the left and the **Cocrico** on the right – stand to either side of the shield. At the base of the coat of arms are the **two islands**, rising out of the sea. The national motto – **Together we aspire, Together we achieve** – is at the bottom of the coat of arms.

Birds

The national bird of Trinidad is the Scarlet Ibis. The largest habitat of the Scarlet Ibis is the Caroni Swamp in central Trinidad. Like the flamingo, the Scarlet Ibis gets its red colour from its diet of red shellfish.

The national bird of Tobago is the Cocrico (*Rufous-vented chachalaca*), also known as the Tobago pheasant. It is a loud bird, with a dawn and evening call. It is said that the bird was named Cocrico because of the sound it makes.

Flower

The Chaconia, also known as the "wild poinsettia" or "Pride of Trinidad and Tobago", is a flaming red forest flower that usually blooms around the time of the nation's anniversary of independence.

Steelpan drums

The steelpan is a musical instrument, first created in Trinidad and Tobago. Traditionally made from a steel drum or container, it is a percussion instrument. The playing surface is divided into convex sections: each section is a note tuned to a particular pitch. Its origins date to the 1930s and 40s.

Pledge

I solemnly pledge
To dedicate my life
To the service of my God
And my country.
I will honour
My parents, my teachers,
My leaders and my elders
And those in authority.
I will be Clean and honest
In all my thoughts,
My words and my deeds.
I will strive in everything I do
To work together with my fellowmen
Of every creed and race
For the greater happiness of all
And the honour and glory
Of my country.

Anthem

Forged from the love of liberty
In the fires of hope and prayer
With boundless faith in our destiny
We solemnly declare:
Side by side we stand
Islands of the blue Caribbean Sea,
This our native land
We pledge our lives to thee.
Here every creed and race find an equal place,
And may God bless our nation.
Here every creed and race find an equal place,
And may God bless our nation.

Government structure

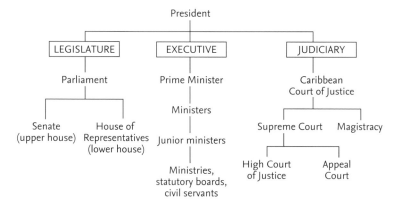

The government of Trinidad and Tobago is divided into three branches – the **legislature**, the **executive** and the **judiciary**.

The Legislature
The Legislature is the **Parliament** of the Republic of Trinidad and Tobago. It consists of two houses, the Upper House (**Senate**), which is presided over by the **President**, and the Lower House (**House of Representatives**). The Legislature makes laws to ensure peace, order and good governance in the state.

The Executive
The Executive is made up of Members of the **Cabinet**. It consists of the **Prime Minister**, or head of government, and the other junior ministers and civil servants. The Cabinet controls the government but is responsible to Parliament.

The Judiciary
The Judiciary ensures that the laws are interpreted and applied fairly. These are the responsibilities of the court system.

First people

The **first people** of Trinidad and Tobago were the **Amerindians**, who settled on the islands roughly 18 000 years ago after migrating from their original settlements in Siberia. First people are the first known population of a place, usually indigenous people.

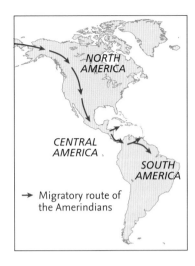

→ Migratory route of the Amerindians

The Caribs and Arawaks

Between 2000 and 2500 years ago, a new group of Amerindians travelled to Trinidad and Tobago from Venezuela. These were the **Caribs** (or Kalinago tribe) and **Arawaks** (or the Taino tribe).

The Caribs lived in the north and west of Trinidad in settlements like Arima and Mucurapo. The Arawaks lived in the southeast and in Tobago. The Arawaks were a peaceful tribe, who were often attacked by the more warlike Caribs. Both established their settlements along the coast, near rivers and at the top of hills.

The indigenous Amerindians' food came from crops such as cassava, maize, potatoes, tomatoes, beans and fruits. They also fished and hunted animals. Cotton was grown to make clothes and bedding, as well as tobacco, which they smoked or chewed. The name Tobago comes from the word tobacco, which shows how important this crop was to them.

A canoe being used by Island Caribs.

European presence in Tobago

Christopher Columbus arriving in the Caribbean and presenting the local people with gifts.

The Spanish had been the first Europeans to become aware of the existence of Trinidad and Tobago when Columbus came across the islands in 1498. He named Trinidad 'La Trinity.' Some Spanish settlers came to live on La Trinity, but the Spanish did not show much interest in either La Trinity or Tobago. After that, various other European powers laid claim to Tobago at different times.

The Assembly of Tobago provided some degree of self-government, although only a small percentage of the population could vote for the elected deputies. Out of every 100 people who lived on the island, 94 were African slaves, who had been brought to the island to work on the plantations.

In 1793, Tobago was captured by the British. The running of the island was given over to the British Crown. All male inhabitants had to take an oath of allegiance to the British Crown, and those who did not were regarded as prisoners of war. In 1802, Tobago was given back to the French, only to be recaptured by the British again the following year. In 1833, Tobago became part of the Windward Islands.

Tobago was a prosperous island as a result of the tobacco plantations and later the sugar and cotton plantations. Slaves were brought from Africa to work on the plantations. Tobago traded with Guyana and Barbados more than with Trinidad.

Location of indigenous peoples' settlements in Tobago

It is known that some Amerindian inhabitants lived close to the mangrove swamps of Bon Accord in the southwest part of Tobago. Some stone artefacts found at this site suggest that Amerindians lived there in approximately 3500/3000 BC. Other important settlements in Tobago include Golden Grove, Courland River, Friendship and Mount Irvine, all in the southwest of Tobago, which were probably inhabited in the period c.300 BC – 650/800 AD. By the time of Columbus' arrival in Tobago, the island was only inhabited by one Amerindian ethnic group – the Caribs. The map shows the location of their settlements on the island.

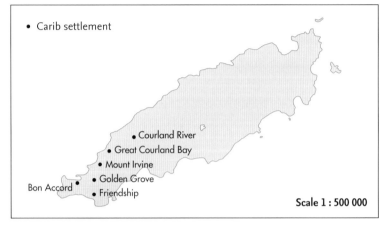

- Carib settlement
- Courland River
- Great Courland Bay
- Mount Irvine
- Golden Grove
- Bon Accord
- Friendship

Scale 1 : 500 000

Treatment of the Amerindians in Trinidad

On his arrival in 1498, Columbus claimed Trinidad as a Spanish colony. His view was that Trinidad now belonged to the Spanish and that the Amerindians had no right to own the land. It took the Spanish almost 100 years before they could make a permanent settlement in Trinidad (in 1592). This was largely because the Amerindians resisted the Spanish and fought back against their occupation.

The Spanish stayed in power in Trinidad until 1797, when they were pushed out by the British. By this time there were very few Amerindians left in either Trinidad or Tobago. Although the Amerindians were not treated as slaves – as the African immigrants would be later on – they were not treated well on either island:
- Thousands died from diseases brought to the islands by the Spanish.
- Others died from being overworked on the Spanish cocoa estates and tobacco plantations.
- Some Amerindians were transported to work in other Spanish colonies.
- Some Amerindians fled to Venezuela or Guyana.

Soon, the numbers of Amerindians in Trinidad began to decline quite dramatically, and by 1800 they were almost extinct.

Tobago timeline

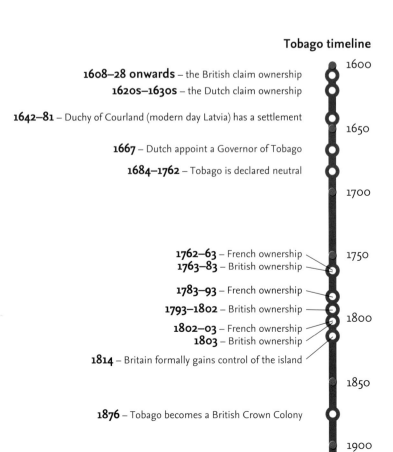

1608–28 onwards – the British claim ownership
1620s–1630s – the Dutch claim ownership

1642–81 – Duchy of Courland (modern day Latvia) has a settlement

1667 – Dutch appoint a Governor of Tobago

1684–1762 – Tobago is declared neutral

1762–63 – French ownership
1763–83 – British ownership

1783–93 – French ownership
1793–1802 – British ownership
1802–03 – French ownership
1803 – British ownership

1814 – Britain formally gains control of the island

1876 – Tobago becomes a British Crown Colony

1600
1650
1700
1750
1800
1850
1900

European settlers

The first European settlers to arrive in Trinidad came from Spain. Spanish explorers sailed into the Caribbean looking for new lands and for gold and silver. Christopher Columbus landed in Trinidad in 1498. For the next 300 years the Spanish ruled Trinidad and they introduced the religion of Roman Catholicism. In 1783, the Spanish encouraged French settlers from other Caribbean islands to come and settle in Trinidad to develop the plantations. In 1797, British forces captured Trinidad. Trinidad was ruled by the British until 1962, when it became an independent country. English replaced French Creole as the most important language, and the Protestant religion was established. The people on the islands developed a lasting love for the sports of cricket and football. The British, the Dutch and the Courland Duchy (Latvia) fought over Tobago for many years before they left.

Migration to Trinidad and Tobago

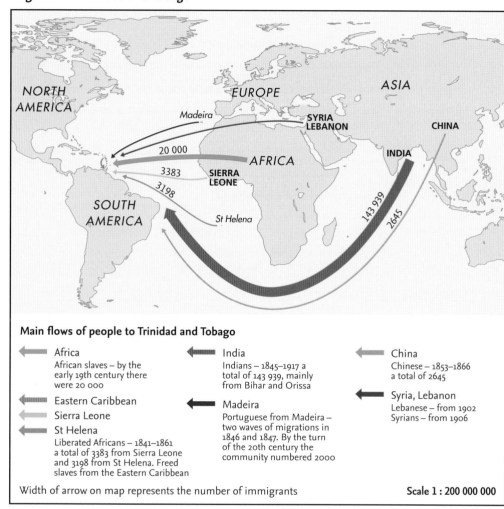

Main flows of people to Trinidad and Tobago

Africa
African slaves – by the early 19th century there were 20 000

Eastern Caribbean

Sierra Leone

St Helena
Liberated Africans – 1841–1861 a total of 3383 from Sierra Leone and 3198 from St Helena. Freed slaves from the Eastern Caribbean

India
Indians – 1845–1917 a total of 143 939, mainly from Bihar and Orissa

Madeira
Portuguese from Madeira – two waves of migrations in 1846 and 1847. By the turn of the 20th century the community numbered 2000

China
Chinese – 1853–1866 a total of 2645

Syria, Lebanon
Lebanese – from 1902
Syrians – from 1906

Width of arrow on map represents the number of immigrants   Scale 1 : 200 000 000

Columbus and his men landing on a Caribbean island.

British colonial period

By 1876, Trinidad was a British **Crown Colony**. The British appointed a **Governor**, who represented the British Crown and under the Crown Colony the Governor had legislative, executive and judicial powers. The people on the island became subject to British law. Trinidad brought great wealth to British companies and to the British government, and it remained a British Colony until **Independence** in 1962.

Cane cutting in Trinidad.

In the first half of the 19th century, sugar was the main industry in Trinidad. After emancipation in 1834, many of the ex-slaves moved away from the plantations. A labour shortage led to the indentureship of immigrants, which helped the sugar industry to remain prosperous. However, by the 1880s, the sugar industry in Trinidad was also in decline.

The Transatlantic slave trade

The transatlantic slave trade was the deportation of people from Africa to the American continent to be sold as slaves in the 18th century. In this period, most of the African people who moved to Trinidad and Tobago came as slaves to provide labour for the sugar plantations.

Until 1780 there were only a few African slaves. When the French settlers arrived from other Caribbean countries they brought slaves and freedmen with them who had been born in the Caribbean. These slaves worked on the plantations. When the sugar industry became more important, and more plantations were started, more labour was needed to work on them, so slaves were brought from Africa.

The African slaves came from Central and West Africa. They came from the Hausa, Yoruba, Congolese, Igbo and Malinké communities. By 1802 there were more than 20 000 African slaves working in Trinidad and Tobago. Today, about 35% of Trinibagonians are of African descent.

Newly arrived indentured labourers from India in Trinidad.

Timeline (slavery and colonialism)

1498 – Christopher Columbus arrives in Trinidad

1583 – Spanish appoint a governor in Trinidad

17th century – Dutch and Duchy of Courland make several attempts to settle in Trinidad and Tobago

1610 – Around 400 African slaves arrive

1783 – Slaves from other Caribbean countries arrive with French settlers

1797 – British capture Trinidad. Spanish surrender. The number of African slaves in Trinidad is 10 000

1802 – Number of African slaves increases to around 20 000

1838 – Slavery is abolished

1839 – First European immigrants arrive

1845 – First Indian labourers arrive aboard the ship *Fatel Razack*

1853-66 – Chinese immigrants arrive

1917 – System of indentured labour comes to an end

1450
1500
1550
1600
1650
1700
1750
1800
1850
1900

Trinidad and Tobago is a republic

A **republic** is a country where the monarch has been replaced by a President as head of state.

Trinidad and Tobago became a republic on 1 August 1976. The table shows a list of the Presidents and Prime Ministers of Trinidad and Tobago and the dates of their terms of office since it became a republic.

Sir Ellis Clarke

Presidents	Prime Ministers
Sir Ellis Clarke (1976–87)	Dr Eric Williams (1976–81)
	George Chambers (1981–86)
Noor Hassanali (1987–97)	A.N.R. Robinson (1986–91)
A.N.R. Robinson (1997–2003)	Patrick Manning (1991–95, 2001–10)
George Maxwell Richards (2003–13)	Basdeo Panday (1995–2001)
Anthony Carmona (2013–2018)	Kamla Persad-Bissessar (2010–15)
Paula-Mae Weekes (2018–present)	Keith Rowley (2015–present)

- The President is the Head of State and Commander in Chief of the Armed Forces of Trinidad and Tobago. The President exercises power in consultation with the Cabinet, including the Prime Minister and the leader of the Opposition in Parliament. The President is elected by the people for a period of five years and has to sign and agree to all bills before they become laws.
- The Prime Minister leads the government and is assisted by a Cabinet.
- The Prime Minister is appointed by the President and is usually the leader of the political party that won the most seats in the House of Representatives in the general election. They form the Executive branch of the government.

The electoral process in Trinidad and Tobago

The government of Trinidad and Tobago is a **representative democracy**, which means that people are elected by voters to serve in the government. **Elections** are held regularly to choose people who will serve in national and local government.

The **electorate** is all the people in the country who are eligible and registered to vote in an election. In the 2010 election in Trinidad and Tobago, 1 040 127 people registered to vote, but only 722 322 people (69%) actually voted.

There are two main types of electoral system: the **first-past-the post** system and the **proportional representation** system. The difference between the two revolves around how votes are counted and the way candidates win elections. The first-past-the-post system is used to elect Members to the House of Representatives in Trinidad and Tobago.

The party that wins the majority of seats in Parliament wins the overall election and therefore forms the government. The Prime Minister is selected from the winning party and the leader of the opposition is selected from the party with the second-highest number of seats.

Independence

Trinidad and Tobago achieved independence on 31 August 1962 and took control of its political and economic affairs, both locally and internationally. Instead of a Governor from Britain, the country now had a Governor-General, who had to be a local citizen. Citizens of Trinidad and Tobago drafted their own Constitution, without being controlled by the British.

Dr Eric Williams, known as the 'Father of the Nation', made a huge contribution to the nation when he led Trinidad and Tobago to independence.

Some of his achievements include:
- free secondary education from 1962 onwards
- the building of many new schools from 1970 onwards
- new infrastructure, including roads and Piarco International Airport, and the improvement of water, electricity, sanitation, housing and health care facilities
- funding for many cultural projects, including Carnival, steelband, dance, drama and sports.

Trinidad and Tobago flag

As a result of his work, Trinidad and Tobago became a republic on 1 August 1976. This ensured the full control of the national and international affairs of the country by the country and its citizens. The country's leaders drafted a new Constitution and Sir Ellis Clarke was elected the first President of the Republic of Trinidad and Tobago to replace the Governor-General.

Dr Eric Williams

The vote in Trinidad and Tobago

From 1797, Trinidad and Tobago was under **Crown Colony** rule from the British. This system had a Governor and a Legislative Council which was made up of people nominated by the Governor. Under this system, citizens did not have the right to vote.

By the 1920s, Trinidad and Tobago had a **limited franchise** system. This means that only some of the people were allowed to take part: men had to be over 21, women had to be over 30, they had to earn a high income or have property above a certain value and had to understand the English language. These rules meant that only about 10% of the population could vote in elections.

After civil disturbances in the 1930s, the call to reform the voting system increased. Finally, in 1945, the right to vote was granted for all citizens over the age of 21. Citizens were allowed to vote in their first general election on 1 July 1946. The age was lowered to 18 in 1962, when Trinidad and Tobago gained independence.

The Caribbean Court of Justice

The **Caribbean Court of Justice (CCJ)** is located in Port of Spain, Trinidad and Tobago. The Court is the highest court of appeal on civil and criminal matters for the national courts of Barbados, Belize, Dominica and Guyana. The CCJ helps to reinforce regional integration by settling commercial disputes. It also brings a single vision to the development of law in the Caribbean region, which has lots of different cultures and historical backgrounds.

As of December 2017, the CCJ has seven judges from St Kitts and Nevis (the President), St Vincent, the United Kingdom, the Netherlands Antilles and Jamaica, and two judges from Trinidad and Tobago.

Tobago House of Assembly

In 1980, the Tobago House of Assembly (THA) was established to manage matters affecting Tobago. It is part of the local government of Trinidad and Tobago.

Some of the Assembly's functions are to:
- collect certain taxes and pay expenses
- promote and regulate tourism
- administer state lands including parks
- administer museums, historical sites and buildings
- promote and support sports, culture and the arts.

Tobago House of Assembly, Division of Sport and Youth Affairs building, Scarborough.

The constitution

Countries have regulations and laws. Laws are a system of rules by which a country is governed. The laws are usually made by the parliament of a country and they are based on the constitution of the country. A constitution is a set of general principles that are drawn up by a country and on which the laws of that country are based. For example, human rights principles, such as equality, may be included in the constitution. Laws are created after consultation with different stakeholders. Once consensus or compromise has been reached, the law can be used. Laws assist with decision-making and the resolution of conflicts.

A member of parliament introduces the bill.

The bill is made available to all members of parliament and to the public for consideration.

Members of the House of Representatives debate, **amend** and vote on the bill.

The bill is referred to a **committee**, who discuss the bill in more detail.

The bill is again discussed and voted on in the House of Representatives.

If the bill is passed (approved) it moves up to the Senate for further debate and amendment.

If approved by the Senate, the bill is sent to the president for signature. This is called **assent**.

The president signs the bill or **vetoes** it. If vetoed, the bill goes back to parliament for further discussion and amendment.

Countries of the Commonwealth Caribbean

The term Commonwealth Caribbean is used to refer to the independent English-speaking islands and dependent and mainland territories around the Caribbean Sea.

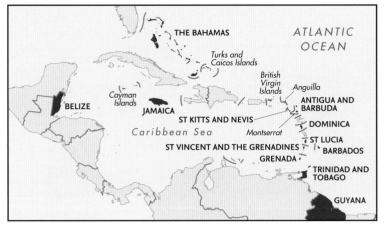

Each Commonwealth Caribbean country has its own flag. They are shown below.

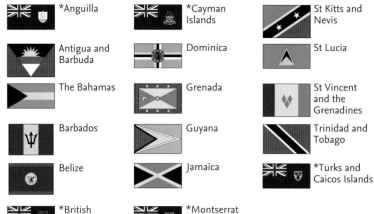

*British Overseas Territory

Physical factors of the Commonwealth Caribbean

- All the countries in the Commonwealth Caribbean are situated in and around the Caribbean Sea. This area has for a long time been a main passageway for ships moving between different continents. As a result, Caribbean islands were among the first to be colonised.
- All of the countries border on the Caribbean Sea and some countries, such as The Bahamas, also border on the Atlantic Ocean.
- The temperature of the Caribbean Sea is quite warm and averages between 21 and 30 degrees Celsius during the year.
- All of the islands share a tropical climate with average annual temperatures of around 25 degrees Celsius.
- The amount of rainfall is not the same on all the islands. The islands to the north tend to be drier than the islands to the south.
- The coastlines of the countries have similar characteristics as most have many natural harbours, bays, beaches, mangroves, cays and coral reefs.
- Trinidad and Tobago are the southernmost islands of the Caribbean archipelago, and are geologically an extension of the South American continent.

Social factors of the Commonwealth Caribbean

Many people in the Caribbean have a common ancestry. For example, it is estimated that more than 2.5 million people in the whole Caribbean region have their roots in India. This is as a result of East Indian people coming to work in the Caribbean sugar plantations as indentured labourers after the abolition of slavery. These workers brought their families to the Caribbean and they played an important part in the economic development of countries in the region.

Economic factors of the Commonwealth Caribbean

CARICOM is a wide association of Caribbean countries.
CARICOM has 15 main members:

- Antigua and Barbuda
- The Bahamas
- Barbados
- Belize
- Dominica
- Grenada
- Guyana
- Haiti
- Jamaica
- Montserrat
- St Kitts and Nevis
- St Lucia
- St Vincent and the Grenadines
- Suriname
- Trinidad and Tobago

Heads of state

The independent nations of the Commonwealth Caribbean have **Heads of State** and **Heads of Government** who are both elected by their own governments. The British Overseas Territories elect their own heads of government only. Queen Elizabeth II is the head of state of the British Overseas Territories.

The **independent** nations choose their own heads of state in different ways. Many heads of state have the title of **President**. The head of state does not have any political power.

The heads of government are elected into their roles through votes. Most heads of government are called **Prime Minister**, but some have other titles such as **President** or **Premier**. The heads of government change from time to time when there are elections.

Country	Capital	Head of government	Title	Status
Anguilla	The Valley	Hubert Hughes	Chief Minister	Dependent territory (UK)
Antigua and Barbuda	St John's	Gaston Browne	Prime Minister	Independent
The Bahamas	Nassau	Hubert Minnis	Prime Minister	Independent
Barbados	Bridgetown	Mi Amor Mottley	Prime Minister	Independent
Belize	Belmopan	Dean Barrow	Prime Minister	Independent
British Virgin Islands	Road Town	Andrew A. Fahie	Premier	Dependent territory (UK)
Cayman Islands	George Town	Aiden McLaughlin	Premier	Dependent territory (UK)
Dominica	Roseau	Roosevelt Skerrit	Prime Minister	Independent
Grenada	St George's	Keith Mitchell	Prime Minister	Independent
Guyana	Georgetown	David Arthur Granger	President	Independent/Mainland Caribbean
Haiti	Port-au-Prince	Jovenel Moise	President	Principal country and territory
Jamaica	Kingston	Andrew Holness	Prime Minister	Independent
Monserrat	Brades	Donaldson Romeo	Premier	Dependent territory (UK)
St Kitts and Nevis	Basseterre	Timothy Harris	Prime Minister	Independent
St Lucia	Castries	Allen Chastanet	Prime Minister	Independent
St Vincent and the Grenadines	Kingstown	Ralph Gonsalves	Prime Minister	Independent
Suriname	Paramaribo	Desiré Delano Bouterse	President	Independent/Mainland Caribbean
Trinidad and Tobago	Port of Spain	Keith Rowley	Prime Minister	Independent
Turks and Caicos Islands	Cockburn Town	Sharlene Cartwright-Robinson	Premier	Dependent territory (UK)

☐ CARICOM members   ▨ CARICOM associate members

Population

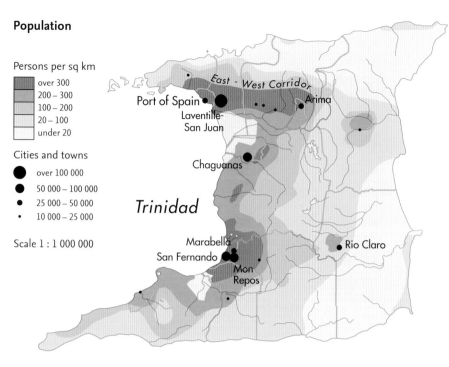

Persons per sq km
- over 300
- 200 – 300
- 100 – 200
- 20 – 100
- under 20

Cities and towns
- ● over 100 000
- ● 50 000 – 100 000
- ● 25 000 – 50 000
- · 10 000 – 25 000

Scale 1 : 1 000 000

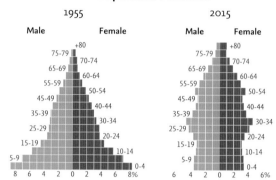

Population structure

Each full square represents 1% of the total population

Population change, 2000–2011

Percentage population change per annum
- over 2.0
- 1.0 – 1.9
- 0.1 – 0.9
- no change
- -0.1 – -0.9
- -1.0 – -1.9
- under -2.0

Scale 1 : 2 000 000

Population increase, 1851–2011

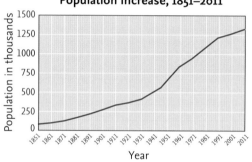

Culture

Trinidad and Tobago is a country that embraces many different cultures and people. This makes it a unique and **multicultural** country.

Some people from Trinidad and Tobago are descended from the Amerindians who first lived on the islands. Others are descended from people who came to live here as **immigrants** later on.

These immigrants came from other Caribbean countries and from Africa, India, China and European countries such as France, Spain, Holland, Britain and Portugal. More recently, around 40 000 refugees and migrants have travelled to Trinidad and Tobago from Venezuela.

Each of these immigrant groups added to the social, religious, ethnic, linguistic and cultural landscape of Trinidad and Tobago. The diverse cultural and religious backgrounds of these groups allow for many festivals and ceremonies throughout the cultural calendar year.

Cultural calendar

Celebrations help to conserve and preserve a country's cultural heritage. The table below provides information about a few of the festivals held in Trinidad and Tobago each year.

Festival	What it commemorates	When it takes place
Emancipation Day	Celebrates the abolition of slavery and the freeing of all slaves in Trinidad and Tobago.	1 August (public holiday)
Double Ten Day	The National Day of the Republic of China (Taiwan). Commemorates the Wuchang Uprising of 1911 which led to the fall of the Qing dynasty.	10 October
Indian Arrival Day	The arrival of East Indian indentured labourers to work on the plantations.	30 May (public holiday)
Tobago Heritage Festival	The cultural heritage of Tobago.	July and August
Carnival	A celebration held before Lent.	Monday and Tuesday before Ash Wednesday (public holidays)
Hosay	Traditionally, an Islamic festival commemorating Husayn, a grandson of the prophet Mohammed.	The 10th day of Muharram: the first month in the Islamic calendar, in August or September (public holiday)
Divali	Hindu 'Festival of Lights'. Lanterns (called "deyas") are lit to celebrate the triumph of good over evil.	(public holiday)
Eid-ul-fitr	Islamic festival commemorating the breaking of the fast at the end of Ramadan.	1st of Shawaal, the tenth month of the Islamic calendar (public holiday)

Ethnic origin, 2011

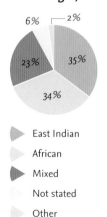

- East Indian
- African
- Mixed
- Not stated
- Other

Religion, 2011

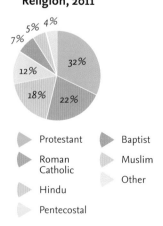

- Protestant
- Roman Catholic
- Hindu
- Pentecostal
- Baptist
- Muslim
- Other

Outstanding personalities and national heroes

Politics

Dr Eric Williams (1911–1981)
- Dr Williams was the first Prime Minister of Trinidad and Tobago after it gained independence from Great Britain in 1962.
- He was educated at Queen's Royal College in Port of Spain and graduated from Oxford University with a First in History in 1935, completing a doctorate a few years later.
- He founded the People's National Movement (PNM) in 1962 and served in government from 1962 until his death in 1981.
- He is popularly known as the 'Father of the Nation'.
- In 2002, he was posthumously awarded the Trinity Cross, Trinidad and Tobago's highest honour.

A.N.R. Robinson (1926–2014)
- Tobago-born A.N.R. Robinson has the unique distinction of having served in three important government offices. Chairman of the Tobago House of Assembly (1980-86), Prime Minister (1986–91) and President of Trinidad and Tobago (1997–2003).
- He was one of the founders of the International Criminal Court, which was established in 2002.

Dr Eric Williams

Business and economics

Sir Arthur Lewis

Sir Arthur Lewis (1915–1991)
- Sir Arthur Lewis was well known for his theories on development economics.
- He helped Ghana draw up a Five-Year Development Plan following its independence in 1957.
- He was appointed Vice Chancellor of the University of the West Indies in 1959 and was knighted for his contributions to economics in 1963.
- He was the first president of the Caribbean Development Bank.
- He won the Nobel Memorial Prize in Economics in 1979.
- Arthur Lewis Community College, St Lucia, is named in his honour.

The Arts

Dr Derek Walcott

Dr Derek Walcott (1930–2017)
- Derek Walcott moved to Trinidad and Tobago aged 23, in 1953.
- He founded the Trinidad Theatre Workshop in 1959 (it still runs today), which puts on theatre shows, as well as offering educational programmes.
- In 1992, he won the highest honour in literature, the Nobel Prize.
- He has written over 20 poetry collections, 25 plays (many of which have been put on at the Trinidad Theatre Workshop) and has won more than a dozen awards.

Sports

Hasley Crawford

Hasely Crawford (born 1950)
- Crawford made history for his record-breaking time of 10.06 seconds for the 100 m race at the 1976 Olympic Games in Montreal.
- He was Trinidad and Tobago's first Olympic champion and the first 100 m champion from a Caribbean country.
- He was awarded Trinidad and Tobago's highest award – the Trinity Cross – in 1978.
- Crawford was named Trinidad and Tobago Athlete of the Millennium in 2000.

Entertainment

Slinger Francisco

Slinger Francisco (born 1935)
- Francisco is also known as 'the Mighty Sparrow', and fondly referred to as "the birdie".
- He has been called the 'King of the Calypso World', as he would regularly beat every other competitor in local calypso singing contests.
- In 1958, he made his first album, Calypso Carnival, and has released over 70 albums and dozens of singles. He has performed at hundreds of shows all over the world.

Keshorn 'Keshie' Walcott

Keshorn 'Keshie' Walcott (born 1993)
- Walcott is an Olympic javelin champion.
- He was the first Caribbean male athlete to win a gold medal in a throwing event at the Olympic Games, in 2012, and was the youngest ever gold medallist in the event.
- Also, at the 2012 Olympics, Trinidad and Tobago's men's 4 x 100 m relay team won a silver medal, which was later upgraded to gold after the initial winners were stripped of their medals. The team consisted of Keston Bledman, Marc Burns, Emmanuel Callender and Richard Thompson.

Science

Professor Courtenay Bartholomew (born 1951)
- Professor Bartholomew has been responsible for important research into Hepatitis A and B, and HIV/AIDS.
- He is also noted for his research on the venom of scorpion stings.
- In 1982, he founded the Trinidad and Tobago Medical Research Foundation, which is dedicated to research on viruses, retroviruses, cancer and AIDS.

Dr Joseph Lennox Pawan (1887–1957)
- Dr Pawan worked at Port of Spain General Hospital and as District Medical Officer in various parts of Trinidad and Tobago.
- He was the first person to isolate the rabies virus and show that it was transmitted by fruit-eating bats and vampire bats.

Brian Lara (born 1969)
- Nicknamed the 'Prince of the Port of Spain', Brian Lara is one of Trinidad and Tobago's most famous sportspeople.
- Until 2008, he held the record as the leading run-scorer in test cricket.
- He holds many records as a batsman, including the highest individual score in first class cricket in 1994 (501 not out) and, in 2004, the highest individual score in test cricket (400 not out).
- The Brian Lara Cricket Academy, in Tarouba, Trinidad and Tobago, is a multi-purpose stadium, named after the world-famous cricketer.

Brian Lara

Historical sites

Port of Spain, the capital city, is home to many places of interest for the people of Trinidad and Tobago. **The House of Parliament, National Museum and Art Gallery** are all places that have special significance for the country's national heritage.

- **The Magnificent Seven** is the name given to a group of seven historical sites along the Queen's Park Savannah in Port of Spain. They were built between 1902 and 1910 and show off a number of different architectural styles including French Colonial and Indian Empire, as well as Caribbean architecture. The buildings are the **Queen's Royal College, Hayes Court, Mille Fleurs, Ambard's House, Archbishop's Palace, Whitehall and Killarney (Stollmeyer's Castle).** All of the Magnificent Seven are listed as heritage sites by the National Trust of Trinidad and Tobago.

Aerial view of Port of Spain, Trinidad.

This house, called Killarney, also known as Stollmeyer's Castle, was built by Charles Fourier Stollmeyer in 1904.

- **Fort King George**, Tobago, is considered a relic. In 1777, the British authorised the building of some barracks to house companies of soldiers. At Fort King George Heritage Park visitors can view the town and see some of the original brick and stone walls, the officers' mess, some cannons and a lighthouse from the days when the fort was in use. The nearby Tobago Museum houses antique maps, African art and artefacts from Amerindian culture.

Churches

The **Roman Catholic Cathedral of the Immaculate Conception** is one of the oldest Catholic churches in Port of Spain. In 1781, the first church in Port of Spain was built where the cathedral stands today.

Other forms of Christianity have smaller and simpler churches. **Greyfriars Church** was built in 1837, marking the introduction of Presbyterianism to Trinidad. It was originally built to offer services to British settlers who were Presbyterians from Scotland. Another example is **La Divina Pastora Catholic Church** in Siparia.

Fort King George barracks, in Scarborough, Tobago, date back to 1777. The fort was named after King George III when under British rule.

Mosques and temples

A **mosque** is a Muslim place of worship, and there are about 65 000 Muslims living in Trinidad and Tobago. There are many mosques on the islands, such as the **Jama Masjid** in San Fernando and the **Bait-ul-Hamid** mosque in the fishing village of Icacos in the southwest of Trinidad.

On the west coast of Trinidad near Waterloo is a Hindu temple known as the **Temple in the Sea**. It was built by Sewdass Sadhu, an indentured Indian.

The Temple in the Sea, Waterloo, Trinidad. Construction was started by one man in 1952, and after 25 years his work was completed. It was rebuilt in 1995.

Civic buildings

- **The Red House** is the seat of Parliament in Trinidad and Tobago. The building was built in the late 1800s, and was renovated in the 1890s, when it was painted red for the Diamond Jubilee of Queen Victoria.
- **The Tobago House of Assembly** is the seat of the Tobago government and is housed in a civic building which is almost 200 years old. The building was renovated in 2011.
- **The President's House** is the official residence of the President of Trinidad and Tobago, in Port of Spain. It was rebuilt between 1873 and 1876 and was once part of a huge sugar plantation. It was the residence of British Governors between 1876 and 1958, and between 1976 and 2010 it was the President's private residence.
- **The Hall of Justice** houses the High Court, the Court of Appeal and the Supreme Court Library.

Recreational facilities

Civic buildings can also be used for recreational facilities in Trinidad and Tobago.
- **The National Academy for the Performing Arts** (NAPA) in Port of Spain is a permanent venue for the development and teaching of the performing arts in Trinidad and Tobago, as well as being a venue for entertainment and the promotion of culture, both past and present. There is also a Southern Academy for the Performing Arts (SAPA) in the city of San Fernando.
- **The Queen's Hall** in Port of Spain is an arts centre that was built in 1959. It is a huge site that provides the facilities for a wide mix of theatre, dance, music and other performing arts.
- **Chacachacare Island**, between Trinidad and Venezuela, has become a centre for adventure activities such as hiking, camping and picnics. The island is 16 km long. It has a long history as a cotton plantation, a whaling station and a leper colony.
- **The Royal Botanic Gardens** in Port of Spain, established in 1819, and the **Scarborough Botanical Garden**, Tobago, established in 1898, are popular destinations for locals as well as tourists.
- **Brian Lara Promenade** is a paved walkway in Port of Spain. It was built in the 1990s and connects the famous Cathedral of the Immaculate Conception with the Cipriani Statue.

The Red House, the seat of Parliament in Trinidad and Tobago. The current building was completed in 1907 after a fire in 1903.

The National Academy for the Performing Arts opened in Port of Spain in 2009.

The Royal Botanic Gardens, Port of Spain, Trinidad, were established in 1818 and contain around 700 trees collected from around the world.

Calypso

Trinidad and Tobago is well known for its **calypso**, steelpan and chutney music. Calypso music has roots in West African tribal songs of the 18th century and became popular in the early 20th century, spreading to the rest of the Caribbean. Originally, calypso was sung in a French creole, led by a **griot** (a storyteller). As English replaced French creole, calypso began to be sung in English. This drew the attention of the British colonial powers, because the calypso song lyrics were often politically critical of the British.

The first calypso recording was made in 1914, and by the 1920s there were permanent bamboo tents where the calypsonians would practise. By the 1930s, some of the big names began to emerge in calypso – Atilla the Hun, Roaring Lion and Lord Kitchener.

In 1939, the Calypso King contest, a singing competition, was first held at the Carnival. A prize was offered for the most original song on a local topic. Growling Tiger won the first contest with 'Trade Union'. The most prolific winners of the Calypso King contest are the Mighty Sparrow and Chalkdust, who both won it eight times.

Indigenous people singing and dancing: the roots of calypso music.

The Asa Wright Nature Centre, Trinidad

The Asa Wright Nature Centre (AWNC) is a 'not-for-profit' trust established in 1967 by a group of naturalists and bird-watchers to "protect part of the Arima Valley in a natural state and to create a conservation and study area for the protection of wildlife and for the enjoyment of all". It was one of the first nature centres to be established in the Caribbean.

Made up of nearly 1500 acres of mainly forested land in the Arima and Aripo Valleys of the Northern Range, the AWNC's properties will be retained under forest cover in perpetuity, to protect the community watershed and provide important wildlife habitat.

Since its inception over 38 years ago, the AWNC has been a leader in ecotourism.

Asa Wright Nature Centre, inside the visitor centre.

Steel band

Trinidad and Tobago is known as the place where steel band originated. In 1880, stick fighting and percussion music were banned in Trinidad and Tobago as a result of the Canboulay riots. The replacements, bamboo sticks, were also banned. In 1937, an orchestra of frying pans, dustbin lids and oil drums emerged in Laventille.

When the US Navy was stationed on the island in 1941, the popularity of steelpan among the soldiers raised the profile of the music. In 1951, the Trinidad All Steel Percussion Orchestra (TASPO) formed to take part in the Festival of Britain. Important names in the development of the steelpan sound include Tony Williams, Bertie Marshall and Ellie Mannette.

Exodus Steel Orchestra performs in Port of Spain.

Food

Food in Trinidad and Tobago has been influenced by the many different cultures that have settled on the islands over the centuries. It is particularly known for its street food, such as the **Double**, a delicious curried chickpea and roti snack.

Certain areas of the country, such as the Western Main Road in St James, or the Queen's Park Savannah in Port of Spain, are famed for their range and quality of street food vendors, selling foods such as coconut, roasted corn, oysters and pholourie (a deep-fried spicy split pea dough with sauce). Roti and curried mango show the influence from India, while there are also strong influences from Spain and China.

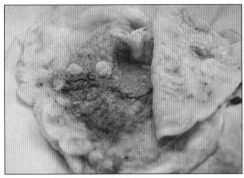

Doubles, delicious street food.

Selling coconuts at a street food stand in Port of Spain.

Chutney

Chutney music first appeared in Trinidad and Tobago in the 1940s, at weddings, religious celebrations and in the sugarcane fields. Originally, chutney songs made reference to deities and were offensive to religious leaders. The up-tempo, rhythmic style of chutney became very popular with Indo-Caribbean people as it blended cultural influences.

As its name suggests, chutney music is a mixture of Indian and local music. The main instruments are the dholak (a hand drum), dhantal (a steel rod) and harmonium. Famous chutney singers include Sundar Popo, Rikki Jai and Sam Boodram.

Dholak drum, a traditional instrument.

World Heritage Sites

A heritage site can have historical, cultural, social or physical significance. It can be a forest, a building, an island, a desert, a lake, or even a whole city. For example, Banwari Trace Archaeological Site, La Brea Pitch Lake, and Main Ridge Forest Reserve are listed on the Tentative List, but none have yet been nominated for consideration or accepted as full UNESCO World Heritage Sites.

To date, in total, 22 sites of historical and natural importance have been identified as World Heritage Sites in the Caribbean. The aim is to ensure the preservation of these sites, as they are part of the heritage of the Caribbean.

Main Ridge Forest Reserve, Tobago, is one of the sites on the UNESCO World Heritage Sites Tentative List.

Folklore

The influences on the country's folklore stretch deep into the islands' Amerindian past. The history of colonialism and immigration to Trinidad and Tobago brought many cultures together. This mixture of people of different faiths and backgrounds led to a mixture in many of their folk legends, particularly those of West Africa and French Creole.

Papa Bois is the mythical 'master of the woods'. He is the protector of the forest and is an old, but very muscular African man, covered in hair with a beard of leaves and with at least one leg ending in a cloven hoof. He can run faster than any forest animal and warns them of human hunters.

Douens are the lost souls of children who died before being baptised. They lure children into the forest, chanting their name and mimicking the voices of the children's parents.

Environment

Trinidad and Tobago has three main types of indigenous flora – the **wetlands, tropical rainforest** and the **savannah**. The biodiversity of Trinidad and Tobago is the most diverse of all the Caribbean.

Environmentally Sensitive Species (ESSs)

Trinidad and Tobago is home to a number of species of plants and animals that are in need of protection. These are classed as Environmentally Sensitive Species (ESSs): the Trinidad piping guan; the West Indian manatee; the white-tailed sabrewing hummingbird; the golden tree frog; the ocelot; and five species of turtle.

Trinidad piping guan, locally known as pawi

The ecological heritage of Trinidad and Tobago

Ecology is the study of the relationships between plants, animals, people and their environment.

There are three **Environmentally Sensitive Areas** (ESAs) that are protected by the government of Trinidad and Tobago:
• Aripo Savannas Strict Nature Reserve
• Matura National Park
• Nariva Swamp Managed Resource Protected Area

There is a wide diversity of species in Trinidad and Tobago:

- 470 birds
- 620 butterflies
- 108 mammals
- 90 reptiles
- 30 amphibians
- 370 trees
- 300 ferns
- 50 freshwater fish
- 950 marine fish
- 3400 plants
- 2500 flowering shrubs including 700 types of orchids

Tobago's unspoilt rainforest

The rainforest of Tobago is one of the oldest nature reserves in the world. It has been legally protected since 1776 when legal protection was secured for it.

As it has been protected for so long, it is one of the few rainforests not damaged by human activities. The Rainforest Reserve Road runs through the unspoilt rainforest, from south of Roxborough through Bloody Bay and passing the entrance to Gilpin Trace, one of the country's best-loved hiking trails.

Leatherback turtle

Reptiles

The golden tree frog is endemic to Trinidad's rainforest. It is one of Trinidad and Tobago's most endangered species.

Flora

Trinidad and Tobago has up to 3400 different types of plants and 2500 different flowering shrubs, including 700 types of orchids.

Habitat	Vegetation
Savannah	Grasses, low shrubs
Rainforests	Tall trees, shrubs, creepers
Swamp	Dense mangrove trees and shrubs
Beach	Tall palm trees, grasses, short shrubs that do not require much water

Trichocentrum lanceanum hybrid flowering in an orchid garden in Trinidad.

Birds

Trinidad and Tobago is home to more than 470 species of birds. Many of these are endangered species, such as the white-tailed sabrewing. The varied vegetation of the islands – rainforests, wetlands, scrubland, marshes and mangroves – offer many important habitats for birds.

The savannah habitat area has rich birdlife. Some of the common savannah and grassland bird species include the red-breasted blackbird (known as soldier bird), blue-black grassquit (or grassie/johnny-jump-up), grey kingbird, forktailed flycatcher, green-rumped parrotlet (or parakeet), striped cuckoo, savannah hawk and red-bellied macaw. Bird sanctuaries are special reserves that protect habitats that are rich in birdlife.

Red-breasted blackbird

White-tailed sabrewing hummingbird

Mammals

Trinidad and Tobago has more than 100 species of mammals, 57 of which are bats.
The savannah habitat is home to many types of mammal, including deer, armadillo, agouti, lappe, opossum and porcupine.

Other mammals in Trinidad and Tobago include:

anteater	lemur	raccoon
ape	manatee	sloth
bat	mongoose	squirrel
cat	monkey	tree rat
dolphin	ocelot	water rat
grass mouse	porpoise	whale

West Indian manatee

Common long-tongued bat

Trinidad resources

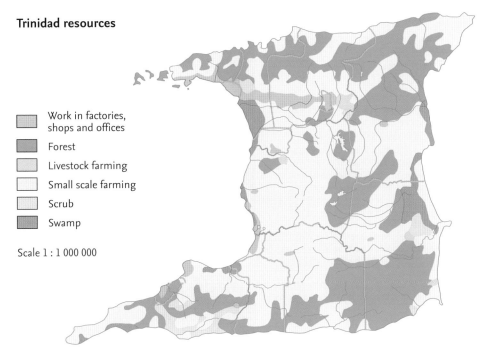

- ▨ Work in factories, shops and offices
- ▨ Forest
- ▨ Livestock farming
- ▨ Small scale farming
- ▨ Scrub
- ▨ Swamp

Scale 1 : 1 000 000

Mangroves

Mangroves are an important part of Trinidad and Tobago's economy. The many organisms that live and reproduce here help to support the populations of birds and fish that form part of the country's environment and economy. Without the mangroves, the islands would be at risk of regular damage from flooding and storms. Mangroves are specially adapted to live in wetlands. They can survive very wet soil with low oxygen and high salt levels. Their dense, tangled roots are called 'prop roots', because they keep the trees standing as the tide moves in and out around them. Most mangroves are flooded with sea or river water at least twice a day.

Mangroves near Manzanilla, Trinidad.

Rainforests

There are two main types of forest in Trinidad and Tobago: dry scrub forests and tropical rainforests.

The slopes of the Northern Range mountains in Trinidad are covered with rainforests, with enormous trees such as silk cotton trees. They support creepers and vines, and tower over the canopy-level trees such as mahogany, balata, palms, poui and immortelle. In Tobago, rainforests are found in the sheltered valleys of the Main Ridge mountains.

Rincon Falls, in the rainforests of the north of Trinidad.

Coral reefs

Coral reefs are the sea's most diverse ecosystems. They support so much plant and animal life that they are known as the rainforests of the sea. The **Buccoo Reef** lies just off the southwestern tip of Tobago and is a protected marine park. The reef system has an area of 12.87 km² and is made up of five reef flats that enclose a shallow reef lagoon and the **Bon Accord Lagoon**.

The reefs support threatened ecological species, such as staghorn coral, brain corals, starlet coral and queen conch. The site also provides habitat and feeding grounds for species such as the critically endangered hawkbill turtle; the endangered green turtle and Nassau grouper; and the vulnerable queen triggerfish, hogfish, lined seahorse, mutton snapper and rainbow parrotfish.

Areas of wetland

(hectares)

- ● >1000
- ● 100 – 1000
- ● 50 – 100
- ● 10 – 50
- ● 1 – 10
- • <1

1 Scotland Bay	22 Los Blanquizales Lagoon
2 Hart's Cut	23 Moruga River
3 Cuesa River	24 St Hilaire River
4 Mucurapo	25 Rushville
5 Sealots	26 Guayaguayare Bay
6 Caroni	27 Mouville
7 Waterloo	28 Ortoire River
8 Orange Valley	29 Nariva Swamp
9 Couva River/Carli Bay	30 L'Ebranche River
10 Lisas Bay	31 North Manzanilla
11 Claxton Bay	32 Manzanilla Windbelt
12 Central Claxton Bay	33 North Oropuche
13 Guaracara River	34 Matura River
14 Marabella River	35 Salybia River
15 Godineau River	36 Balandra River
16 Rousillac	37 Grande Riviere
17 La Brea	38 Marianne River
18 Guapo River	39 Yarra River
19 Irois Bay	40 Las Cuevas
20 Los Gallos Point	41 Tyrico Bay
21 Icacos	42 Maracas Bay

Tobago

A	Black Rock Pond
B	Buccoo Bay Freshwater Marsh
C	Bon Accord Lagoon
D	Kilgwyn
E	Friendship
F	Petit Trou
G	Little Rockly Bay
H	Minister Bay
I	Fort Granby
J	Lucy Vale
K	Bloody Bay
L	Parlatuvier
M	Courland Bay

Trinidad

Scale 1 : 1 610 000

Fishing beds

Like many islands and coastal cities around the world, Trinidad and Tobago has a long history of fishing. The waters around Trinidad and Tobago are home to tuna, snapper, flying fish, kingfish, carite, croakers, bechine and shrimp. However, fish populations all over the world are under threat because of trawling, overfishing and pollution.

Pitch Lake

A pitch lake is like a lake, except it is formed from a thick, black, sticky mineral substance called pitch. Asphalt is a type of pitch used for constructing roads. **La Brea Pitch Lake**, located on Trinidad's southwestern coast, is the largest deposit of asphalt in the world. About 20 000 people visit the pitch lakes each year.

Coral reef

Transport carriages crossing the Pitch Lake, La Brea.

Deforestation

Deforestation is the process of clearing land of natural or planted trees and forest woodland for housing, industry, farming or any other use. According to the Food and Agriculture Organization of the United Nations (FAO), 44.1% of Trinidad and Tobago is forested. Of this, 27.4% is primary forest, which includes the most biodiverse and carbon-dense form of forest.

Global warming

The addition of industrial chemicals to the air changes the composition of the atmosphere. Chemicals such as carbon monoxide, sulphur oxides and dioxides create a thick chemical blanket at the top of the Earth's atmosphere, preventing some of the Earth's heat from escaping into space. This produces the **greenhouse effect**, in which the Earth's average temperature is gradually rising. Global warming can have very negative impacts on the environment such as melting of glaciers, increase in sea levels, higher temperatures, drought and an increase in hurricanes.

Pollution

Solid waste includes organic waste from food, as well as waste materials from packaging. Most waste is dumped in **landfills**. Some sewage systems also dispose of solid waste in landfills. Consequences can be that harmful chemicals leak out from products; chemicals dissolve into the water in the soil, adding to water pollution. Chemicals taken up by food crops may cause illnesses in people and animals.

Some farmers use pesticides, insecticides, herbicides and chemical fertilizers on their crops. However, these products can reduce biodiversity by killing insects or weeds that they were not intended for, and can add to water pollution.

Air pollution

Air pollution comes from many different human activities:
- Fire produces smoke, dust and soot.
- Internal combustion engines burn gasoline. By-products of the burning process include carbon monoxide, lead and particulates, which are released into the air.
- Some factories release gases such as sulphur oxides, sulphur dioxides and nitrous oxides.
- Cement and chemical factories, as well as quarries and mines, emit large quantities of dust into the air.

Effects of air pollution
- Polluted air can cause many types of illnesses and even death. In cities with heavy smog, there are higher rates of lung cancer, chest infections, respiratory diseases and asthma than in rural areas.
- Breathing in carbon monoxide lowers the amount of oxygen in the body. This can lead to headaches, dizziness, nausea and even unconsciousness.
- Sulphur dioxides cause poor growth in plants and can prevent the plants from producing fruit.
- Air pollution can cause haziness and reduce visibility.

Water pollution

Untreated sewage carries bacteria and viruses, which cause diseases such as cholera, typhoid and hepatitis. Industrial waste such as lead, mercury and other chemicals that are highly toxic (poisonous) to animals and humans can cause many illnesses if they come into contact with them through polluted water. Water pollution also includes solid wastes, such as plastics that do not degrade in water. During the wet season, solid waste and litter in rivers can cause flooding.

Water pollution

Two Liberian oil tankers collided close to Tobago on 19 July 1979, spilling vast amounts of crude oil into the sea.

Industrial pollution

Industrial processes use large quantities of physical resources and release many different chemicals into the environment.

Trinidad and Tobago oil spills

In 1979, Trinidad and Tobago suffered a severe oil spill after two tankers collided 16 km off the coast of Tobago. This caused 280 000 tonnes of oil to leak into the Caribbean Sea.

In 2013, Trinidad and Tobago suffered another spill when 11 oil spills occurred from a pipeline off the coast of Trinidad. Several kilometres of coastline were coated in oil. Spilled oil cannot dissolve or disperse in water. It sits on the surface and prevents light and air from reaching the plants that live in the water. It also coats fish, causing suffocation. It gets stuck on the feathers of sea birds, preventing them from flying. Many animals and plants die as a result of oil spills.

Effects of pollution

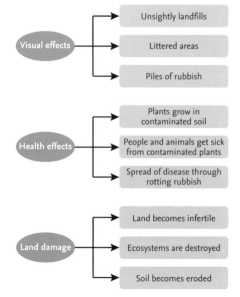

Visual effects
- Unsightly landfills
- Littered areas
- Piles of rubbish

Health effects
- Plants grow in contaminated soil
- People and animals get sick from contaminated plants
- Spread of disease through rotting rubbish

Land damage
- Land becomes infertile
- Ecosystems are destroyed
- Soil becomes eroded

Fire burning in the forested mountains of Trinidad.

The burning of fossil fuels contributes to global warming.

Controlling pollution

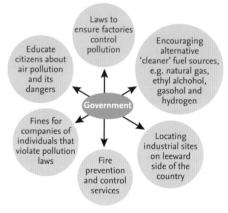

Government
- Educate citizens about air pollution and its dangers
- Laws to ensure factories control pollution
- Encouraging alternative 'cleaner' fuel sources, e.g. natural gas, ethyl alchohol, gasohol and hydrogen
- Fines for companies of individuals that violate pollution laws
- Fire prevention and control services
- Locating industrial sites on leeward side of the country

Industry
- Using special burners and filters designed to purify waste gases before releasing them
- Using tall chimneys to release gases higher into the atmosphere, far from people

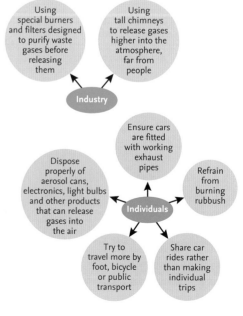

Individuals
- Dispose properly of aerosol cans, electronics, light bulbs and other products that can release gases into the air
- Ensure cars are fitted with working exhaust pipes
- Refrain from burning rubbush
- Try to travel more by foot, bicycle or public transport
- Share car rides rather than making individual trips

Mining

- ▲ Asphalt
- △ Gypsum
- ✕ Limestone
- ▨ Oilfield
- ▨ Gasfield
- —— Oil pipeline
- —— Gas pipeline

Scale 1 : 1 500 000

Fossil fuels

Fossil fuels include **oil, natural gas** and **coal**. The manufacturing sector processes each of these fossil fuels to produce a wide range of products. Oil and gas production have become the country's most important industries. In 2012, the petroleum sector accounted for over 40% of the country's economy. Extensive pipelines carry the fossil fuels from the offshore oil and gas fields, located to the north, west and east of Trinidad, to refineries at Pointe-à-Pierre and at Point Fortin.

Oil

The **refining process** separates oil into different chemicals. Most of the oil is refined into fuel, but the refining process also leaves many residual **petrochemicals** that are used to produce a huge range of products. These include chemical products (e.g. pesticides and fertilizers), plastics, lubricating oils, synthetic fibres, bitumen, paints, detergents and cosmetics.

Natural gas

The **methane** content of the gas mined in Trinidad and Tobago makes it useful in the production of **methanol** and **ammonia**. As a result, the country is one of the world's largest exporters of these chemicals.

Exploitation

Exploitation means using too much of something and making the resource unavailable for future generations. In Trinidad and Tobago, the current known oil reserves will run out by around 2050, presenting a challenge to the country's economy.

Cocoa is a crop grown over much of Trinidad.

Aerial view of fields near Valencia, Trinidad.

Large-scale farming

Advantages

- Large-scale farming is less work for the farmer, for example driving a tractor is less work than using a hand plough and a farmer can irrigate a much larger area with a sprinkler system than a hand watering system.
- Cheaper than labour – using technology and chemicals reduces the number of workers the farmer employs.
- Very high yields – chemical fertilizers, insecticides and pesticides allow the farmer to get more crops out of each square unit of land. Conventional agriculture can also damage the main resource it relies on – the land.

Disadvantages

- Clearing land for farming destroys habitats for many animals and plants.
- Monocropping destroys biodiversity and can wipe out many local crop varieties.
- Once crops are harvested, the land is bare. Bare soil easily becomes eroded by wind and rain.
- Insecticides and pesticides pollute the environment.
- Fertilizers run off into the water cycle and can cause unnatural amounts of algae to grow in seas and rivers. This uses up oxygen in the water, causing the death of many aquatic plants and animals.

Agriculture

- ▨ Livestock farming
- ☐ Crop farming
- ▨ Sugar cane
- ▙ Sugar factory
- ◍ Cocoa
- ⬡ Coconuts
- ⬭ Citrus fruits
- ✓ Rice

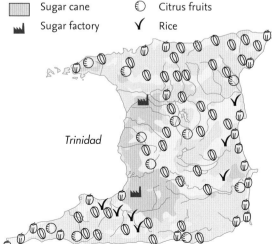

Scale 1 : 1 500 000

Sustainable agriculture practices

There are many ways that farmers around the world are working towards making agriculture more **sustainable**.

- **Crop rotation** – planting different crops each season helps to replenish some of the nutrients in the soil.
- **Natural forms of fertilizer** instead of chemical fertilizers.
- Using **local varieties** of crops with greater resistance to local pests and diseases than imported varieties.
- Planting **different varieties** of the same species instead of monocropping, e.g. several varieties of rice in one paddy make it more likely they will not be destroyed by a single pest attack.
- **Mulching** prevents water from evaporating so it reduces the need for irrigation.

Tourism

Tourism is the practice of visiting places for pleasure. One of the most important industries in the Caribbean is tourism. Tourism in Trinidad and Tobago is not as developed as some of the other Caribbean islands, such as Barbados and The Bahamas, but it is very important to the country's economy.

Hundreds of thousands of people work in the tourism industry. In total, 16.7% of the population is employed in tourist-related industries. However, it is not the same for both islands: nearly 50% of Tobago's total employment comes from the tourist industry and here, 98% of the island's exports are related to travel and tourism. In Tobago, the contribution of the tourism industry to Gross Domestic Product (GDP) is an estimated 39.6% (2019). In comparison, in Trinidad, only 10% of GDP and 13% of employment are related to travel and tourism.

Recently there has been a focus on ecotourism in Trinidad and Tobago, a type of tourism that allows tourists into a country or area but focuses on protecting the environment and local culture.

Maracas Beach is very popular with tourists, surfers, and lovers of the street food available there.

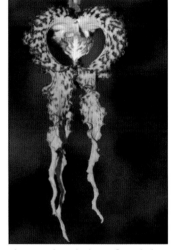

Plants, such as the butterfly orchid, attract tourists to the islands.

Fort King George and the Tobago Museum – this is the most well-preserved fort on the island. It has many original features still remaining such as stone walls, cannons and a lighthouse.

Pigeon Point – this is a beautiful, sandy beach on Tobago. It has crystal clear waters and white sands.

ASA Wright Nature Centre & Lodge – this is 1500 acres of dense forest in the Arima and Aripo Valleys. It is home to a diverse amount of wildlife such as hummingbirds, trogons and oilbirds.

Main Ridge Forest Reserve – this is home to more than half of the island's bird species. There is plenty to see and do here.

Maracas Bay – this is a beautiful, sandy beach just north of Port of Spain.

Little Tobago Island – this is an uninhabited bird sanctuary just off the coast of Tobago.

Port of Spain – Trinidad and Tobago's capital city. There are many entertainment facilities and hotels here.

Aripo Caves – these are limestone caves in the north of Trinidad. They are home to many species of birds including the oilbird. The caves have many interesting features such as stalactites and stalagmites.

Caroni Bird Sanctuary – this is just south of Port of Spain and is home to Trinidad and Tobago's national bird, the scarlet ibis. There is a lot to see within this sanctuary.

Mount St Benedict Monastery – home to Benedictine monks, this monastery is a popular tourist destination.

Pointe-à-Pierre Wildfowl Trust – this is an unusual but very popular bird sanctuary.

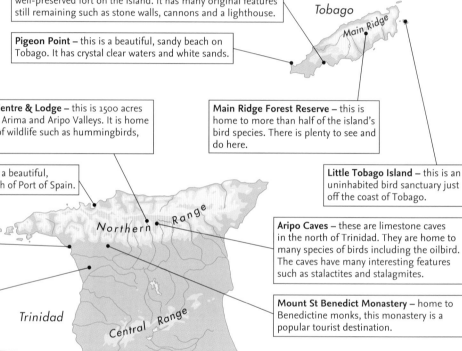

Year	Total tourist arrivals
2014	412 447
2015	439 749
2016	408 782
2017	394 650
2018	375 485

Scale 1 : 1 200 000

Climate

Trinidad and Tobago has an attractive climate for tourists. It has both a tropical maritime climate and an equatorial climate. A tropical maritime climate is characterised by warm temperatures, some rainfall and moderate to strong winds. An equatorial climate typically has much more rainfall and hot temperatures, forming humid conditions and calmer winds. The two climate types are evident from the two seasons in Trinidad – the wet season (July to December) and the dry season (January to June).

Natural sites

The country's rainforests support unique ecosystems that have a wide array of plant species. These areas are very attractive to visitors. Other natural sites that are popular tourist destinations: sandy beaches such as Maracas Bay and Englishman's Bay; lakes such as La Brea Pitch Lake; and waterfalls such as Avocat Falls.

Damage to historical sites

As with any fragile environment, whether it is natural or man-made, an increase in the number of people visiting that place, or area, puts a huge amount of pressure on the attraction in question. Quite often historical sites of interest can be damaged by increased visitor numbers. Organisations, such as the **Caribbean Conservation Association**, work with local governments to help create a greater awareness and value of the Caribbean's natural resources.

Avocat Falls, a destination for nature tourists.

Trinidad and Tobago are in the tropics, and have a pleasant sub-tropical climate all year round, influenced by the northeast trade winds.

Trinidad has an annual mean temperature of 26°C, and an average maximum temperature of 34°C, with high humidity, especially in the rainy season when it can reach 85%. The hottest and coldest temperatures experienced on Trinidad are recorded as 39°C and 16°C respectively. Tobago is very similar but just a little cooler.

The rainy season runs from July to December for both islands, and this season is punctuated with frequent short but intense rain showers. Most of the rainfall is on Trinidad's Northern Range, however in the dry season it is known for there to be drought in other parts of the centre of the island. Trinidad averages 2110 mm of rain in a year, and Tobago slightly more at 2500 mm.

The islands lie outside the regular hurricane belt of the Caribbean, but despite this, they were damaged by Hurricane Flora in 1963 and Tropical Storm Alma in 1974.

Average rainfall

Average temperature

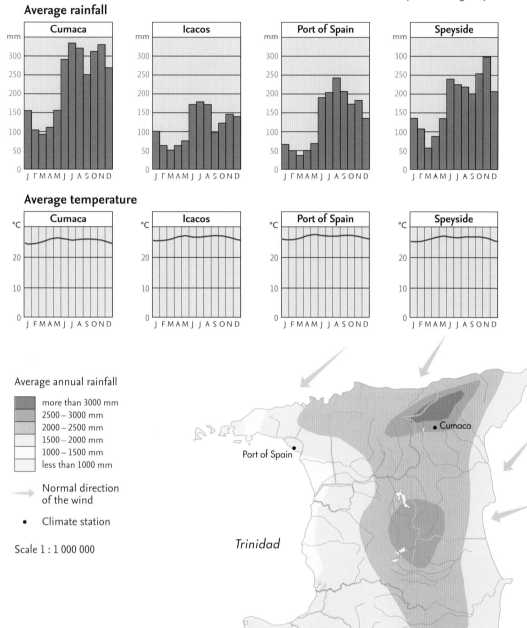

Average annual rainfall

- more than 3000 mm
- 2500 – 3000 mm
- 2000 – 2500 mm
- 1500 – 2000 mm
- 1000 – 1500 mm
- less than 1000 mm

→ Normal direction of the wind

• Climate station

Scale 1 : 1 000 000

Remote weather station with rain gauge, using solar power.

Wet weather living up to the name in the rainforest, Tobago.

A thunderstorm brewing at Pigeon Point, Tobago.

Imports

The main imports into Trinidad and Tobago include both refined and unrefined petroleum. Sugar, cars, other motor vehicles, machinery and equipment also account for many imports. Trinidad and Tobago also imports goods such as mobile phones and clothing. These products come from all over the world, but the biggest trading partners for Trinidad and Tobago are the United States and Brazil. The total value of imports in 2015 was estimated to be around $7.9 billion.

Exports

Trinidad and Tobago exports more than it imports, mainly as a result of petroleum and natural gas products. This has made the country very wealthy, with a very favourable balance of trade.

Trinidad and Tobago exports mainly to other countries in the Caribbean and to North and South America, but it also exports to countries in Europe and in Asia. In 2015, Trinidad and Tobago exported $8.166 billion worth of goods, which included petroleum and petroleum products, liquefied natural gas, methanol, ammonia, urea, steel products, beverages, cereal and cereal products, cocoa, fish, preserved fruits, cosmetics, household cleaners and plastic packaging.

Imports by country, 2015

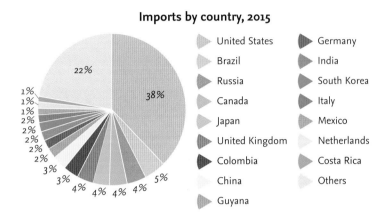

United States | Germany
Brazil | India
Russia | South Korea
Canada | Italy
Japan | Mexico
United Kingdom | Netherlands
Colombia | Costa Rica
China | Others
Guyana

Exports by country, 2015

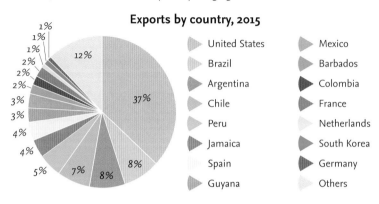

United States | Mexico
Brazil | Barbados
Argentina | Colombia
Chile | France
Peru | Netherlands
Jamaica | South Korea
Spain | Germany
Guyana | Others

Imports by commodity, 2015

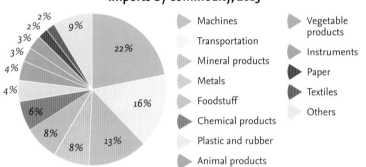

Machines | Vegetable products
Transportation | Instruments
Mineral products | Paper
Metals | Textiles
Foodstuff | Others
Chemical products
Plastic and rubber
Animal products

Value of the top six exports, 2015

Export	Value in US$	% of total exports
Petroleum gas	4 877 668 055	41
Ammonia	2 262 616 643	19
Refined petroleum	1 643 265 597	14
Iron reductions	936 520 936	8
Nitrogenous fertilizers	569 998 933	5
Acyclic alcohols (such as ethanol)	478 554 499	4

Containers being loaded or unloaded onto a transport ship at the port, Port of Spain.

Banknotes used in Trinidad and Tobago.

Transport and economic development

Roads
- the movement of goods from the place where they are produced to places where they can be sold is permitted
- roads make remote access more accessible
- different types of vehicle can use roads (e.g. trucks, cars, buses)
- roads allow workers to get to and from work, and traders to move goods

Water
- water allows the transport of heavy and bulky items
- goods can be imported and exported through ports
- inland waterways are often naturally occurring and generally do not need many repairs
- transporting by water means less traffic congestion
- in the Caribbean, the presence of cruise ships encourages tourism

How can our transport system help economic development?

Rail
- rail allows the transportation of heavy and bulky items
- rail travel can be relatively quick, as there is less congestion on the rail networks
- the rail network can carry passengers and cargo
- the rail network can carry large numbers of passengers in one trip – for example, to work

Air
- access to any part of the world is provided in a relatively short amount of time
- cargo can easily be transported between countries or within large countries
- air travel encourages tourism

Trinidad and Tobago is the largest **oil and natural gas producer** in the Caribbean. The oil and gas companies, in the primary sector, make a significant contribution to the economy of Trinidad and Tobago.

Share of industry

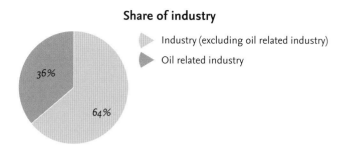

Industry (excluding oil related industry)

Oil related industry

36%

64%

Primary sector workers in **agriculture, fishing, mining and forestry** also contribute to the economic development of Trinidad and Tobago. Farmers and fishermen provide food security for the nation, which is key to economic development, as well as providing employment opportunities and spinoff industries, such as locally salted fish.

The value of the **secondary sector** to economic development is related to the satisfaction of human needs from **products that are created by the manufacturing sector**. Electricity production enables the use of labour-saving devices such as washing machines, water pumps, ovens, and other small appliances, while manufactured goods earn export revenue for the country.

Tertiary sector work includes **personal services** such as medical, dental and optical services, private transport, domestic help, food delivery; and **services to trade** such as banking, transport, canning, labelling, packaging, delivery, machine repair, toolmaking, security, cleaning and maintenance.

The **quaternary sector** includes the **information, or knowledge industries**, such as education, research and development, medicine and the media.

Employment by sector

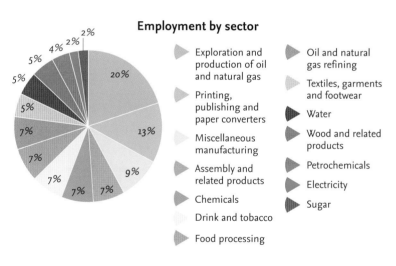

2%
2%
4%
5%
5%
5%
5%
7%
7%
7%
7%
7%
9%
13%
20%

Exploration and production of oil and natural gas

Printing, publishing and paper converters

Miscellaneous manufacturing

Assembly and related products

Chemicals

Drink and tobacco

Food processing

Oil and natural gas refining

Textiles, garments and footwear

Water

Wood and related products

Petrochemicals

Electricity

Sugar

Nicholas Tower, Port of Spain. This building houses the Trinidad and Tobago Stock Exchange, and Ministry of Trade and Industry, among many other economic and government tenants.

Gross Domestic Product per capita, 1960–2018

Eric Williams Plaza

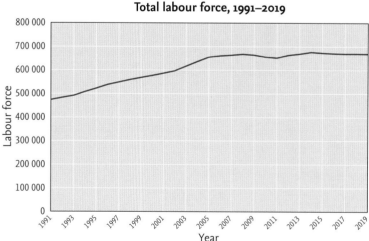

Eric Williams Plaza, Port of Spain, locally known as the Twin Towers. One tower houses the Central Bank of Trinidad and Tobago, and the other houses the Ministry of Finance.

Total labour force, 1991–2019

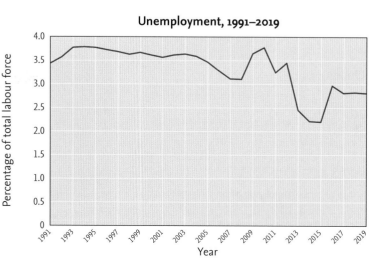

Unemployment, 1991–2019

BELIZE

Population (2010) 312 971
Capital city Belmopan
Area 22 965 sq km
Languages English, Spanish, Mayan, creole
National flower Black Orchid
National bird Keel-billed Toucan
National animal Baird's Tapir

Occupied by the Mayans until conquest and settlement

Progressively conquered and partially occupied by the Spanish from **1544** onwards

From the early **1600s** British settlers cut and exported logwood, and later mahogany

In **1787** some 2000 British refugees from the Mosquito Coast of Nicaragua settled in Belize, and by **1854** the British had total possession

In **1862** the British declared Belize a colony which it named British Honduras

The name was changed to Belize in **1973**, and Belize became independent on 21 September **1981**

Features

- ⬤ National park
- ★ Point of interest
- ☐ Major resort
- ✈ Main airport
- ⚓ Port
- 🚢 Cruise ships
- 🐟 Fishing port

Belize City:
Museum of Belize
Maritime Museum
Baron Bliss Lighthouse

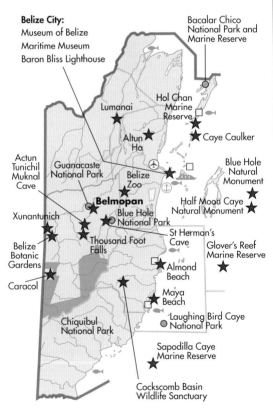

Bacalar Chico National Park and Marine Reserve
Lumanai
Altun Ha
Hol Chan Marine Reserve
Caye Caulker
Actun Tunichil Muknal Cave
Guanacaste National Park
Belize Zoo
Blue Hole Natural Monument
Xunantunich
Belmopan
Blue Hole National Park
Half Moon Caye Natural Monument
St Herman's Cave
Glover's Reef Marine Reserve
Belize Botanic Gardens
Thousand Foot Falls
Caracol
Almond Beach
Maya Beach
Laughing Bird Caye National Park
Chiquibul National Park
Sapodilla Caye Marine Reserve
Cockscomb Basin Wildlife Sanctuary

Scale 1 : 3 000 000

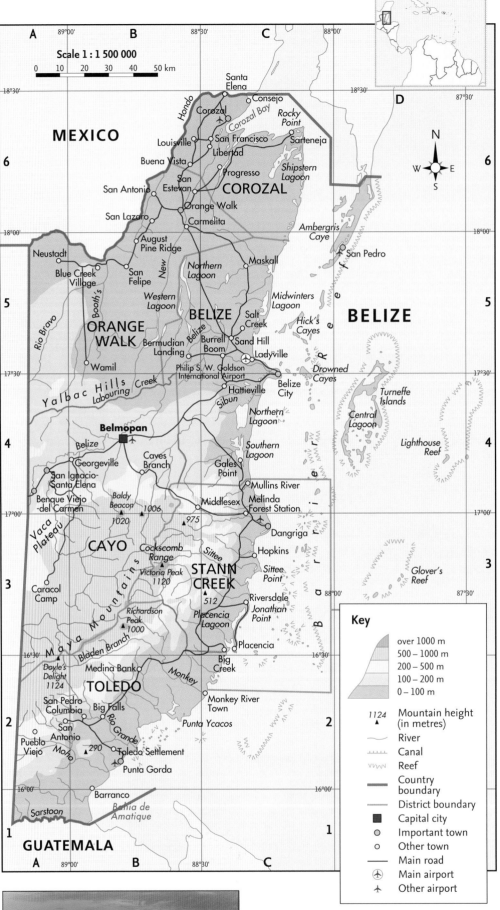

Scale 1 : 1 500 000
0 10 20 30 40 50 km

MEXICO

Santa Elena
Consejo
Corozal
Rocky Point
Louisville
San Francisco
Sarteneja
Buena Vista
Libertad
Progresso
Shipstern Lagoon
San Antonio
San Estevan
Orange Walk
Ambergris Caye
San Lazaro
Carmelita
San Pedro
Neustadt
August Pine Ridge
Blue Creek Village
San Felipe
Northern Lagoon
Maskall
COROZAL
Midwinters Lagoon
Western Lagoon
BELIZE
Salt Creek
Hick's Cayes
BELIZE
ORANGE WALK
Burrell Boom
Sand Hill
Bermudian Landing
Ladyville
Wamil
Philip S. W. Goldson International Airport
Drowned Cayes
Turneffe Islands
Hattieville
Belize City
Yalbac Hills
Labouring Creek
Sibun
Central Lagoon
Belmopan
Northern Lagoon
Georgeville
Caves Branch
Gales Point
Southern Lagoon
Lighthouse Reef
San Ignacio-Santa Elena
Benque Viejo -del Carmen
Baldy Beacon
1006
1020
Mullins River
Middlesex
Melinda Forest Station
Vaca Plateau
975
Dangriga
CAYO
Cockscomb Range
Sittee
Hopkins
Caracol Camp
Victoria Peak
1120
STANN CREEK
Sittee Point
Glover's Reef
Richardson Peak
1000
512
Riversdale
Jonathan Point
Placencia Lagoon
Placencia
Maya Mountains
Bladen Branch
Big Creek
Doyle's Delight
1124
Medina Bank
Monkey
Monkey River Town
San Pedro Columbia
Big Falls
TOLEDO
Punta Ycacos
San Antonio
Rio Grande
290
Pueblo Viejo
Moho
Toledo Settlement
Punta Gorda
Barranco
Sarstoon
Bahia de Amatique
GUATEMALA

Key

▨	over 1000 m
▨	500 – 1000 m
▨	200 – 500 m
▨	100 – 200 m
▨	0 – 100 m
1124 ▲	Mountain height (in metres)
∿	River
⊥⊥⊥	Canal
⌄⌄⌄	Reef
━━	Country boundary
────	District boundary
■	Capital city
◉	Important town
○	Other town
──	Main road
✈	Main airport
✈	Other airport

Chewing gum

- Chewing gum was originally made from chicle, the sap of the sapodilla tree
- The sapodilla tree is common throughout the Caribbean, commonly called the 'Dilly' tree. It is widespread in Belize
- In the 1880s American companies, including Wrigley's and Beechnut, bought large amounts from local sap collectors, known as 'chicleros'
- In the 1960s chewing gum began to be made from a cheaper chemical product related to synthetic rubber, and the chicle industry collapsed
- Chewing gum is a worldwide pollution agent (it is banned in Singapore). It cannot be cleaned up easily as it does not dissolve in water

The Great Blue Hole is a large solution hole (315 m wide and 124 m deep), now flooded since sea level rose after the ice ages. It is surrounded by coral reefs which are a World Heritage site popular with tourists.

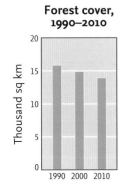

Forest cover, 1990–2010

Thousand sq km
20
15
10
5
0
1990 2000 2010

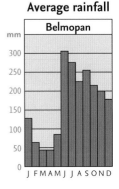

Average rainfall

Belmopan

mm
300
250
200
150
100
50
0
J F M A M J J A S O N D

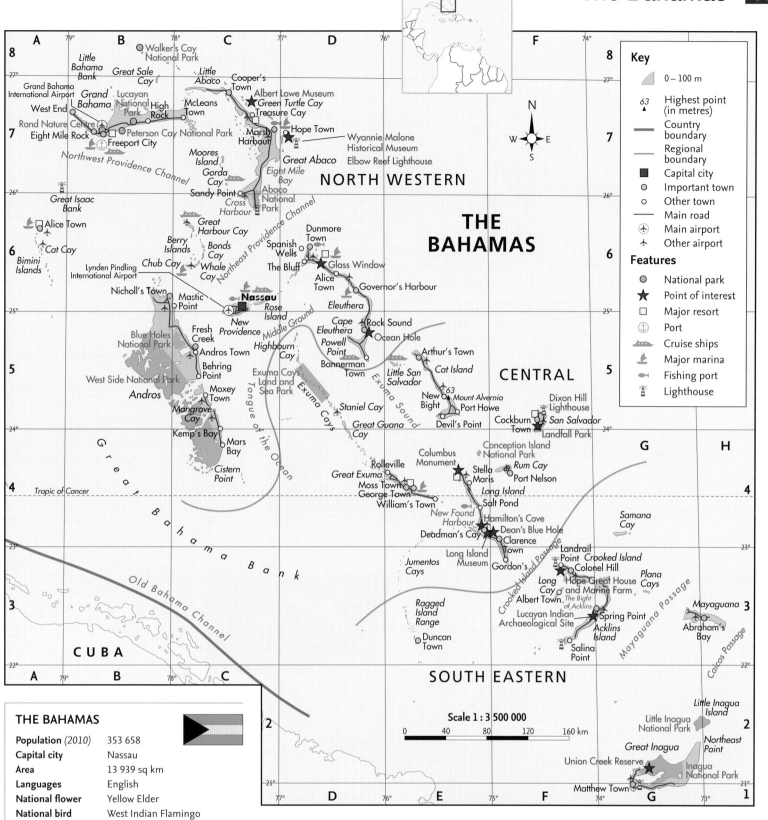

THE BAHAMAS

Population (2010)	353 658
Capital city	Nassau
Area	13 939 sq km
Languages	English
National flower	Yellow Elder
National bird	West Indian Flamingo
National animal	Blue Marlin

Columbus's first landfall in the New World was on San Salvador on 14 October **1492**

Columbus visited four islands in The Bahamas before travelling on

The prehistoric inhabitants were the Lucayans, a branch of the Taino people, but all were wiped out within 50 years of the country's first sighting

The first settlers were religious refugees from Bermuda who settled on Eleuthera in **1648**

The Bahamas became a British colony in **1718** and remained British until independence in **1973**

The Bahamas had a small cotton plantation economy with the arrival of the Loyalists, but also subsisted on shifting cultivation and fishing, and occasionally from wrecking, blockade running and other opportunistic enterprises

New Providence is the most densely populated island in the Caribbean region

The extent of the archipelago is the same as the distance from Antigua to Trinidad

The current economy is dependent on tourism and offshore finance

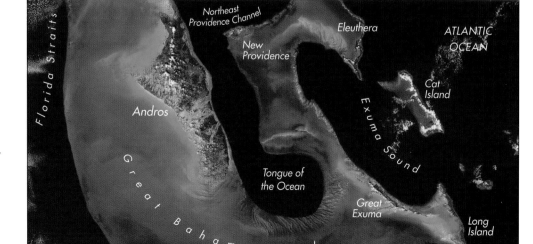

This satellite view shows the shallow waters (in lighter blue) of the Great Bahama Bank.

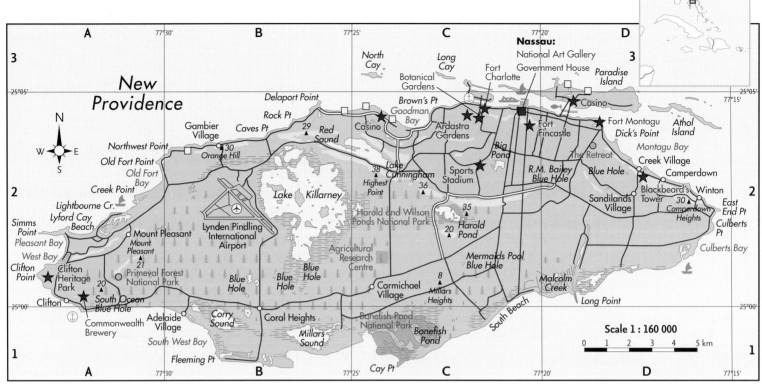

Key

over 12 m		
0 – 12 m		
38 ▲	Mountain height (in metres)	
	River	
■	Capital city	
○	Other town	

Features

═══	Highway
────	Main road
✈	Main airport
	Mangrove
	Pine forest
	National park

●	National park
★	Point of interest
□	Major resort
⚓	Port
🚢	Cruise ships
⛵	Major marina
🐟	Fishing port

Average rainfall

Nassau

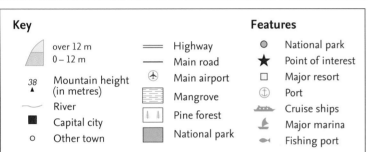

The Bahamas population growth

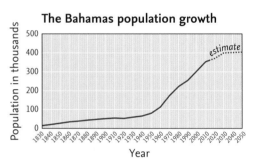

Blue holes

- These are deep solution holes in the flat limestone islands and shallow seas
- Those in the sea are known as ocean holes
- Some exist in The Cockpit Country of Jamaica and many in the Yucatán area of Mexico
- There are hundreds in The Bahamas, many over 100 metres deep
- The deepest blue hole is Dean's Blue Hole on Long Island, 202 metres deep
- This blue hole has been the scene of a number of recent free diving record attempts
- Many artifacts from the original Amerindian inhabitants (known as the Lucayans) have been found in the blue holes which these people used as burial sites

Hoffman's Cay Blue Hole, in the southern Berry Islands, is a popular spot with tourists, scuba divers and swimmers.

The Bahamas population distribution, 2010

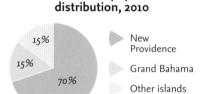

- New Providence
- Grand Bahama
- Other islands

THE BAHAMAS island data	Area (sq km)	Population (2010)	Pop. density (per sq km)
TOTAL	13 939	353 658	25
New Providence	207	248 948	1203
Grand Bahama	1373	51 756	38
Abaco	1681	16 692	10
Acklins	497	560	1
Andros	5957	7386	1
Berry Islands	31	798	26
Bimini Islands	23	2008	87
Cat Island	389	1503	4
Cay Sal Bank	5	0	0
Crooked Island/ Long Cay	241	323	1
Eleuthera	518	11 065	21
Exuma and Cays	290	7314	25
Inagua	1551	911	1
Long Island	596	3024	5
Mayaguana	285	271	1
Ragged Island	36	70	2
Rum Cay	78	99	1
San Salvador	163	930	6

Cruise ships docked in Nassau, the main port for tourist arrivals. The tourism industry is the biggest source of income in The Bahamas, with about half of the labour force working in tourism, supplying 70 per cent of tax revenue.

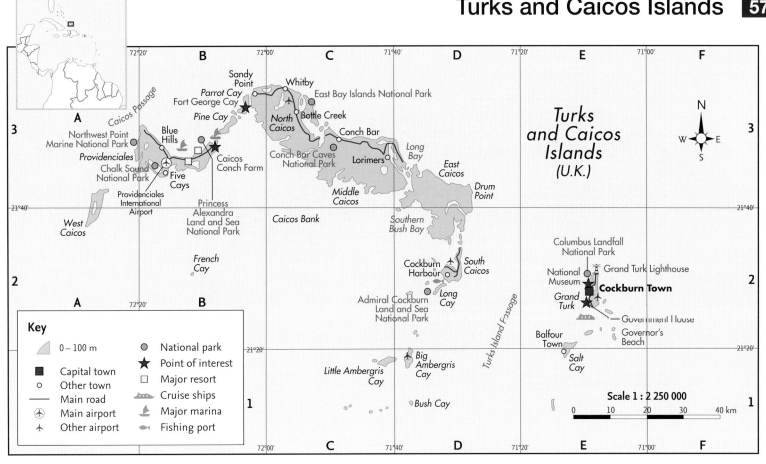

TURKS & CAICOS island data	Area (sq km)	Population (2012)	Pop. density (per sq km)
TOTAL	616	31 458	51
Grand Turk	17	4831	284
Middle Caicos	144	168	1
North Caicos	116	1312	11
Parrot Cay	6	131	22
Providenciales	122	23 769	195
Salt Cay	7	108	15
South Caicos	21	1139	54

Average rainfall

Turks and Caicos population distribution, 2012

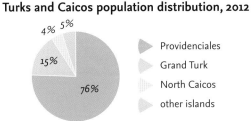

- Providenciales — 76%
- Grand Turk — 15%
- North Caicos — 4%
- other islands — 5%

Cockburn Town, on Grand Turk Island, was founded on the sea salt industry. Cockburn Town is the capital city of the Turks and Caicos Islands, and Duke Street (above) is a historic street in the city lined with British colonial architecture.

TURKS AND CAICOS ISLANDS

British Overseas Territory

Population (2012) 31 458
Capital town Cockburn Town
Area 616 sq km
Languages English
National flower Turk's Head Cactus
National bird Brown Pelican
National animal Rock Iguana

The prehistoric inhabitants were the Taino
First sighted by Ponce de León in **1512**
Settled by Bermudans collecting salt after **1680**
Occupied by the French **1765–1799**
Became part of the British Bahamas in **1799**
Governed variously by Jamaica and The Bahamas until **1973** when it became a British Overseas Territory

Grace Bay, Providenciales, Turks and Caicos Islands is one of the most pristine beaches in the world.

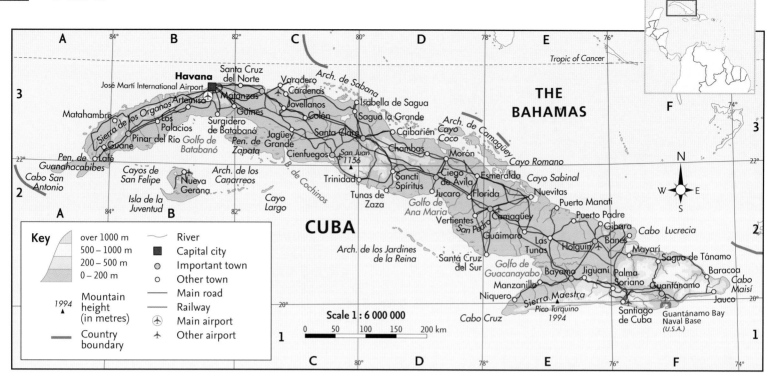

Key

over 1000 m		River
500 – 1000 m	■	Capital city
200 – 500 m	⊙	Important town
0 – 200 m	○	Other town
		Main road
▲ 1994 Mountain height (in metres)		Railway
	✈	Main airport
Country boundary	✈	Other airport

Scale 1 : 6 000 000

0   50   100   150   200 km

Tropic of Cancer

THE BAHAMAS

CUBA

Features

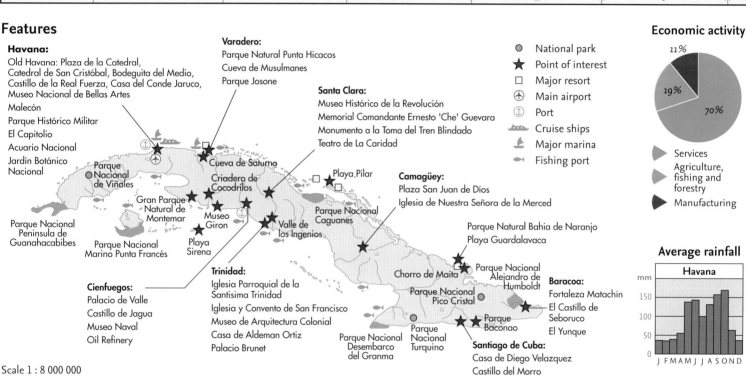

Havana:
Old Havana: Plaza de la Catedral,
Catedral de San Cristóbal, Bodeguita del Medio,
Castillo de la Real Fuerza, Casa del Conde Jaruco,
Museo Nacional de Bellas Artes
Malecón
Parque Histórico Militar
El Capitolio
Acuario Nacional
Jardín Botánico Nacional

Parque Nacional Península de Guanahacabibes

Cienfuegos:
Palacio de Valle
Castillo de Jagua
Museo Naval
Oil Refinery

Scale 1 : 8 000 000

Varadero:
Parque Natural Punta Hicacos
Cueva de Musulmanes
Parque Josone

Santa Clara:
Museo Histórico de la Revolución
Memorial Comandante Ernesto 'Che' Guevara
Monumento a la Toma del Tren Blindado
Teatro de La Caridad

Trinidad:
Iglesia Parroquial de la Santisima Trinidad
Iglesia y Convento de San Francisco
Museo de Arquitectura Colonial
Casa de Aldeman Ortiz
Palacio Brunet

Camagüey:
Plaza San Juan de Díos
Iglesia de Nuestra Señora de la Merced

Baracoa:
Fortaleza Matachín
El Castillo de Seboruco
El Yunque

Santiago de Cuba:
Casa de Diego Velazquez
Castillo del Morro

⊙	National park
★	Point of interest
□	Major resort
✈	Main airport
⚓	Port
🚢	Cruise ships
⚓	Major marina
🐟	Fishing port

Economic activity

11%
19%
70%

▸ Services
▸ Agriculture, fishing and forestry
▸ Manufacturing

Average rainfall

Havana

mm
150
100
50
0
J F M A M J J A S O N D

Fulgencio Batista was president of Cuba from 1940 to 1944. He came back to power in 1952 through a military coup and remained dictator of Cuba until deposed by the Cuban Revolution in 1959. He died in exile in Spain in 1973.

Fidel Castro was the ruler of Cuba from 1959 until 2008. He gained power through the Cuban Revolution, which he led with Che Guevara and his brother Raúl Castro. Due to failing health he passed the presidency to his brother in 2008, and died in 2016.

CUBA

Population (2012)	11 167 325
Capital city	Havana
Area	110 860 sq km
Languages	Spanish
National flower	White Mariposa
National bird	Tocororo
National animal	Cuban Trogon

First sighted by Columbus on his first voyage in **1492**. Columbus thought he had reached Japan (Cipangu)

Original inhabitants were the Taino and Ciboney. Both groups had died out, mainly from disease, by **1600**

Cuba was a Spanish colony from its sighting by Columbus until **1898**

The Spanish-American war of **1898** led to the independence of Cuba, but until **1902** it was governed by the USA

In **1959** the Cuban Revolution took over the government and founded a socialist state, and by **1965** a communist state

In **1961** a US supported invasion at the Bay of Pigs was repelled by the Cubans

A US embargo on trade and travel to Cuba was begun in **1960**, but was partly reduced in **2015**

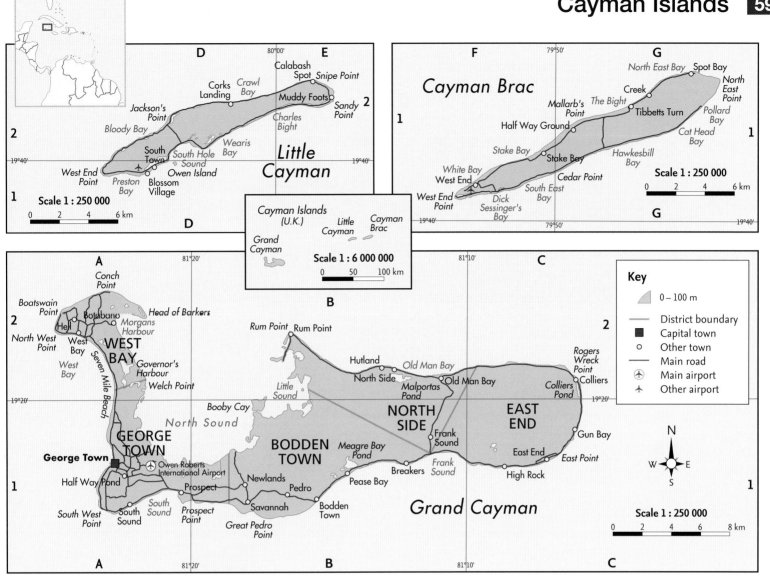

Little Cayman

D — E

Calabash Spot — Snipe Point
Corks Landing — Crawl Bay
Muddy Foots
Jackson's Point — Sandy Point
Charles Bight
Bloody Bay — Wearis Bay
South Town — South Hole Sound
West End Point — Owen Island
Preston Bay — Blossom Village

Scale 1 : 250 000
0 2 4 6 km

Cayman Brac

F — 79°50' — G

North East Bay — Spot Bay
Creek — North East Point
Mallarb's Point — The Bight
Tibbetts Turn — Pollard Bay
Half Way Ground
Cat Head Bay
Stake Bay
White Bay — Stake Bay — Hawkesbill Bay
West End — Cedar Point
West End Point — South East Bay
Dick Sessinger's Bay

Scale 1 : 250 000
0 2 4 6 km

Cayman Islands (U.K.)

Grand Cayman   Little Cayman   Cayman Brac

Scale 1 : 6 000 000
0 50 100 km

Grand Cayman

A — B — C

Conch Point
Boatswain Point
Head of Barkers
Botabano — Morgans Harbour
Hell — WEST BAY
North West Point — West Bay
West Bay
Governor's Harbour
Welch Point
Booby Cay
Little Sound
North Sound
GEORGE TOWN
George Town
Seven Mile Beach
Half Way Pond
Owen Roberts International Airport
Prospect
South Sound
South West Point — South Sound
Prospect Point
Great Pedro Point
Newlands — Pedro
Savannah
Bodden Town
BODDEN TOWN
Meagre Bay Pond
Breakers — Pease Bay
Rum Point
Hutland
North Side
Old Man Bay
Malportas Pond
Old Man Bay
NORTH SIDE
Frank Sound
Frank Sound
Rogers Wreck Point
Colliers
Colliers Pond
EAST END
Gun Bay
East End — East Point
High Rock

Key

▨	0 – 100 m
—	District boundary
■	Capital town
○	Other town
—	Main road
✈	Main airport
✈	Other airport

N W E S

Scale 1 : 250 000
0 2 4 6 8 km

CAYMAN ISLANDS

British Overseas Territory

Population (2010)	55 036
Capital town	George Town
Area	264 sq km
Languages	English
National flower	Wild Banana Orchid
National bird	Cayman Parrot

No prehistoric settlement is known

Little Cayman and Cayman Brac were first sighted by Columbus in **1503**

Occasional European settlements were attempted on Grand Cayman in the **17th** century

The Cayman Islands formally became British in **1670**, and permanent settlement was established after **1730**

The Caymans were governed as a British colony with Jamaica until **1962**, when it became a separate crown colony, and subsequently a British Overseas Territory

It has since become a tax haven and a major tourist destination in the modern era

Features

● National park	✈ Main airport
★ Point of interest	Port
□ Major resort	Cruise ships
	Major marina
	Fishing port

Barker's National Park
Hell Rock Formations
Stingray City
Cayman Turtle Farm
Cemetery Beach and Reef
Kittiwake Shipwreck and Artificial Reef
Seven Mile Beach
Government House
Devil's Grotto
Davinoff's Concrete Sculpture Garden
Mastic Trail
Blue Iguana Nature Reserve
Queen Elizabeth II Botanic Park
East End Lighthouse Park
Pedro St James National Historic Site

George Town:
Fort George
Government Buildings
National Museum
National Gallery

Scale 1 : 400 000

	Area (sq km)	Population (2010)	Population density (per sq km)
Grand Cayman	197	52 740	268
Cayman Brac	39	2098	54
Little Cayman	28	198	7

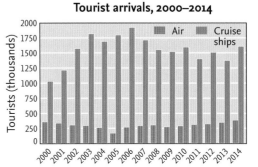

Tourist arrivals, 2000–2014

Air — Cruise ships
Tourists (thousands)
2000 2001 2002 2003 2004 2005 2006 2007 2008 2009 2010 2011 2012 2013 2014

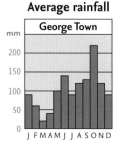

Average rainfall

George Town
mm
J F M A M J J A S O N D

The Blue Iguana is found only on Grand Cayman. It can reach 1.5 metres in length and live for over 60 years. It is an endangered species and only 750 are believed to exist.

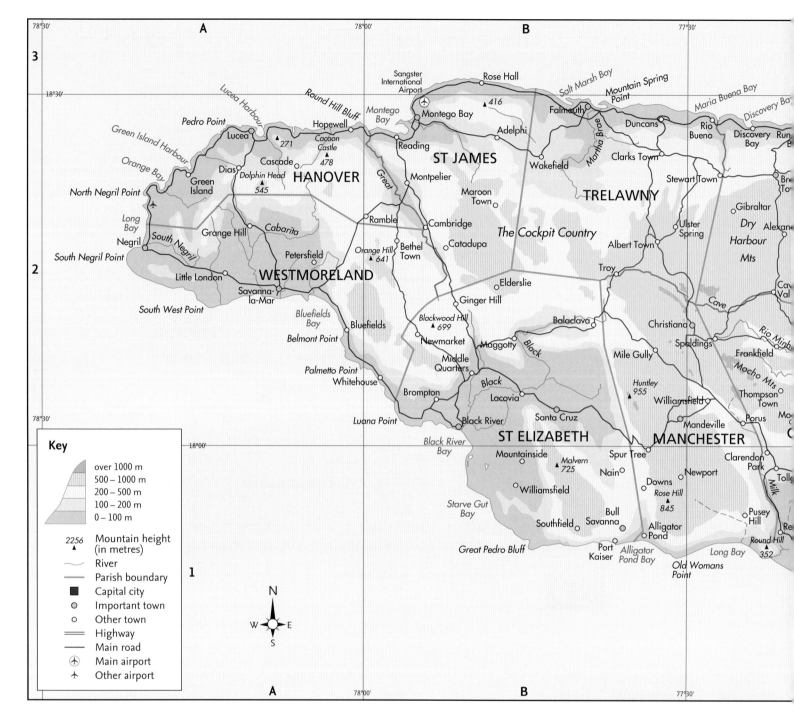

Key

	over 1000 m
	500 – 1000 m
	200 – 500 m
	100 – 200 m
	0 – 100 m
▲ 2256	Mountain height (in metres)
	River
	Parish boundary
■	Capital city
◉	Important town
○	Other town
⚌	Highway
—	Main road
✈	Main airport
✈	Other airport

JAMAICA

Population (2016)	2 730 894
Capital city	Kingston
Area	10 991 sq km
Languages	English, creole

National flower	Lignum Vitae
National fruit	Ackee
National tree	Blue Mahoe
National bird	Red-billed Streamertail (Doctor Bird)

Counties and parishes

	County boundary
	Parish boundary
○	Parish capital

Scale 1 : 2 000 000

Salt fish and ackee is the traditional dish of Jamaica. The ackee (top) is the national fruit, originally from West Africa, while the salt fish is dried and salted cod from Canada, and originally imported as a food for the population during slavery.

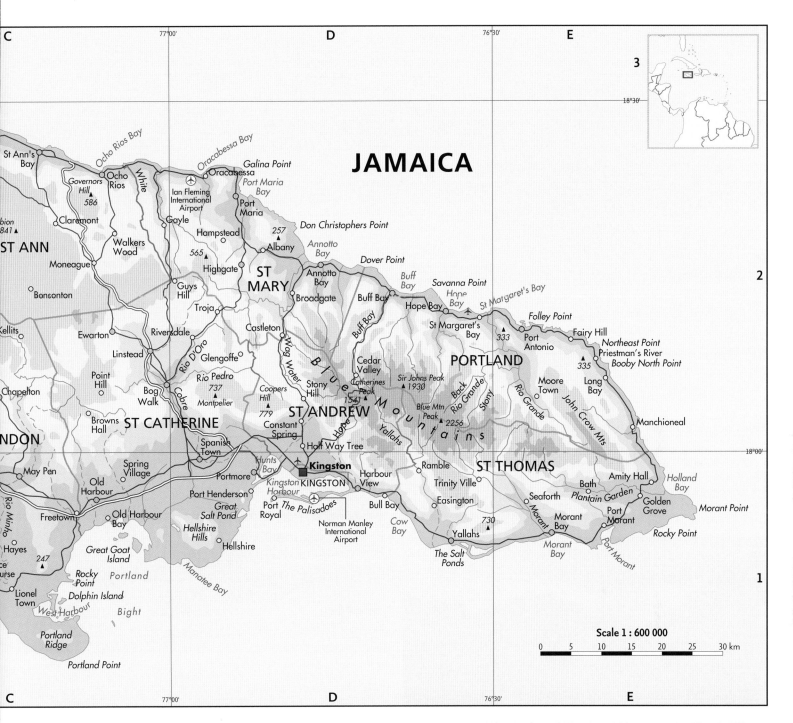

C 77°00' D 76°30' E

3

18°30'

JAMAICA

St Ann's Bay
Governors Hill 586
Ocho Rios
Ocho Rios Bay
White
Oracabessa Bay
Oracabessa
Galina Point
Port Maria
Port Maria Bay
bion 841
Claremont
Walkers Wood
Ian Fleming International Airport
Gayle
Hampstead
257
Albany
Don Christophers Point
Annotto Bay
Dover Point
ST ANN
Moneague
565
Highgate
ST MARY
Annotto Bay
Buff Bay
Savanna Point
Hope Bay
St Margaret's Bay
2
Bonsonton
Guys Hill
Troja
Broadgate
Buff Bay
Hope Bay
St Margaret's Bay
Folley Point
Kellits
Ewarton
Riversdale
Castleton
Buff Bay
Port Antonio
333
Fairy Hill
Northeast Point
Linstead
Rio D'Oro
Glengoffe
Wog Water
Cedar Valley
Sir Johns Peak 1930
PORTLAND
335
Priestman's River
Booby North Point
Point Hill
Rio Pedro
737
Catherines Peak 1541
Stony Hill
Blue Mtn Peak 2256
Back Rio Grande
Stony
Moore Town
Rio Grande
Long Bay
Chapelton
Bog Walk
Coopers Hill
Montpelier
Blue Mountains
John Crow Mts
Manchioneal
NDON
Browns Hall
ST CATHERINE
779
Constant Spring
ST ANDREW
Hope
Yallahs
18°00'
Spanish Town
May Pen
Spring Village
Old Harbour
Portmore
Hunts Bay
Kingston
KINGSTON
Kingston Harbour
Harbour View
Ramble
Trinity Ville
ST THOMAS
Bath
Amity Hall
Holland Bay
Port Henderson
Great Salt Pond
Port Royal
The Palisadoes
Bull Bay
Easington
Seaforth
Plantain Garden
Golden Grove
Morant Point
Freetown
Old Harbour Bay
Hellshire Hills
Norman Manley International Airport
Cow Bay
730
Morant
Morant Bay
Port Morant
Rocky Point
Rio Minho
Hayes
ce urse
247
Great Goat Island
Rocky Point
Portland
Dolphin Island
Hellshire
Yallahs
The Salt Ponds
Morant Bay
Port Morant
1
Lionel Town
West Harbour
Manatee Bay
Bight
Portland Ridge
Portland Point

Scale 1 : 600 000
0 5 10 15 20 25 30 km

C 77°00' D 76°30' E

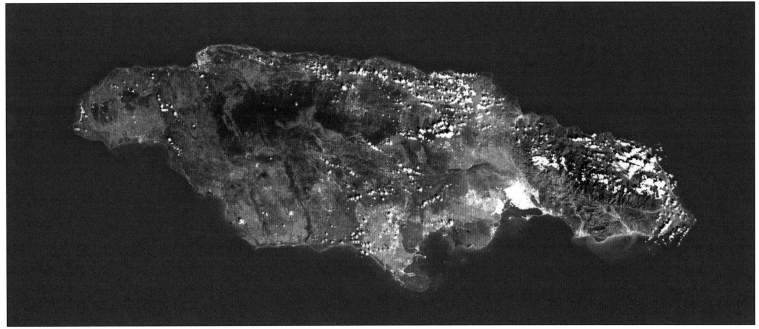

This satellite image shows Kingston and nearby Spanish Town as bright white areas, while the red patches are the bauxite workings in the interior. To the far east the rugged Blue Mountains can be seen, and in the west the very dark green represents the forests of the Cockpit Country. Note the clouds along the north coast, the wetter side of Jamaica as opposed to the drier south coast.

Features

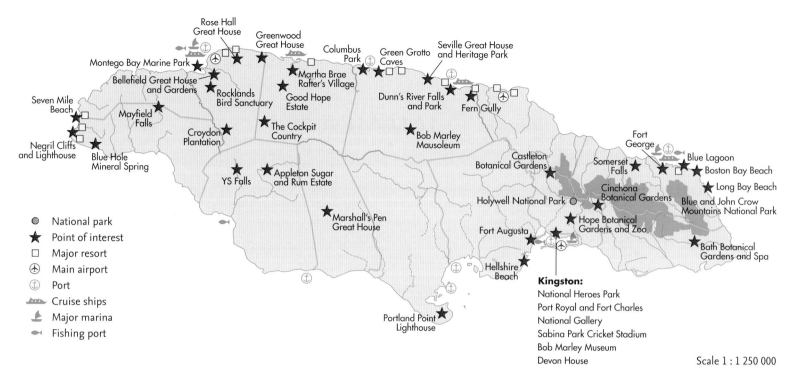

- National park
- ★ Point of interest
- □ Major resort
- ✈ Main airport
- ⊕ Port
- 🚢 Cruise ships
- ⚓ Major marina
- 🐟 Fishing port

Kingston:
National Heroes Park
Port Royal and Fort Charles
National Gallery
Sabina Park Cricket Stadium
Bob Marley Museum
Devon House

Scale 1 : 1 250 000

The Cockpit Country

- Severely eroded limestone district in northwest Jamaica
- The area is a wilderness of conical hills and deep hollows
- It contains the largest area of rainforest in Jamaica
- It is a proposed National Park and World Heritage site
- It was a hideout for escaped slaves (known as the maroons) in the 18th century
- It is still largely inaccessible today

In the last 50 years, Ocho Rios has grown from a fishing village to a major resort city and cruise port. It benefits from its attractive coastal setting and the nearby Dunn's River Falls, Jamaica's most visited tourist site.

The Cockpit Country is an area of heavily weathered limestone. It is a network of conical hills separated by deep sinkholes. It has been described as 'one of the world's most dramatic examples of karst topography'. Due to its difficult access it is still heavily forested.

Average rainfall
Kingston

mm
200
150
100
50
0
J F M A M J J A S O N D

Average rainfall
Montego Bay

mm
200
150
100
50
0
J F M A M J J A S O N D

Average rainfall
Port Antonio

mm
350
300
250
200
150
100
50
0
J F M A M J J A S O N D

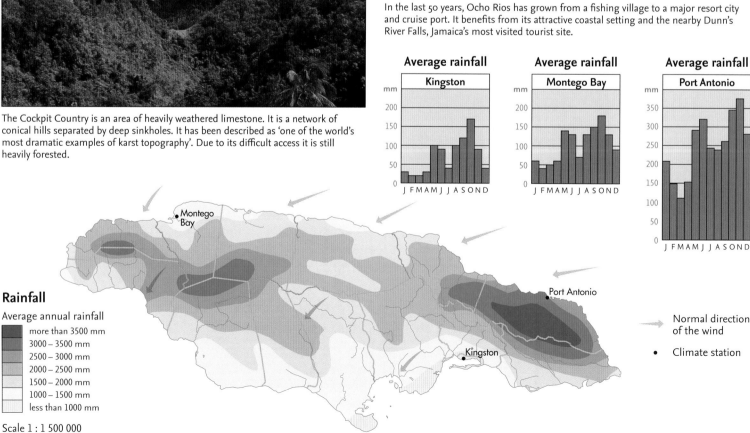

Rainfall

Average annual rainfall

- more than 3500 mm
- 3000 – 3500 mm
- 2500 – 3000 mm
- 2000 – 2500 mm
- 1500 – 2000 mm
- 1000 – 1500 mm
- less than 1000 mm

Scale 1 : 1 500 000

→ Normal direction of the wind

• Climate station

Population density, 2016

Persons per sq km

- over 500
- 250 – 500
- 200 – 250
- 150 – 200
- under 150

• Parish capital

Scale 1 : 2 500 000

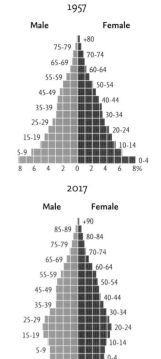

Population structure

1957

Male | Female

+80
75-79
70-74
65-69
60-64
55-59
50-54
45-49
40-44
35-39
30-34
25-29
20-24
15-19
10-14
5-9
0-4

8 6 4 2 0 2 4 6 8%

2017

Male | Female

+90
85-89
80-84
75-79
70-74
65-69
60-64
55-59
50-54
45-49
40-44
35-39
30-34
25-29
20-24
15-19
10-14
5-9
0-4

6 4 2 0 2 4 6%

Each full square represents 1% of the total population

Population change, 2001–2016

Percentage population change 2001–2016

- over 7.0
- 5.0 6.9
- 4.0 – 4.9
- 3.0 – 3.9
- 2.0 – 2.9

Scale 1 : 2 500 000

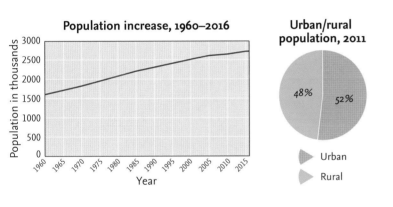

Population increase, 1960–2016

(graph: Population in thousands vs Year, 1960–2015)

Urban/rural population, 2011

48% | 52%

▸ Urban
▸ Rural

A busy street scene in Downtown, Kingston.

Kingston-Spanish Town conurbation

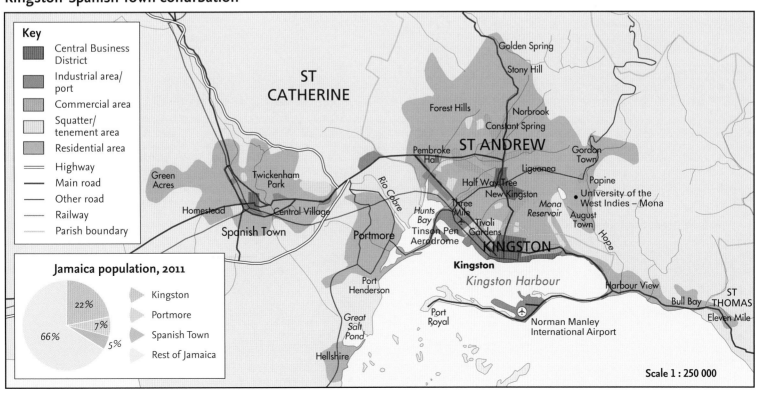

Key

- Central Business District
- Industrial area/ port
- Commercial area
- Squatter/ tenement area
- Residential area
- Highway
- Main road
- Other road
- Railway
- Parish boundary

Jamaica population, 2011

22%
7%
5%
66%

▸ Kingston
▸ Portmore
▸ Spanish Town
▸ Rest of Jamaica

Scale 1 : 250 000

Agriculture

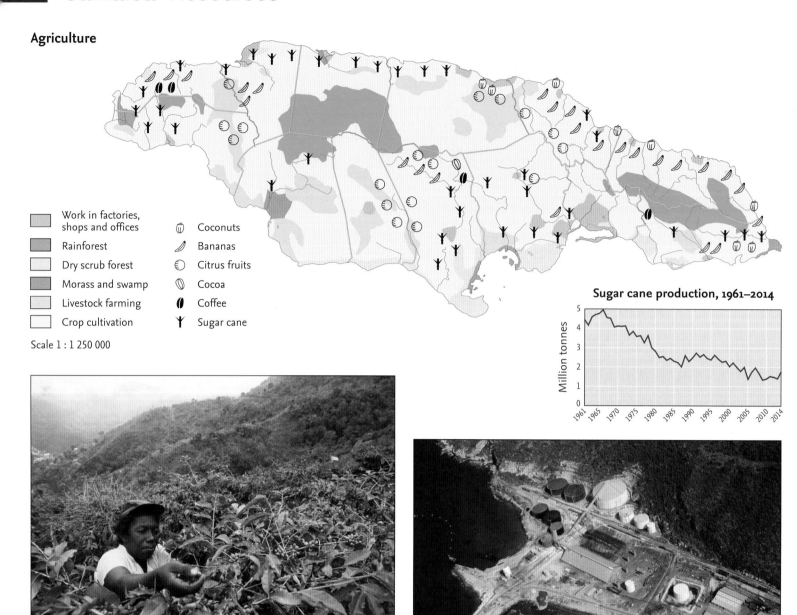

Legend:
- Work in factories, shops and offices
- Rainforest
- Dry scrub forest
- Morass and swamp
- Livestock farming
- Crop cultivation

- Coconuts
- Bananas
- Citrus fruits
- Cocoa
- Coffee
- Sugar cane

Scale 1 : 1 250 000

Sugar cane production, 1961–2014

Million tonnes (y-axis: 0 to 5)
Years: 1961, 1965, 1970, 1975, 1980, 1985, 1990, 1995, 2000, 2005, 2010, 2014

The cool humid atmosphere of the Blue Mountains ensures that the finest coffee can grow here. Blue Mountain Coffee has a limited production, but it is considered one of the world's finest (and most expensive) coffees.

Port Kaiser is the export point for bauxite and alumina being shipped from Alpart's mines at Nain. The port was closed until 2015 when the mines were re-opened, and the first exports went to the Ukraine.

Industry

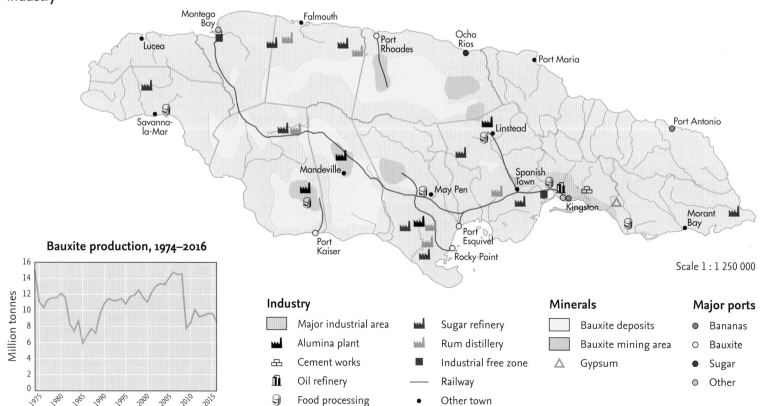

Bauxite production, 1974–2016

Million tonnes (y-axis: 0 to 16)
Years: 1975, 1980, 1985, 1990, 1995, 2000, 2005, 2010, 2015

Industry
- Major industrial area
- Alumina plant
- Cement works
- Oil refinery
- Food processing
- Sugar refinery
- Rum distillery
- Industrial free zone
- Railway
- Other town

Minerals
- Bauxite deposits
- Bauxite mining area
- Gypsum

Major ports
- Bananas
- Bauxite
- Sugar
- Other

Scale 1 : 1 250 000

History

- Between **4000** and **1000** BC Arawak and Taino peoples from South America migrated northwards. Some of these migrants settled in Jamaica
- Christopher Columbus arrived in **1494** and claimed Jamaica for Spain. The first Spanish settlement was established in **1509**. Spanish Town was settled by the Spanish in **1534**
- In **1655** the British captured Jamaica from the Spanish and ruled the island until **1962**
- Under British rule Jamaica became one of the world's main producers and exporters of sugar using a plantation economy and African slave labour
- With the full abolition of slavery in **1838** the British did not have a large enough work force for their plantations and so hired Indian and Chinese contract labourers
- Since **1952** bauxite has replaced sugar and other agricultural products as Jamaica's main export
- Jamaica gained full independence in **1962**

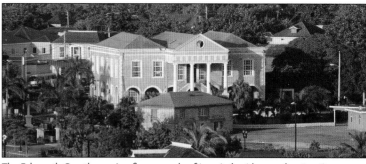

The Falmouth Courthouse is a fine example of Jamaica's widespread restoration projects. The Courthouse was built in 1815, but eventually deteriorated and was gutted by fire in 1926. Between 2007 and 2011 the windows and portico were rebuilt, and today the building presents a fine prospect for vessels entering the harbour.

Culture

Music

- Jamaica has had a big impact on the development of popular music worldwide. Musical styles such as ska, reggae and dancehall all originated in Jamaica and these in turn influenced the development of punk rock and American rap and hip hop music
- Many internationally known musicians were born in Jamaica, one of the most famous being the reggae artist Bob Marley who died in 1981. There is a museum dedicated to his life in Kingston

Musical innovation and musicians are not only a Jamaican characteristic, but they are also a valuable export, attracting many thousands to the country. Chronixx specialises in reggae, but is a young and versatile artist.

Literature

- The author of the James Bond novels, Ian Fleming, lived in Jamaica and set some of his stories on the island
- Marlon James, a Jamaican-born writer, won the 2015 Man Booker Prize for his novel *A Brief History of Seven Killings*

Sport

- Sport is an important part of life for Jamaicans. The most popular sports include athletics, cricket, soccer and basketball
- Jamaica is one of the top nations in sprinting. The current World and Olympic record holder in the 100 m and 200 m is the Jamaican-born Usain Bolt
- Veronica Campbell-Brown won the Olympic gold for the 200 m in both 2004 and 2008, becoming the first Caribbean woman to win this event and also to retain the title. In 2008 Shelly-Ann Fraser-Pryce matched this feat and became the first Caribbean woman to win the 100 m sprint
- Some of the world's most famous cricketers have come from Jamaica including Michael Holding, Courtney Walsh and Chris Gayle. Jamaica provides players for the West Indies cricket team and the Test venue is at Sabina Park in Kingston

Shelly-Ann Fraser-Pryce won the women's Olympic 100 m in 2008 and repeated the achievement in 2012, only the third woman ever to have done this. In 2012 she also won the Olympic silver medal for the 200 m and 4 x 100 m races. She is seen here anchoring a 4 x 100 m relay race in Philadelphia, USA.

Tourism

Stop-over visitor arrivals, 2001–2016

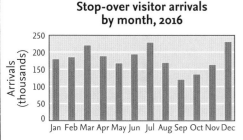

Stop-over visitor arrivals by country of origin, 2016

- USA 64%
- Canada 17%
- Europe 14%
- Caribbean 3%
- Rest of the world 2%

Cruise passenger arrivals, 2001–2016

Stop-over visitor arrivals by month, 2016

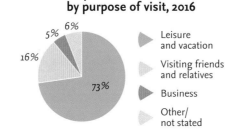

Stop-over visitor arrivals by purpose of visit, 2016

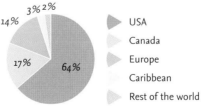

- Leisure and vacation 73%
- Visiting friends and relatives 16%
- Business 5%
- Other/ not stated 6%

Cruise passenger arrivals by month, 2016

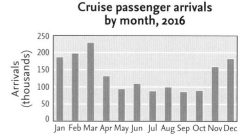

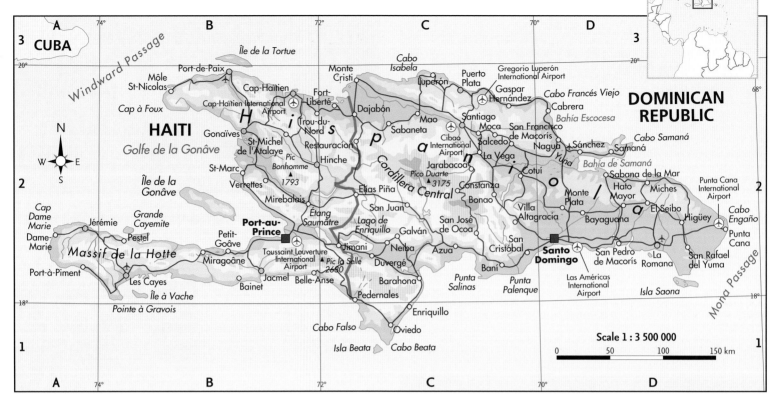

A 74° **B** 72° **C** 70° **D**

3 CUBA

Windward Passage

Île de la Tortue

Môle St-Nicolas
Port-de-Paix
Cap-Haïtien
Monte Cristi
Cabo Isabela
Luperón
Puerto Plata
Gregorio Luperón International Airport
Gaspar Hernández
Cabo Francés Viejo
Cabrera
Bahía Escocesa

DOMINICAN REPUBLIC

Cap à Foux
Cap-Haïtien International Airport
Fort-Liberté
Dajabón
Mao
Santiago
Moca
San Francisco de Macorís
Nagua
Sánchez
Samaná
Cabo Samaná

HAITI
Gonaïves
St-Michel de l'Atalaye
Trou-du-Nord
Restauración
Sabaneta
Cibao International Airport
Salcedo
La Vega
Cotuí
Bahía de Samaná
Sabana de la Mar

Golfe de la Gonâve
St-Marc
Pic Bonhomme 1793
Hinche
Jarabacoa
Pico Duarte ▲ 3175
Constanza
Bonao
Monte Plata
Hato Mayor
Miches
Punta Cana International Airport

2
Cap Dame Marie
Jérémie
Grande Cayemite
St-Marc
Verrettes
Mirebalais
Étang Saumâtre
Elías Piña
San Juan
Lago de Enriquillo
Galván
San José de Ocoa
Villa Altagracia
Bayaguana
El Seibo
Higüey
Cabo Engaño
Punta Cana

Dame Marie
Pestel
Île de la Gonâve
Port-au-Prince
Petit-Goâve
Jimaní
Neiba
Azua
San Cristóbal
Santo Domingo
San Pedro de Macorís
La Romana
San Rafael del Yuma

Massif de la Hotte
Toussaint Louverture International Airport
Miragoâne
Pic la Selle 2680
Duvergé
Baní
Punta Salinas
Punta Palenque
Las Américas International Airport
Isla Saona

Port-à-Piment
Les Cayes
Jacmel
Belle-Anse
Barahona
Pedernales

1
Île à Vache
Pointe à Gravois
Bainet
Enriquillo
Scale 1 : 3 500 000

Cabo Falso
Oviedo
0   50   100   150 km

Isla Beata
Cabo Beata

Mona Passage

A 74° **B** 72° **C** 70° **D**

Features

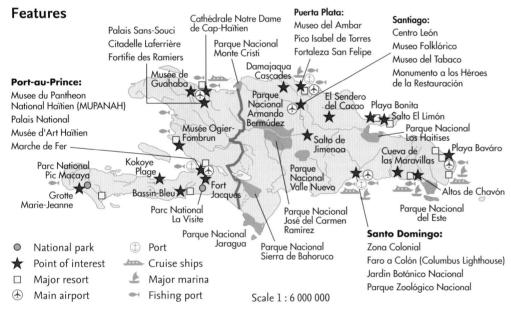

Port-au-Prince:
Musee du Pantheon National Haïtien (MUPANAH)
Palais National
Musée d'Art Haïtien
Marche de Fer

Palais Sans-Souci
Citadelle Laferrière
Fortifie des Ramiers

Cathédrale Notre Dame de Cap-Haïtien

Parque Nacional Monte Cristi

Musée de Guahaba

Damajagua Cascades

Parque Nacional Armando Bermúdez

Puerta Plata:
Museo del Ambar
Pico Isabel de Torres
Fortaleza San Felipe

Santiago:
Centro León
Museo Folklórico
Museo del Tabaco
Monumento a los Héroes de la Restauración

El Sendero del Cacao
Playa Bonita
Salto El Limón
Parque Nacional Los Haitises

Musée Ogier-Fombrun
Salto de Jimenoa
Cueva de las Maravillas
Playa Bávaro

Parc National Pic Macaya
Kokoye Plage
Parque Nacional Valle Nuevo
Altos de Chavón

Grotte Marie-Jeanne
Bassin-Bleu
Fort Jacques
Parque Nacional José del Carmen Ramírez
Parque Nacional del Este

Parc National La Visite

Santo Domingo:
Zona Colonial
Faro a Colón (Columbus Lighthouse)
Jardin Botánico Nacional
Parque Zoológico Nacional

Parque Nacional Jaragua
Parque Nacional Sierra de Bahoruco

● National park
★ Point of interest
☐ Major resort
⊛ Main airport

⊕ Port
⛴ Cruise ships
⚓ Major marina
🐟 Fishing port

Scale 1 : 6 000 000

Key

over 3000 m	～ River
2000 – 3000 m	━ Country boundary
1000 – 2000 m	
500 – 1000 m	■ Capital city
200 – 500 m	⊚ Important town
0 – 200 m	○ Other town
	— Main road
▲ 3175 Mountain height (in metres)	⊛ Main airport
	✦ Other airport

Average rainfall

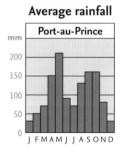

Port-au-Prince

mm
200
150
100
50
0
J F M A M J J A S O N D

Average rainfall

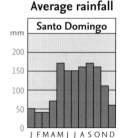

Santo Domingo

mm
200
150
100
50
0
J F M A M J J A S O N D

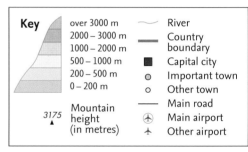

HAITI

Population (2013 est.)	10 320 000
Capital city	Port-au-Prince
Area	27 750 sq km
Languages	French, creole
National flower	Hibiscus
National bird	Hispaniolan Trogon

First sighted by Columbus, who thought he had reached India, on his first voyage in **1492**

The original inhabitants were the Taino who died out mainly from disease in the next 100 years

Initially part of the larger Spanish colony of Hispaniola, the whole island was ceded to France in **1625**. In **1697** Hispaniola became a French colony called Saint-Domingue

The French created a sugar plantation economy for their new colony

In **1804** the Haitian Revolution (began **1791**) created the Republic of Haiti, the first independent country in the Caribbean

From **1915** until **1934** the country was occupied by the United States

On 12 January **2010** a major earthquake destroyed much of the capital Port-au-Prince and killed an estimated 100 000 people

DOMINICAN REPUBLIC

Population (2010)	9 445 281
Capital city	Santo Domingo
Area	48 442 sq km
Languages	Spanish, creole
National flower	Bayahibe Rose
National bird	Palm Chat

First sighted by Columbus on his first voyage in **1492**

The original inhabitants were the Taino who died out mainly from disease in the next 100 years

The colony of Hispaniola remained Spanish until the French took over in **1625**

French rule continued after the Haitian revolution until **1809** when the present Dominican Republic's boundaries were established

The Dominican Republic, part of Saint-Domingue, again became Spanish, until **1821**, when it was occupied by Haiti, and the whole island became Haitian until **1844**

The modern Dominican Republic was created as an independent country on 27 February **1844** (independence from Haiti), but was commonly called Santo Domingo

From **1861** until 16 August **1865** the Dominican Republic was again a Spanish colony, so there are two independence days (independence from Spain)

Street sellers are often the main sellers of food in Haiti.

Spanish historic remains in Santo Domingo.

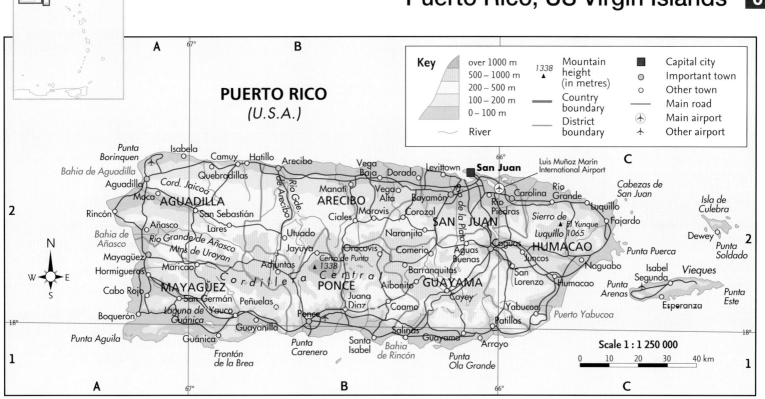

PUERTO RICO (U.S.A.)

Key
- over 1000 m
- 500 – 1000 m
- 200 – 500 m
- 100 – 200 m
- 0 – 100 m
- River
- 1338 ▲ Mountain height (in metres)
- Country boundary
- District boundary
- ■ Capital city
- ● Important town
- ○ Other town
- Main road
- ✈ Main airport
- ✈ Other airport

Scale 1 : 1 250 000

0 10 20 30 40 km

Features

- ● National park
- ★ Point of interest
- □ Major resort
- ⊕ Main airport
- ⚓ Port
- ⛴ Cruise ships
- ⛵ Major marina

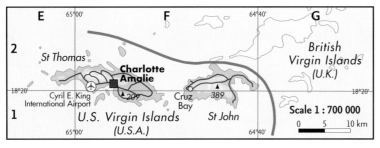

Faro de Punta Higuero
Bosque Estatal de Guajataca
Arecibo Radio Telescope Observatory
Arecibo Lighthouse and Historical Park
Cueva del Indio
Museo del Café
Parque de las Cavernas del Río Camuy
Zoologico
Jardín Botánico y Cultural de Caguas
Centro Ceremonial Indígena de Tibes
Hacienda Buena Vista
Reserve Natural de Humacao
El Yunque National Forest
Reserva Natural de las Cabezas de San Juan
Culebra National Wildlife Refuge
Vieques National Wildlife Refuge
Fortín Conde de Mirasol
Reserve Natural Laguna de Joyuda
Bosque Estatal de Guánica

Scale 1 : 2 500 000

San Juan:
San Juan National Historic Site:
La Fortaleza; Castillo San Cristóbal;
Castillo San Felipe del Morro
Catedral San Juan Bautista
Museo de Arte de Puerto Rico
Museo de Las Americas

Ponce: Museo de Arte de Ponce;
Parque de Bombas; Museo de la Historia de Ponce;
Museo de la Música Puertorriqueña

PUERTO RICO

United States Commonwealth

Population (2010)	3 725 789
Capital city	San Juan
Area	9104 sq km
Languages	Spanish, English
National flower	Flor de Maga
National bird	Stripe-headed Tanager
National animal	Coqui Frog

First sighted by Columbus on his second voyage in **1493**

The original inhabitants were the Taino who died out mainly from disease in the next 100 years

Puerto Rico remained a Spanish colony until **1898**

In **1898** Puerto Rico was invaded by the USA and became a US possession

In **1952** the island became self-governing under its own constitution, but remains an unincorporated US territory

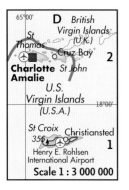

Scale 1 : 3 000 000

Features

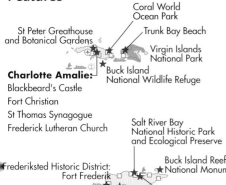

Coral World Ocean Park
St Peter Greathouse and Botanical Gardens
Trunk Bay Beach
Virgin Islands National Park
Buck Island National Wildlife Refuge

Charlotte Amalie:
Blackbeard's Castle
Fort Christian
St Thomas Synagogue
Frederick Lutheran Church

Salt River Bay National Historic Park and Ecological Preserve
Buck Island Reef National Monument

Frederiksted Historic District:
Fort Frederik

Sandy Point National Wildlife Refuge
Cruzan Rum Distillery
Christiansted National Historic Site:
Fort Christiansvaern
Steeple Building
Danish Custom House

Scale 1 : 2 000 000

U.S. VIRGIN ISLANDS

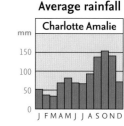

United States Unincorporated Territory

Population (2010)	106 405
Capital city	Charlotte Amalie
Area	347 sq km
Languages	English, Spanish
National flower	Yellow Cedar
National bird	Bananaquit

First sighted and named by Columbus on his second voyage in **1493**

The Taino (Arawaks and Caribs) were the original inhabitants

Spain and France at times colonized the islands, but permanent settlement only came when the Danish settled in St Thomas in **1672**, followed by St John in **1694**. Denmark also bought St Croix from the French in **1733**. From **1754** the islands were officially Royal Danish colonies with sugar plantations

Denmark sold the islands to the United States which took possession on 31 March **1917**, now known as Transfer Day, a public holiday

Average rainfall
San Juan

Average rainfall
Charlotte Amalie

The busy harbour of San Juan with the skyline of the city across the bay.

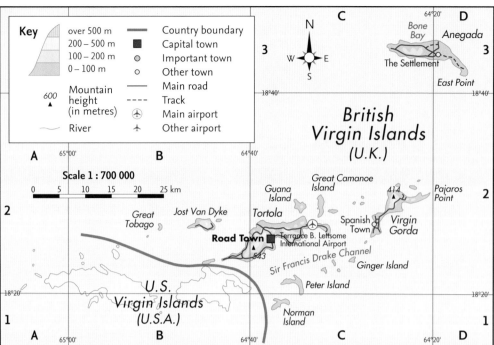

Key

over 500 m	
200 – 500 m	
100 – 200 m	
0 – 100 m	

▲ 600 Mountain height (in metres)

~ River

━━ Country boundary
■ Capital town
◉ Important town
○ Other town
── Main road
--- Track
✈ Main airport
✈ Other airport

Scale 1 : 700 000

0 5 10 15 20 25 km

British Virgin Islands (U.K.)

Bone Bay
Anegada
The Settlement
East Point

Great Camanoe Island
Guana Island
Jost Van Dyke
Great Tobago
Tortola
414
Pajaros Point
Spanish Town
Virgin Gorda
Road Town
Terrance B. Lettsome International Airport
543
Sir Francis Drake Channel
Ginger Island
Peter Island
Norman Island

U.S. Virgin Islands (U.S.A.)

Features

◉ National park
★ Point of interest
□ Major resort
⊕ Main airport
⊕ Port
🚢 Cruise ships
⚓ Major marina

Scale 1 : 500 000

Diamond Cay
Shark Bay National Park
Mount Healthy National Park
Road Town
Callwood Distillery
J.R. O'Neal Botanic Gardens
Smuggler's Cove
Fort Burt
Folk Museum
Sage Mountain National Park
Tortola
Sugar Works Museum

Shoal Bay East
Shoal Bay-Island Harbour Marine Park
Little Bay Marine Park
The Valley
Heritage Collection Museum
Wallblake Historic House
Anguilla
Meads Bay
Rendezvous Bay

Marigot
Fort Louis
St-Martin's Museum
St-Martin
National Nature Reserve
Baie Orientale
Loterie Farm
St Maarten Zoo and Botanical Park
Mullet Beach
Fort Amsterdam
Philipsburg
St Maarten Museum
The Courthouse
Sint Maarten

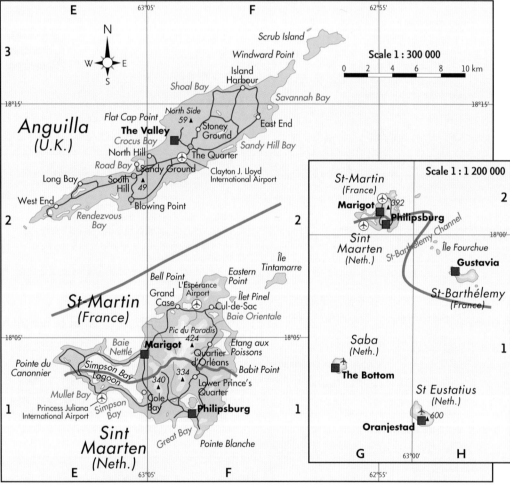

Anguilla (U.K.)

Scrub Island
Windward Point
Island Harbour
Shoal Bay
Savannah Bay

Flat Cap Point
North Side 59▲
Stoney Ground
East End
The Valley
Crocus Bay
North Hill
The Quarter
Sandy Hill Bay
Road Bay
Sandy Ground
Clayton J. Lloyd International Airport
Long Bay
South Hill 49▲
West End
Blowing Point
Rendezvous Bay

Scale 1 : 300 000

0 2 4 6 8 10 km

St-Martin (France)

Bell Point
Eastern Point
L'Espérance Airport
Île Tintamarre
Grand Case
Îlet Pinel
Cul-de-Sac
Baie Orientale
Pic du Paradis 424▲
Baie Nettlé
Marigot
Quartier d'Orléans
Etang aux Poissons
Pointe du Canonnier
Simpson Bay Lagoon
340▲ 334▲
Babit Point
Lower Prince's Quarter
Mullet Bay
Cole Bay
Princess Juliana International Airport
Simpson Bay
Philipsburg
Sint Maarten (Neth.)
Great Bay
Pointe Blanche

Scale 1 : 1 200 000

St-Martin (France)
Marigot 392▲
Philipsburg
Sint Maarten (Neth.)
St-Barthélemy Channel
Île Fourchue
Gustavia
St-Barthélemy (France)

Saba (Neth.)
The Bottom

St Eustatius (Neth.)
600▲
Oranjestad

Saba can be seen from Fort Oranje on St Eustatius. Both islands have a volcanic origin.

	BRITISH VIRGIN ISLANDS	ANGUILLA	ST-MARTIN	SINT MAARTEN	SABA	ST EUSTATIUS	ST-BARTHÉLEM
	British Overseas Territory	British Overseas Territory	French Overseas Collectivity	Self-governing Netherlands Territory	Netherlands Special Municipality	Netherlands Special Municipality	French Overseas Collectivity
Population	28 054 (2010)	13 037 (2011)	36 286 (2011)	33 609 (2011)	1971 (2014 est.)	3791 (2014 est.)	9072 (2010)
Capital town	Road Town	The Valley	Marigot	Philipsburg	The Bottom	Oranjestad	Gustavia
Area	153 sq km	91 sq km	54 sq km	34 sq km	13 sq km	21 sq km	21 sq km
Languages	English	English	French	Dutch, English	Dutch, English	Dutch, English	French
National flower	White Cedar Flower	White Cedar	Hibiscus	Orange-yellow Sage	Black-eyed Susan	Morning Glory	Lily
National bird	Zenaida Dove	Zenaida Dove	Brown Pelican	Brown Pelican	Audubon's Shearwater	Nahamaya	-

Economic activity

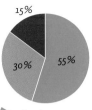

15%
30%
55%

- Services
- Agriculture, fishing and forestry
- Manufacturing

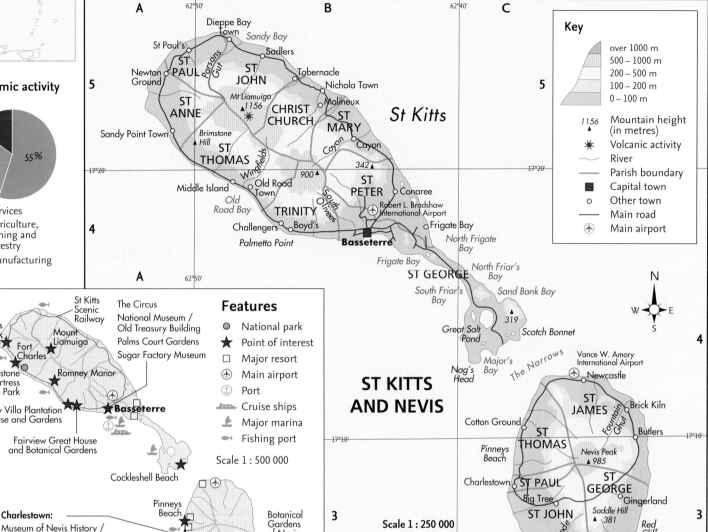

Key

- over 1000 m
- 500 – 1000 m
- 200 – 500 m
- 100 – 200 m
- 0 – 100 m

1156 ▲ Mountain height (in metres)
✳ Volcanic activity
River
Parish boundary
■ Capital town
o Other town
Main road
✈ Main airport

St Kitts

Dieppe Bay Town
Sandy Bay
St Paul's
Sadlers
ST PAUL
ST JOHN
Tabernacle
Newton Ground
Nichola Town
ST ANNE
Mt Liamuiga ▲1156
CHRIST CHURCH
Molineux
ST MARY
Sandy Point Town
Brimstone Hill
Cayon
Cayon
ST THOMAS
Middle Island
Old Road Town
900▲
342▲
Old Road Bay
TRINITY
South Olivees
ST PETER
Challengers
Boyd's
Conaree
Palmetto Point
Robert L. Bradshaw International Airport
Basseterre
Frigate Bay
North Frigate Bay
Frigate Bay
ST GEORGE
North Friar's Bay
South Friar's Bay
Sand Bank Bay
Great Salt Pond
319▲
Scotch Bonnet
Nag's Head
Major's Bay

ST KITTS AND NEVIS

Nevis

Vance W. Amory International Airport
Newcastle
The Narrows
ST JAMES
Brick Kiln
Cotton Ground
ST THOMAS
Fountain Ghut
Butlers
Pinneys Beach
Nevis Peak ▲985
Charlestown
ST PAUL
ST GEORGE
Fig Tree
Gingerland
ST JOHN
Saddle Hill ▲381
Grande Ghut
Red Cliff

Scale 1 : 250 000
0 2 4 6 8 km

St Kitts Scenic Railway
St Kitts Eco-Park
The Circus
National Museum / Old Treasury Building
Palms Court Gardens
Sugar Factory Museum
Mount Liamuiga
Fort Charles
Romney Manor
Brimstone Hill Fortress National Park
Clay Villa Plantation House and Gardens
Basseterre
Fairview Great House and Botanical Gardens
Cockleshell Beach

Features

- ● National park
- ★ Point of interest
- ☐ Major resort
- ✈ Main airport
- ⚓ Port
- Cruise ships
- Major marina
- Fishing port

Scale 1 : 500 000

Charlestown:
Museum of Nevis History / Alexander Hamilton House
Horatio Nelson Museum
Government House
Pinneys Beach
Botanical Gardens of Nevis
Bath Hotel and Spring House
Montpelier House

ST KITTS AND NEVIS

Population (2014 est.) 54 940
Capital town Basseterre
Area (St Kitts) 168 sq km
Area (Nevis) 93 sq km
Languages English, creole
National flower Flamboyant
National bird Brown Pelican

First sighted by Columbus **1493**
Occupied by Arawaks and later Caribs
Jointly settled by English in **1623** and French in **1625**
Alternately occupied by English and French until became British in **1783**
A sugar colony into the **20th** century. Sugar cultivation ended in **2005**

MONTSERRAT

British Overseas Territory

Population (2011) 4922
Capital town Brades
Area 102 sq km
Languages English
National flower Heliconia
National bird Montserrat Oriole

First sighted by Columbus **1493**
Occupied by Irish settlers **1632**
Sugar, and later lime, plantations were established, but none exist today
In **1995** the Soufrière Hills volcano erupted. Ultimately the town of Plymouth was buried and two thirds of the island was abandoned
The island remains a British Overseas Territory

Features

Rendezvous Beach
Cultural Centre
Blake's Estate Stadium
National Museum
Jack Boy Hill Viewpoint
Woodlands Bay
National Trust Botanical Gardens
Centre Hills
Montserrat Volcano Observatory
Chances Peak

Scale 1 : 350 000

Average rainfall

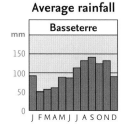

Basseterre

mm
200
150
100
50
0
J F M A M J J A S O N D

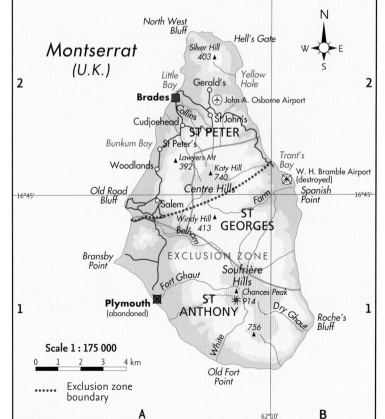

Montserrat (U.K.)

North West Bluff
Hell's Gate
Silver Hill ▲403
Little Bay
Yellow Hole
Gerald's
Brades
John A. Osborne Airport
Cudjoehead
St John's
Collins
ST PETER
Bunkum Bay
St Peter's
Trant's Bay
Woodlands
Lawyers Mt ▲392
Katy Hill ▲740
W. H. Bramble Airport (destroyed)
Old Road Bluff
Centre Hills
Spanish Point
Salem
Farm
Windy Hill ▲413
ST GEORGES
Belham
Bransby Point
EXCLUSION ZONE
Fort Ghaut
Soufrière Hills
Chances Peak ✳914
Plymouth (abandoned)
ST ANTHONY
Dry Ghaut
756▲
Roche's Bluff
White
Old Fort Point

Scale 1 : 175 000
0 1 2 3 4 km

•••••• Exclusion zone boundary

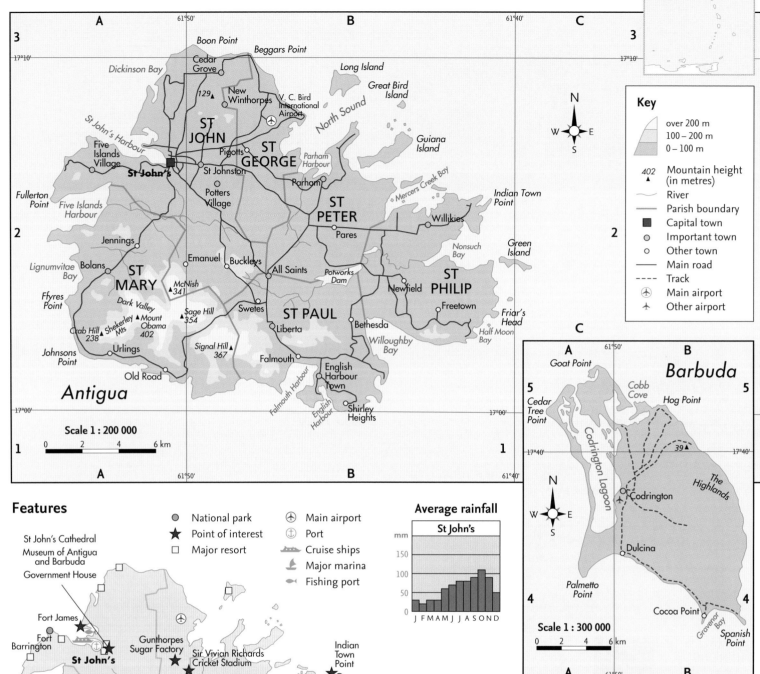

Key

over 200 m
100 – 200 m
0 – 100 m

402 ▲ Mountain height (in metres)
River
Parish boundary
■ Capital town
◉ Important town
○ Other town
Main road
---- Track
✈ Main airport
✈ Other airport

Antigua

Scale 1 : 200 000

0   2   4   6 km

Barbuda

Scale 1 : 300 000

0   2   4   6 km

Features

◉ National park
★ Point of interest
□ Major resort
⊕ Main airport
⊕ Port
Cruise ships
Major marina
Fishing port

St John's Cathedral
Museum of Antigua and Barbuda
Government House
Fort James
Fort Barrington
St John's
Gunthorpes Sugar Factory
Sir Vivian Richards Cricket Stadium
Betty's Hope Sugar Estate
Indian Town Point
Devil's Bridge
Harmony Hall
Green Castle Hill
Jolly Harbour
Mount Obama
Potworks Dam
Montpelier Sugar Factory
Monk's Hill
Dow's Hill Interpretation Centre
Nelson's Dockyard
Shirley Heights

Scale 1 : 275 000

Average rainfall

St John's

mm

150

100

50

0

J F M A M J J A S O N D

Tourist arrivals by country, 2014

10 %
11 %
12 %
29 %
38 %

United States
United Kingdom
Caribbean
Canada
Other

ANTIGUA AND BARBUDA

Population (2011)   81 799
Capital town   St John's
Area (Antigua)   281 sq km
Area (Barbuda)   161 sq km
Languages   English, creole
National flower   Dagger Log
National bird   Magnificent Frigatebird

Prehistoric inhabitants: Arawaks then Caribs
First sighted and named by Columbus **1493**
British sugar colony **1632–1981**
British naval base **1725–1889**
Sugar cultivation ceased **1971**
Independent 1 November **1981**

Nelson's Dockyard was the Royal Navy's naval base in the Caribbean for over 100 years. It is now a national park and includes a dockyard museum and an active yacht club and marina.

GUADELOUPE

Department of France

Population *(2014 est.)* 403 750
Capital town Basse-Terre
Area 1780 sq km
Languages French, creole
National flower Lily
National bird Gallic Rooster

Original inhabitants: Caribs

First sighted and named by Columbus **1493**

Occupied by the French **1635**

Annexed by France **1674**

Became a major French sugar colony, but occupied by the British at times in the **17th** century

In **1946** became a department (an integral part) of France, and therefore is part of the European Union

Sugar is still exported, along with bananas

Map

3 Pointe de la Grande Vigie
Anse-Bertrand
Massioux
Campêche
Pointe d'Antigues
Gros-Cap
Port-Louis
Beauport
Les Mangles
Petit-Canal
Vieux-Bourg
Grande-Terre
Morne-à-l'Eau
Le Moule
Pointe-à-Pitre (Le Raizet) International Airport
Ilet à Fajou
Grand Cul-de-Sac Marin
Bosrédon
Château-Gaillard
Pointe Allègre
Ste-Rose
Monplaisir
Goyaves
Lamentin
Baie-Mahault
Salée
Les Abymes
Douville
St-François
Basse-Terre
Pointe-Noire
Morne Jeanneton 744 ▲
Pointe-à-Pitre
Besson
Ste-Anne
Pointe des Châteaux
Mahaut
Petit-Bourg
Petit Cul-de-Sac Marin
Le Gosier
Pigeon
Pitons de Bouillante 1088 ▲
Vernou
Montebello
Guadeloupe (France)
Bouillante
La Lézarde
Goyave
Marigot
Vieux-Habitants
▲ 1354 Sans Toucher
Ste-Marie
Capesterre
Carangaise
Vieux-Habitants
La Soufrière ☀ 1467 ▲
Capesterre-Belle-Eau
Baillif
St-Claude
Basse-Terre ■
Gourbeyre
Bananier
Trois-Rivières
Vieux-Fort
Pointe de Vieux-Fort

Scale 1 : 500 000
0 5 10 15 km

Grosse Pointe
St-Louis
Marie-Galante
St Louis
Capesterre
Grand-Bourg
Pointe des Basses

Îles des Saintes
Terre-de-Bas
Petites-Anses
Terre-de-Haut

Key

over 1000 m
500 – 1000 m
200 – 500 m
100 – 200 m
0 – 100 m

1467 ▲ Mountain height (in metres)
☀ Volcanic activity
〜 River
■ Capital town
◉ Important town
○ Other town
— Main road
✈ Main airport
✈ Other airport

Features

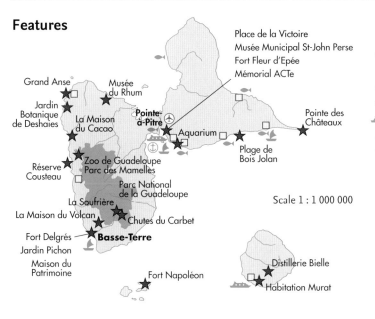

Place de la Victoire
Musée Municipal St-John Perse
Fort Fleur d'Epée
Mémorial ACTe
Grand Anse
Musée du Rhum
Jardin Botanique de Deshaies
La Maison du Cacao
Pointe-à-Pitre
Aquarium
Pointe des Châteaux
Plage de Bois Jolan
Réserve Cousteau
Zoo de Guadeloupe Parc des Mamelles
Parc National de la Guadeloupe
La Soufrière
La Maison du Volcan
Chutes du Carbet
Fort Delgrés **Basse-Terre**
Jardin Pichon
Maison du Patrimoine
Scale 1 : 1 000 000
Fort Napoléon
Distillerie Bielle
Habitation Murat

◉ National park
★ Point of interest
□ Major resort
✈ Main airport
⚓ Port
🚢 Cruise ships
⚓ Major marina
🐟 Fishing port

Average rainfall

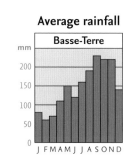

Basse-Terre
mm
200
150
100
50
0
J F M A M J J A S O N D

Economic activity

13%
27%
60%

▶ Services
▶ Agriculture, fishing and forestry
▶ Manufacturing

Although Basse-Terre is the capital of Guadeloupe, Pointe-à-Pitre is the largest city, commercial capital, and the main port. Its population is over 132 000, compared with less than 40 000 for Basse-Terre.

Traditional dishes

- *Matete* – a hot crab curry
- *Colombo* – a curry made with chicken or cabri (goat)
- *Callaloo* – a soup made with bacon and leafy greens
- *Bébélé* – a tripe soup with dumplings and green bananas
- *Blaff* – seafood cooked in a seasoned soup
- *Accras* – cod or vegetable fritters
- *Ouassou* – large freshwater shrimp

Chicken Colombo, one of the traditional dishes of Guadeloupe.

DOMINICA

Population (2011)	71 293
Capital town	Roseau
Area	750 sq km
Languages	English, creole
National flower	Carib Wood
National bird	Imperial Parrot (Sisserou)

Prehistoric inhabitants: Arawaks followed by Caribs

First sighted and named by Columbus **1493**

Some minor Spanish attempts at settlement resisted by the Caribs in **16th** and **17th** centuries

Colonised by the French as a sugar colony **1690–1763**

British colony **1763–1978**

Occupied by the French **1778–1783**

The sugar plantations were replaced by bananas in the **1960s**

Became independent 3 November **1978** and declared itself a Republic with a President

Banana production

Thousand tonnes

80 70 60 50 40 30 20 10 0

1961 1971 1981 1991 2001 2013

Average rainfall

Roseau

mm

200 150 100 50 0

J F M A M J J A S O N D

Features

- ● National park
- ★ Point of interest
- □ Major resort
- ✈ Main airport
- ⚓ Port
- 🚢 Cruise ships
- ⚓ Major marina
- 🐟 Fishing port
- ● Carib Territory

Cabrits National Park
Fort Shirley
Batibou Beach
Morne Diablotins National Park
Kalinago Barana Autê (Culture Village)
Coconut Products Factory
Morne Trois Pitons National Park
Museum of Rum
Middleham Falls
Trafalgar Falls
Roseau
Boiling Lake
Victoria Falls
Botanical Gardens
Morne Bruce
Champagne Beach and Reef
Dominica Museum
Bois Cotlette Estate
Government House

Scale 1 : 600 000

Key

over 1000 m
500 – 1000 m
200 – 500 m
100 – 200 m
0 – 100 m

1447 ▲	Mountain height (in metres)
✹	Volcanic activity
～	River
⋎	Waterfall
—	Parish boundary
■	Capital town
●	Important town
○	Other town
—	Main road
✈	Main airport

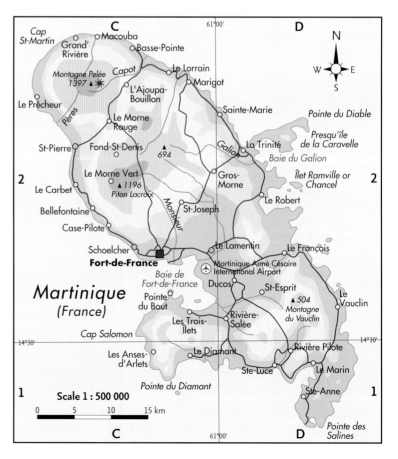

Cape Capucin
Carib Point
Pennville
Vieille Case
Cottage
Morne Aux Diables 861
Anse De Mai
Calibishie
Cabrits
La Source
Larey
Portsmouth
ST JOHN
Wesley
Prince Rupert Bay
Glanvillia
ST ANDREW
Marigot
Picard
Douglas–Charles Airport
Pagua Bay
Melville Hall
Dublanc
ST PETER
▲ 1447
Morne Diablotins
Pagua
Colihaut
Batalie
Coulibistrie
Morne Rachette
ST JOSEPH
ST DAVID
Castle Bruce
Salisbury
Belles
Belle Fille
St Joseph
Layou
Pont Cassé
Rosalie
Rosalie
Belfast
Morne Trois Pitons 1386
Boeri Lake
Rosalie Bay
Mahaut
ST PAUL
Massacre
Morne Macaque 1221
Freshwater Lake
Canefield Airport
Ouayeneri
La Plaine
Canefield
ST GEORGE
Trafalgar
Morne Watt ▲ 1224
Boetica
Roseau
Roseau
Delices
Giraudel
ST PATRICK
Loubière
Bellevue Chopin
Pointe Michel
ST LUKE
Berekua
Petite Savanne
Scale 1 : 300 000
ST MARK
Soufrière
Grand Bay
Scotts Head
DOMINICA

0 2 4 6 km

MARTINIQUE

Department of France

Population (2014 est.)	381 326
Capital town	Fort-de-France
Area	1079 sq km
Languages	French, creole
National flower	Lily
National bird	Gallic Rooster

Prehistoric inhabitants: Arawaks followed by Caribs

First sighted and named by Columbus **1493**, visited and named by him in **1502** ('Martinica')

Settled by the French from St Kitts **1635**

The French conquered the Caribs and the survivors fled to Dominica

Mainly occupied by the British **1794–1815**

In **1946** became a department of France

Distillerie J M
Montagne Pelée
Les Gorges de la Falaise
La Maison Regionale des Volcans
Le Figuier
Musée Volcanologique
Musée Gauguin
Jardin de Balata
Presqu'île de la Caravelle
Fort-de-France
Habitation Clement
Fort St-Louis
La Savane
Cathédrale St-Louis
Bibliothèque Schoelcher
Musée de la Pagerie
Musée Regional d'Histoire et d'Ethnographie
Le Diamant
Les Salines

Scale 1 : 1 000 000

Montagne Pelée

- This active volcano exploded on 2 May 1902
- About 30 000 persons were killed
- The town of St-Pierre, capital of Martinique, was destroyed
- The capital was later moved to Fort-de-France, far from the volcano
- The nature of the explosion was an incandescent gas cloud known as a Nuée Ardente, which incinerated everything in its path
- Only two persons survived, one in a dungeon and one on a ship

St-Pierre, at the foot of Montagne Pelée.

Cap St-Martin
Macouba
Grand' Rivière
Basse-Pointe
Montagne Pelée 1397
Capot
Le Lorrain
Le Prêcheur
L'Ajoupa-Bouillon
Marigot
Pères
Le Morne Rouge
Sainte-Marie
Pointe du Diable
St-Pierre
Fond-St-Denis
▲ 694
Galion
La Trinité
Presqu'île de la Caravelle
Baie du Galion
Le Carbet
Le Morne Vert
▲ 1196
Piton Lacroix
Gros-Morne
St-Joseph
Îlet Ramville or Chancel
Bellefontaine
Monsieur
Le Robert
Case-Pilote
Schoelcher
Le Lamentin
Le François
Fort-de-France
Martinique Aimé Césaire International Airport
Ducos
St-Esprit
Martinique (France)
Baie de Fort-de-France
Pointe du Bout
Le Vauclin
▲ 504
Montagne du Vauclin
Rivière-Salée
Les Trois-Îlets
Cap Salomon
Les Anses-d'Arlets
Le Diamant
Rivière Pilote
Ste-Luce
Le Marin
Pointe du Diamant
Ste-Anne
Scale 1 : 500 000
Pointe des Salines

0 5 10 15 km

Average rainfall

Castries

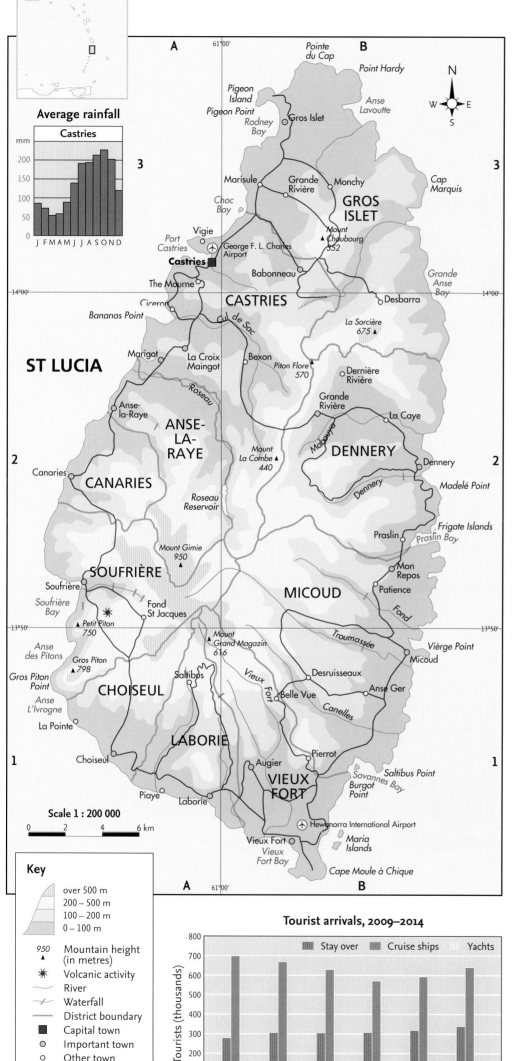

ST LUCIA

Population (2010)	166 526
Capital town	Castries
Area	617 sq km
Languages	English, creole
National flower	Rose
National bird	St Lucian Parrot

Prehistoric inhabitants: Arawaks followed by Caribs

First sighted and named by Columbus **1493**

Many failed attempts at settling the island were made by French, Dutch and British colonists from **1550** until **1640**

Colonised by the French as a sugar colony **1643–1803**. This period included several British occupations

British colony **1803–1979**

The sugar plantations were replaced by bananas in the **1960s**

Independent 22 February **1979**

Two St Lucians have won Nobel Prizes. The Nobel Prize for Economics was won by Sir Arthur Lewis in **1979**, and the Nobel Prize for Literature by Derek Walcott in **1992**

Features

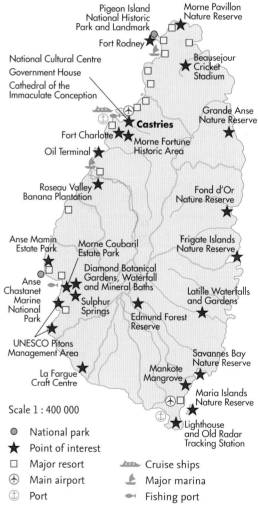

Scale 1 : 400 000

●	National park
★	Point of interest
▢	Major resort
⊕	Main airport
⚓	Port

🚢	Cruise ships
⚓	Major marina
🐟	Fishing port

Key

	over 500 m
	200 – 500 m
	100 – 200 m
	0 – 100 m
950 ▲	Mountain height (in metres)
✳	Volcanic activity
∿	River
⤳	Waterfall
⸽	District boundary
■	Capital town
◉	Important town
○	Other town
—	Main road
⊕	Main airport

Tourist arrivals, 2009–2014

Stay over   Cruise ships   Yachts

Tourists (thousands)

2009   2010   2011   2012   2013   2014

The *Carnival Valor* in Castries. This cruise ship can carry 3000 passengers and has a crew of over 1100.

Key

- over 1000 m
- 500 – 1000 m
- 200 – 500 m
- 100 – 200 m
- 0 – 100 m

- *1234* ▲ Mountain height (in metres)
- 🎇 Volcanic activity
- River
- Waterfall
- Parish boundary
- ■ Capital town
- ◉ Important town
- ○ Other town
- Main road
- ✈ Main airport
- ✈ Other airport

ST VINCENT AND THE GRENADINES

Population (2011)	109 991
Capital town	Kingstown
Area (St Vincent)	344 sq km
Area (Grenadines)	45 sq km (15 islands)
Languages	English, creole
National flower	Soufrière Tree
National bird	St Vincent Parrot

Prehistoric inhabitants: Caribs

First sighted and named by Columbus **1498**

Colonised by the French as a plantation colony **1719–1783**

British colony **1793–1979**

Sugar cane cultivation was replaced by bananas in the **1950s**

Soufrière volcano erupted in **1902** causing 1680 deaths

Independent 27 October **1979**

Scale 1 : 200 000

0   2   4   6 km

Features

- ◉ National park
- ★ Point of interest
- ☐ Major resort
- ✈ Main airport
- ⚓ Port
- 🚢 Cruise ships
- ⚓ Major marina
- 🐟 Fishing port

Scale 1 : 300 000

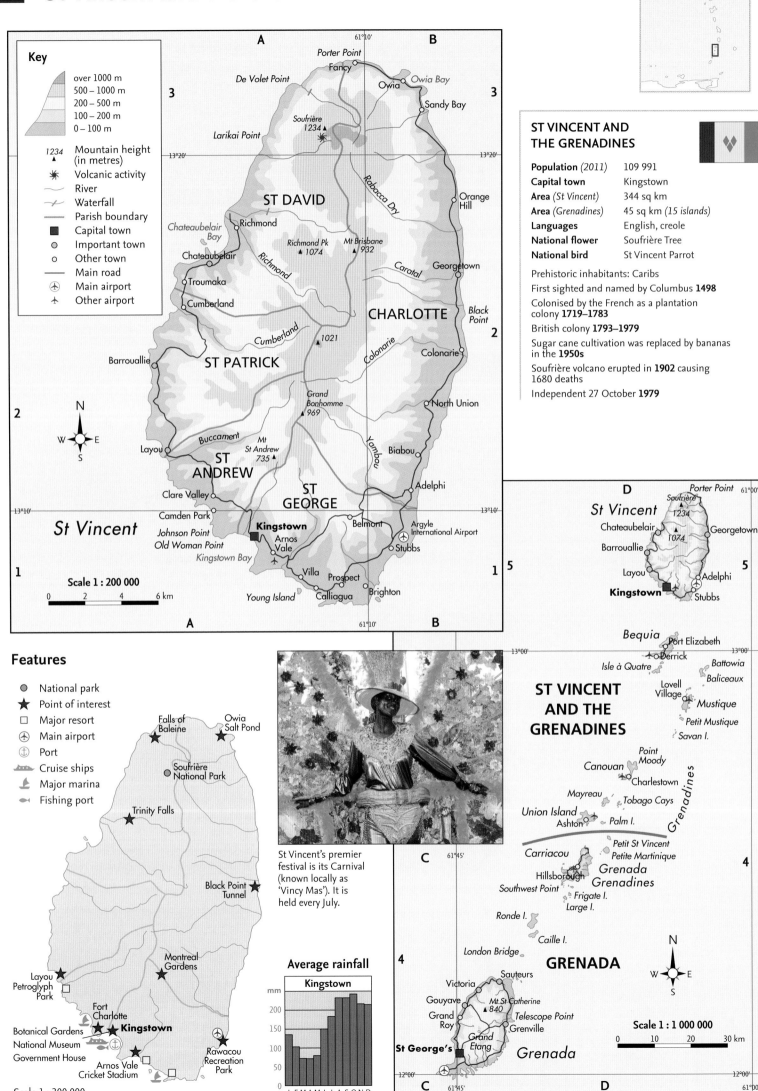

St Vincent's premier festival is its Carnival (known locally as 'Vincy Mas'). It is held every July.

Average rainfall

Kingstown

mm
250
200
150
100
50
0
J F M A M J J A S O N D

Scale 1 : 1 000 000

0   10   20   30 km

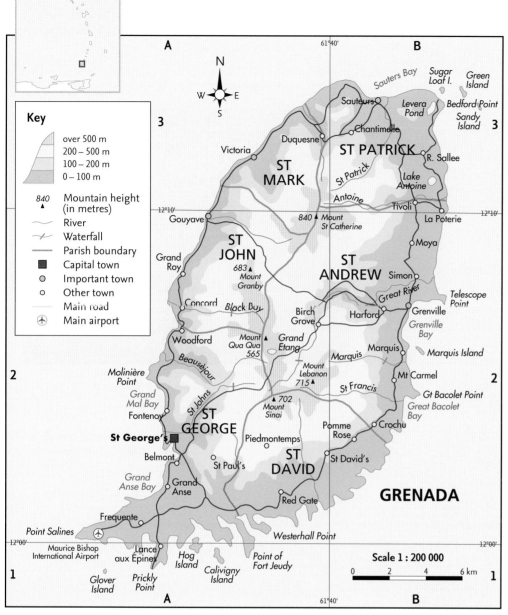

GRENADA

Population (2011)	103 328
Capital town	St George's
Total area	348 sq km
Area (Grenada)	313 sq km
Area (Carriacou)	33 sq km
Area (Petite Martinique)	2 sq km
Languages	English, creole
National flower	Bougainvillea
National bird	Grenada Dove

Prehistoric inhabitants: Caribs

First sighted and named by Columbus **1498**

Colonised by the French as a sugar colony **1649–1763**

British colony **1793–1974**

Sugar soon gave way to cocoa production and later bananas

Independent 7 February **1974**

Invaded by USA in **1983**

World renowned producer of nutmeg and other spices. Sugar cane cultivation has largely ceased and bananas are a minor crop

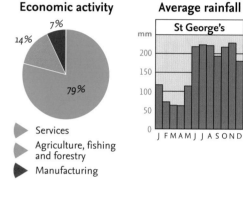

Economic activity

- Services 79%
- Agriculture, fishing and forestry 14%
- Manufacturing 7%

Average rainfall — St George's

Features

- National park
- Point of interest
- Major resort
- Main airport
- Port
- Cruise ships
- Major marina
- Fishing port

Scale 1 : 300 000

Grenada is known as the Spice Island

- *Nutmeg and Mace* – second largest producer after Indonesia (also called 'Spice Islands'). Mace is a coating on the outside of the nutmeg
- *Cinnamon* – production has increased in recent years
- *Cloves* – production has increased in recent years
- *Ginger* – versatile root widely grown
- *Cocoa* – used locally to make cocoa tea and exported as organic dark chocolate
- *Pimento* – also known as allspice, an easily grown tree
- *Turmeric* – produced from a root, also known as saffron. Used in curries and popular for its medicinal value

Tramping through cocoa beans at the Belmont Estate to ensure they dry evenly.

A   59°35'   B   59°30'   C

59°40'

5

N
W   E
S

13°20'

Archers Bay

North Point

The Spout

Seaview

Archers
Greenidge

Spring Hall

Harrison Point

Bromefield

Babbs

Fustic

ST LUCY

Nesfield

Pie Corner

Cockold Point

Paul's Point

Boscobelle

4

13°20'

harbour

Carlisle Bay

Satellite view of Bridgetown, showing the deep-water harbour and Constitution River ('The Careenage'), which flows into Carlisle Bay.

Six Men's Bay

Mile and a Quarter

ST PETER

Mount Stepney 245 ▲

▲ 147

Greenland

Speightstown

13°15'

Long Pond

Belleplaine

13°15'

Mullins

Lower Carlton

Westmoreland

Alleynes Bay

The Garden

Holetown

Sunset Crest

169

277 ▲

Upper Carlton

ST JAMES

Orange Hill

Hillaby

Mose Bottom

Mount Hillaby 340 ▲

Mount Misery 326 ▲

Welchman Hall

Rock Hall

Arch Hall

ST ANDREW

Chalky Mount 167

Bruce Vale

Joe's River

ST JOSEPH

Chimborazo

Castle Grant 338

Coffee Gully

Clifton Hill

Venture

Cattlewash

Bathsheba

Hillcrest

306 ▲

Hothersal

Newcastle

Clifton Hall

Glebe

Coach Hill

St Marks

Congor Rocks

Conset Bay

Conset Point

Bell Point

3

ST THOMAS

ST JOHN

3

59°25'

Key

over 200 m
100 – 200 m
0 – 100 m

340 ▲ Mountain height (in metres)

~~~ River

—— Parish boundary
■ Capital town
◉ Important town
○ Other town
═ Highway
— Main road
✈ Main airport

Paynes Bay

Sandy Lane

Bagatelle

Thorpes

Fitts Village

Prospect

▲ 228

Redman's

Bridgefield

Belair

Ashbury

Four Cross Roads

Massiah Street

164 ▲

Bayfield

Thicket

Wellhouse

Robinsons

Ragged Point

Marley Vale

Kitridge Point

13°10'

13°10'

Warrens

123

Jackson

Black Rock

Hothersal Turning

ST MICHAEL

Brighton

Bush Hall

Howells

Constitution

Mount Friendship

▲ 83

Rowans

Hilbury

Mapp Hill

Dash Valley

St Davids

Boarded Hall

Ellerton

Melverton

ST GEORGE

St Patricks

Cottage Vale

Church Village

Marchfield

Brereton

Six Cross Roads

Four Roads

62

St Martins

ST PHILIP

The Crane

Cobbler's Rock

Foul Bay

2

2

Carlisle Bay

Bridgetown

Garrison

Needham's Point

Rockley

Hastings

Worthing

St Lawrence

Welches

Oistins

Oistins Bay

Sargeants Village

Vauxhall

Lodge Road

Pegwell

Scarborough

Enterprise

Inch Marlowe

South Point

CHRISTCHURCH

Newton Terrace

Providence

Charnocks

Chancery Lane

Long Bay

✈ Grantley Adams International Airport

Salt Cave Point

BARBADOS

13°05'

13°05'

1

Scale 1 : 145 000

0   1   2   3   4   5 km

1

59°40'

A   59°35'   B   59°30'   C   59°25'

Constitution River

BARBADOS

Population *(2010)*	277 821
Capital town	Bridgetown
Area	430 sq km
Languages	English, creole
National flower	Pride of Barbados
National animal	Dolphin (the fish, also known as Mahi-mahi)

The original inhabitants were various Amerindians (Arawaks and Caribs), the last tribe being the Kalingo (Caribs). Barbados was uninhabited when it was settled

Unlike most Caribbean islands Barbados was not first sighted by Columbus – rather, it was by unknown Spanish mariners. The first recorded visit was by the Portuguese in **1536**

From **1625** English settlers arrived and the country became, and remained, a British colony until **1966**

Initially the colony grew tobacco and cotton and other non plantation crops

In **1640** the economy changed to one of sugar plantations

Internal self-government was granted from **1961** until independence on 30 November **1966**

The economy diversified by the **1980s** to include tourism, and sugar is no longer the main source of income

Economic activity

6% 3%

91%

- Services
- Manufacturing
- Agriculture, fishing and forestry

Average rainfall

Bridgetown

mm

150

100

50

0

J F M A M J J A S O N D

Fishing industry

- Flying fish account for over half the total catch
- Flying fish and dolphin (the fish) are major restaurant dishes for the tourist industry
- Kingfish (wahoo) and shark are also popular
- Oistins and Bridgetown have the two largest fish markets
- About 6000 people are employed in the fisheries industry
- The white sea egg is a local delicacy with a fishing season limited to September through December

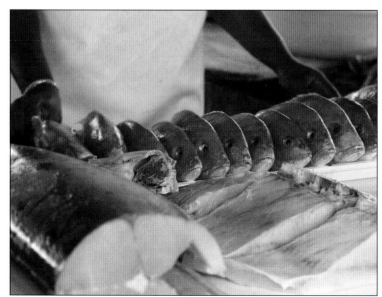

Berinda Cox Fish Market, Oistins.

Features

●	National park
★	Point of interest
□	Major resort
✈	Main airport
⚓	Port
🚢	Cruise ships
⚓	Major marina
⛵	Fishing port
🗼	Lighthouse

Animal Flower Cave
Mount Gay Distillery
St Nicholas Abbey
Barbados Wildlife Reserve
Morgan Lewis Sugar Mill
Farley Hill National Park
Arlington House Museum Gallery of Caribbean Art
Flower Forest Park
Bathsheba Beach
Welchman Hall Gully
Andromeda Botanical Gardens
Folkestone Marine Park and Museum
Sir Frank Hutson Sugar Museum
Hunte's Gardens
Clifton Hall
Harrison's Cave
Gun Hill Signal Station
Sunbury Plantation House and Museum
West Indies Rum Distillery
Mount Gay Visitor Centre
Kensington Oval
Bridgetown
Crane Beach
Foursquare Rum Distillery and Heritage Park
Parliament Buildings
Government House
Graeme Hall Nature Sanctuary
Concorde Experience

Garrison Historic Area:
St Ann's Fort
George Washington House
Barbados Museum
Garrison Savannah Racetrack

Scale 1 : 250 000

Sugar and rum

- Barbados is noted for its sugar and rum. Over the years the sugar industry has declined, but rum has been very successful
- In the 19th century there were 12 **sugar** factories that crushed the cane, but as sugar sales declined these were closed one by one
- By 2000 there were only two factories still working, Andrew's and Portvale
- In 2014 the Andrew's Factory closed and is being dismantled. A new factory to produce multiple sugar products will eventually be built
- The Portvale Factory is now the only working factory in Barbados. There is a Sugar Museum in the grounds of the factory and both are open to visitors
- Foursquare Factory closed in the 1980s and is now a museum and park, with a modern rum distillery built on the site
- There are 3 **rum** distilleries in Barbados
- Mount Gay in the north in St Lucy has had great success in exporting its rum worldwide. It is now owned by the French Rémy Cointreau liquor company
- The West Indies Distillery is located in Brighton and is used by several rum companies to produce Cockspur and other rums
- Foursquare is the newest distillery, built on the site of the old sugar factory in St Philip, and produces a variety of popular and quality rums. It is open for tours

Crop Over in Barbados is a harvest festival which first began in the 17th century, celebrating the end of the sugar cane season. It is now the island's biggest event running from June until the first Monday in August, ending with the Grand Kadooment Day Parade.

GUYANA

Population (2012)	747 884
Capital city	Georgetown
Area	214 969 sq km
Languages	English, creole, Amerindian
National flower	Victoria Regia Lily
National bird	Hoatzin or Canje Pheasant
National animal	Jaguar

Original inhabitants included coastal Arawaks and inland Caribs, and other Amerindian tribes

Sighted by Columbus in **1498**

Settled by Dutch from **1616** in three separate colonies

Also settled by British from **1746**, and ceded by Netherlands to Britain in **1814**

Became a British colony named British Guiana in **1831**

Became independent on 26 May **1966** and renamed Guyana

Declared a Cooperative Republic on 23 February **1970**

Economic activity

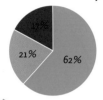

- 17%
- 21%
- 62%

▷ Services

▷ Agriculture, fishing and forestry

▷ Manufacturing

Average rainfall

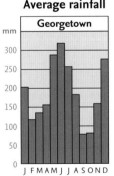

Georgetown

Provinces

ESSEQUIBO

DEMERARA

BERBICE

Scale 1 : 14 000 000

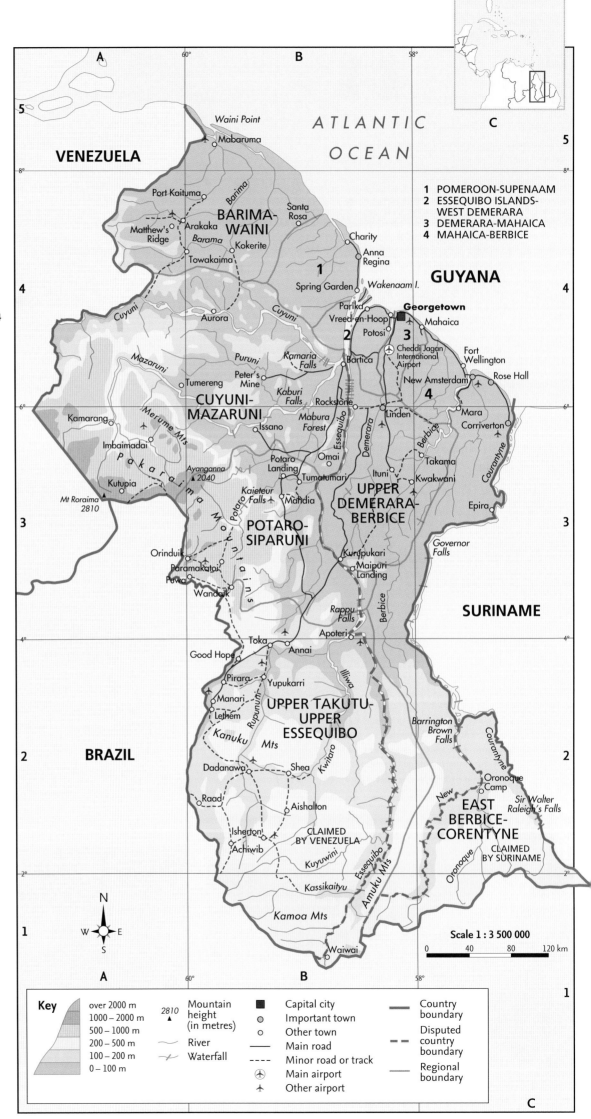

VENEZUELA

ATLANTIC OCEAN

GUYANA

Waini Point

Mabaruma

Port Kaituma

Santa Rosa

BARIMA-WAINI

Charity

Anna Regina

Matthew's Ridge

Arakaka

Kokerite

1

Spring Garden

Wakenaam I.

Towakaima

Barama

Aurora

Parika

Vreed-en-Hoop

Georgetown

Mahaica

Cuyuni

Cuyuni

2

Potosi

3

Cheddi Jagan International Airport

Fort Wellington

Mazaruni

Puruni

Kamaria Falls

Bartica

New Amsterdam

Rose Hall

Peter's Mine

Kaburi Falls

Rockstone

4

Tumereng

CUYUNI-MAZARUNI

Linden

Mara

Corriverton

Kamarang

Issano

Mabura Forest

Berbice

Takama

Imbaimadai

Merume Mts

Potaro Landing

Omai

Ituni

Kwakwani

Ayanganna ▲2040

Tumatumari

UPPER DEMERARA-BERBICE

Epira

Kutupia

Kaieteur Falls

Mahdia

Mt Roraima ▲2810

POTARO-SIPARUNI

Governor Falls

Orinduik

Kurupukari

Paramakatoi

Maipuri Landing

Puwa

Wandaik

Rappu Falls

Berbice

SURINAME

Toka

Apoteri

Good Hope

Annai

Pirara

Yupukarri

Illiwa

Manari

UPPER TAKUTU-UPPER ESSEQUIBO

Barrington Brown Falls

Lethem

Kanuku Mts

Rupununi

Kwitaro

Oronoque Camp

Sir Walter Raleigh's Falls

Dadanawa

Shea

New

Raad

EAST BERBICE-CORENTYNE

Aishalton

CLAIMED BY VENEZUELA

CLAIMED BY SURINAME

Isherton

Essequibo

Achiwib

Kuyuwini

Oronoque

BRAZIL

Kassikaityu

Amuku Mts

Kamoa Mts

Waiwai

Scale 1 : 3 500 000

0   40   80   120 km

1 POMEROON-SUPENAAM
2 ESSEQUIBO ISLANDS-WEST DEMERARA
3 DEMERARA-MAHAICA
4 MAHAICA-BERBICE

Key

over 2000 m	
1000 – 2000 m	
500 – 1000 m	
200 – 500 m	
100 – 200 m	
0 – 100 m	

2810 ▲ Mountain height (in metres)

∼ River

↯ Waterfall

■ Capital city

◉ Important town

○ Other town

✈ Main airport

✈ Other airport

Main road

Minor road or track

Country boundary

Disputed country boundary

Regional boundary

Features

- ● National park
- ★ Point of interest
- ☐ Major resort
- ⊕ Main airport
- ⚓ Port
- ⛴ Cruise ships
- 🐟 Fishing port

Georgetown:
St George's Cathedral
National Museum
Promenade Gardens
Parliament Building
Guyana Zoo and Botanical Gardens
Walter Roth Museum of Anthropology
Museum of African Heritage
International Conference Centre
Providence Cricket Stadium

Scale 1 : 7 000 000

Minerals

- ☐ Bauxite
- ■ Diamonds
- ◻ Oil
- ● Gold
- ● Manganese
- ● Clay

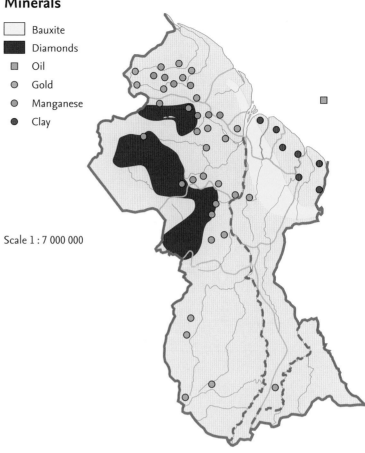

Scale 1 : 7 000 000

Bauxite mining in Guyana

- Guyana has the oldest bauxite industry in the Caribbean, started in 1916 south of Georgetown
- A settlement named Mackenzie grew up and the workers excavated the bauxite (aluminium ore) by hand, and later with steam-powered machinery
- The ore was loaded into barges and sent down the Demerara River where it was transferred to ships at Georgetown
- The ore then travelled to smelters in Canada for refining into metal. Guyana (then British Guiana) did not have the energy to run smelters, but Canada had developed very cheap HEP on its large rivers
- Over the years more companies came to Guyana and bauxite is still the country's main export

Mashramani, often abbreviated to 'Mash', takes place on 23 February each year to celebrate Republic Day when Guyana gained independence. There are float parades, spectacular costumes and masquerade bands and dancing in the streets.

Gold and diamond mining is widespread in the interior of Guyana. Unfortunately the widely-used system of alluvial mining (panning, or sifting the river sediment) is very destructive.

Aruba (Neth.)

Scale 1 : 300 000
0 2 4 6 8 km

Cudarebe
A — California Lighthouse
Arashi
Hadikurari
Westpunt
Alto Vista 70 ▲
Bubali Bird Sanctuary
Noord
Bushiribana Gold Mine Ruins
Eagle Beach
Druif
Paradera
Noordkaap
Oranjestad
Casibari Rock Formations
Ayo Rock Formations
Natural Pool
Santa Cruz
Simeon Antonio
Jamanota ▲188
Fort Zoutman
National Archaeological Museum
Trinidad Stadium
Balcadera
Pos Chiquito
De Palm Reef Island
Savaneta
Lourdes Grotto
Queen Beatrix International Airport
Commandeursbaai
Sint Nicolaas
Seroe Colorado
Oil refinery and terminal
St Nicolaasbaai
Punta Basora
Baby Beach

Scale 1 : 5 000 000
0 25 50 75 km

Aruba (Neth.)
Oranjestad
Curaçao (Neth.)
Kralendijk
Willemstad
VENEZUELA
Bonaire (Neth.)

Bonaire (Neth.)

Scale 1 : 300 000
0 2 4 6 8 km

Malmok
Playa Funchi
Brandaris ▲240
Boca Slagbaai
Goto Meer
Rincón
Boca Olivia
Punt'l Wecúa
Oil terminal
Fort Oranje
Bonaire Museum
Pasangrahan (Parliament House)
Hato
Noord Salina
Antriol
Boven Bolivia
Boka Chikitu
Lagun
Kralendijk
Klein Bonaire
Sabana
Nikiboko
Tera Kora
Punt Vierkant
Donkey Sanctuary
Mangrove Information and Kayaking Centre
Lac Bay
Flamingo (Bonaire) International Airport
Salt Works
Pekelmeer
Flamingo Sanctuary
Lacre Punt

Curaçao

Noordpunt
Westpunt
Sabana Westpunt
Boca Tabla Caves
Boca Tabla
St Christoffelberg ▲372
Lagun
Barber
Boca Santa Cruz
Soto
Boca Ascención
Ascensión
Santa Martabaai
San Juanbaai
Punta Halvedag
Playa Cas Abou
Tera Kora
St Willibrordus
Salina Santa Marie
Bocht Van Hato

Curaçao (Neth.)

Scale 1 : 300 000
0 2 4 6 8 10 km

Kaap Santa Marie
Bullenbaai
Grote Berg
Curaçao International Airport
Hato Caves
Santa Catarina
Juliandorp
Rio Canario
Boca Sami
St Michiel
Emmastad
Zoo Parke Tropikal
Ostrich Farm
St Jorisbaai
Isla Oil Refinery
Schottegat
Santa Rosa
Piscaderabaai
Otrobanda
Bottelier
Maritime Museum
Punda
Willemstad:
Fort Amsterdam
Rif Fort
Handelskade
Kura Hulanda Museum
Jewish Cultural Historical Museum
Dolphin Academy
Sea Aquarium
Lagun Jan Thiel
Spaanse Water
Jan Thiel
Santa Barbara
New Port
Curaçao Underwater Marine Park
Oostpunt

(National parks inset)

Arikok National Park
Washington Slagbaai National Park
Shete Boka National Park
Christoffel National Park
Bonaire National Marine Park
● National park
Scale 1 : 1 000 000

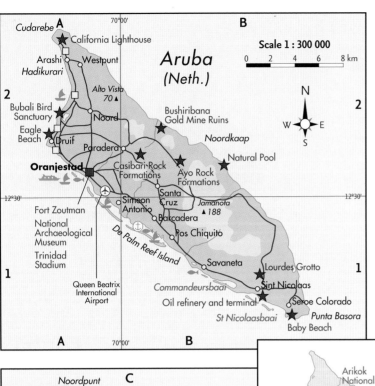

A diver examines a wreck on the Front Porch dive site, Bonaire.

Key

over 200 m
100 – 200 m
0 – 100 m

372 Mountain height (in metres) ▲
River
Capital town ■
Important town ◎
Other town ○
Main road
Main airport ✈

Features

★ Point of interest
□ Major resort
Port
Cruise ships
Major marina
Fishing port

Oil refineries

- The large Isla refinery was built on Curaçao in 1918
- It was the largest refinery in the world for many years
- It is still operating and contributes 90% of the export earnings to the economy
- Copying Curaçao, two large refineries were built on Aruba in 1929 and 1930
- They refined oil from Venezuela, and later Brazil
- The Eagle refinery closed in 1950
- The Lago refinery was attacked by a U-Boat in 1942
- The Lago refinery, once one of the world's largest, closed in 2009
- Due to the loss of jobs from the closed refineries, Aruba started its modern tourist industry

Aruba and Curaçao are Self-governing Netherlands Territories. Bonaire is a Netherlands Special Municipality

	ARUBA	CURAÇAO	BONAIRE
Population	101 484 (2010)	150 563 (2011)	16 541 (2014 est.)
Capital town	Oranjestad	Willemstad	Kralendijk
Area	193 sq km	444 sq km	288 sq km
National flower	Wanglo Flower	Kibrahacha	Divi-divi
National bird	Burrowing Owl	Majestic Oriole	Greater Flamingo
Languages	Dutch, Papiamento, English		

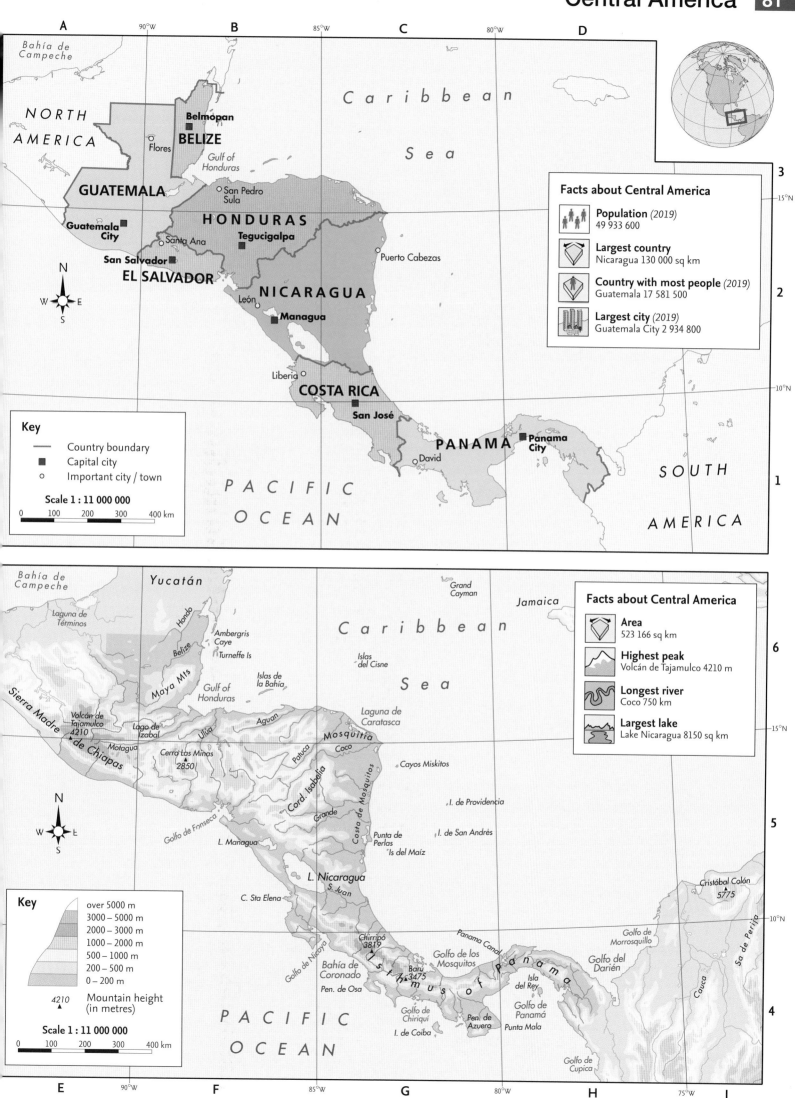

Lambert Conformal Conic projection

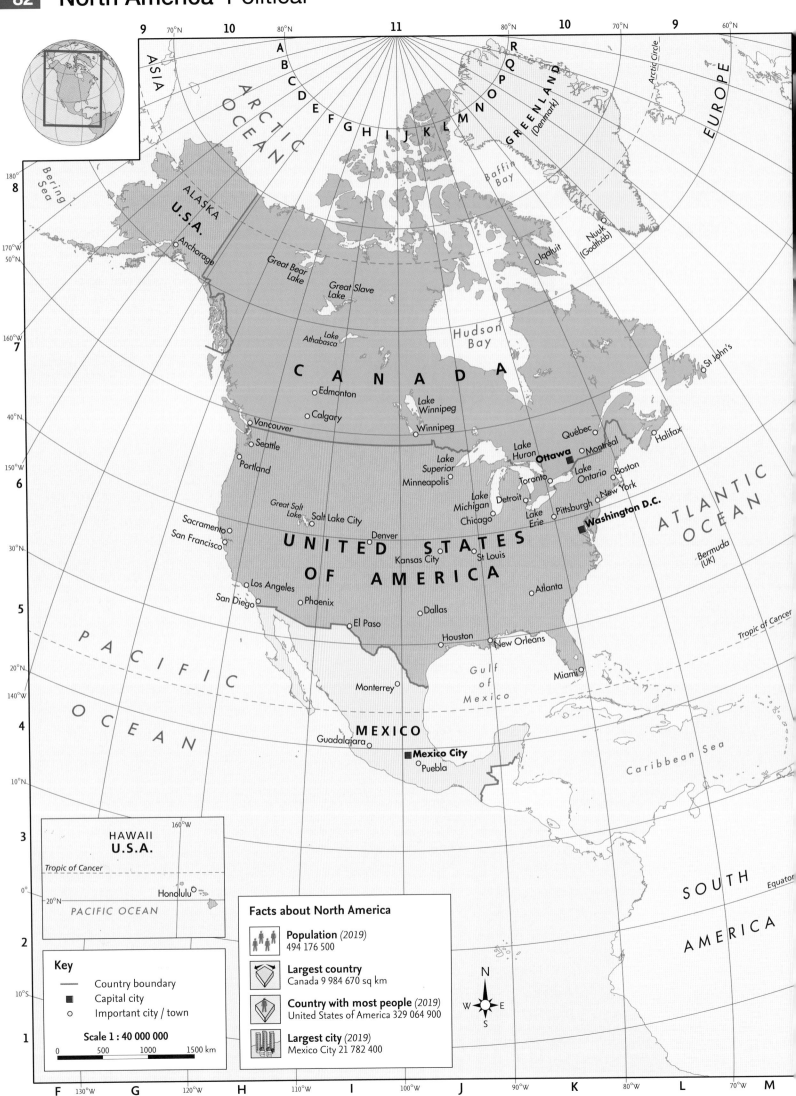

ASIA

ARCTIC OCEAN

EUROPE

Arctic Circle

GREENLAND (Denmark)

Bering Sea

ALASKA
U.S.A.

Anchorage

Baffin Bay

Iqaluit

Nuuk (Godthab)

Great Bear Lake

Great Slave Lake

Hudson Bay

Lake Athabasca

C A N A D A

St John's

Edmonton

Lake Winnipeg

Calgary

Vancouver

Winnipeg

Québec

Halifax

Seattle

Lake Superior

Ottawa

Montréal

Portland

Minneapolis

Toronto

Lake Huron

Lake Ontario

Boston

Great Salt Lake

Salt Lake City

Lake Michigan

Detroit

Chicago

Lake Erie

Pittsburgh

New York

ATLANTIC OCEAN

Sacramento

Denver

U N I T E D   S T A T E S

Washington D.C.

San Francisco

O F   A M E R I C A

Kansas City

St Louis

Bermuda (UK)

Los Angeles

Phoenix

Atlanta

San Diego

Dallas

P A C I F I C

El Paso

Houston

New Orleans

Tropic of Cancer

O C E A N

Gulf of Mexico

Miami

Monterrey

Caribbean Sea

M E X I C O

Guadalajara

Mexico City

Puebla

HAWAII
U.S.A.

Tropic of Cancer

Honolulu

PACIFIC OCEAN

SOUTH

AMERICA

Equator

Facts about North America

Population (2019)
494 176 500

Largest country
Canada 9 984 670 sq km

Country with most people (2019)
United States of America 329 064 900

Largest city (2019)
Mexico City 21 782 400

Key

—— Country boundary

■ Capital city

○ Important city / town

Scale 1 : 40 000 000
0   500   1000   1500 km

N
W   E
S

Lambert Azimuthal Equal Area projection

ARCTIC OCEAN

Wrangel I.
Point Barrow
Beaufort Sea
Queen Elizabeth Islands
Ellesmere Island
Greenland
Arctic Circle
Iceland
Denmark Strait
Cape Farewell

St Lawrence Island
Bering Strait
Nunivak I.
Brooks Range
Yukon
Banks Island
Victoria Island
Parry Islands
Baffin Bay
Davis Strait
Baffin Island

Bering Sea
Bristol Bay
Alaska Peninsula
Alaska Range
Denali (Mt McKinley) 6190
Mt Logan 5959
Kodiak Island
Gulf of Alaska
Mackenzie Mts
Mackenzie
Great Bear Lake
Southampton Island
Foxe Basin
Hudson Strait
Labrador Sea

PACIFIC OCEAN

Alexander Archipelago
Haida Gwaii (Queen Charlotte Islands)
Coast Mountains
Great Slave Lake
Peace
Churchill
Nelson
Hudson Bay
Belcher Islands
Labrador
Newfoundland

Vancouver Island
Fraser
Columbia
Rocky Mountains
Missouri
Yellowstone
Snake
Lake Athabasca
Lake Winnipeg
Canadian Shield
Lake Superior
St Lawrence
Gulf of St Lawrence
Cape Breton Island
Cape Sable

Cascade Range
Great Salt Lake
Great Basin
Sierra Nevada
Gannett Peak 4202
Colorado
Death Valley
Mount Whitney 4418
Grand Canyon
Colorado Plateau
Mount Elbert 4401
Great Plains
Arkansas
Mississippi
Missouri
Ohio
Lake Michigan
Lake Huron
Lake Erie
Lake Ontario
Niagara Falls
Appalachian Mountains
Chesapeake Bay
Cape Cod
Cape Hatteras
Bermuda

ATLANTIC OCEAN

Guadalupe
Baja California
Gulf of California
Rio Grande
Sierra Madre Occidental
Sierra Madre Oriental
Edwards Plateau
Red
Ozark Plateau
Mississippi
Cape Fear
Cape Canaveral
Tropic of Cancer

Cabo Falso
Altiplano Mexicano
Volcán Popocatépetl 5452
Bahía de Campeche
Mississippi Delta
Gulf of Mexico
Str. of Florida
Bahamas
Cuba
Yucatán Channel
Greater Antilles
Hispaniola
Puerto Rico
Lesser Antilles

Sierra Madre del Sur
Sierra Madre
Yucatán
G. of Honduras
Jamaica
Caribbean Sea
Curaçao

I. Clarión
Île Clipperton
Lake Nicaragua
Isla de Coco
Isthmus of Panama
Golfo del Darién
Orinoco
Guaviare
Equator

Islas Galapagos
Cordillera Occidental
Cordillera Central
Cordillera Oriental
Caquetá
Amazon
Marañón
Selvas
Andes
Cordillera Central
Cordillera Occidental
Cordillera Oriental
Lake Titicaca

Hawaiian Islands (inset)

Kure Atoll
Midway Is
Laysan I.
Tropic of Cancer
Necker I.
Kauai
Oahu
Maui
Hawaii
Johnston Atoll
PACIFIC OCEAN

Key

- over 5000 m
- 3000 – 5000 m
- 2000 – 3000 m
- 1000 – 2000 m
- 500 – 1000 m
- 200 – 500 m
- 0 – 200 m
- land below sea level

Ice cap

6190 ▲ Mountain height (in metres)

Scale 1 : 40 000 000

0   500   1000   1500 km

Facts about North America

Area
23 959 746 sq km

Highest peak
Denali 6190 m

Lowest point
Death Valley -86 m

Longest river
Mississippi-Missouri 5969 km

Largest lake
Lake Superior 82 100 sq km

N
W   E
S

Lambert Azimuthal Equal Area projection

80°W C 70°W D 60°W E 50°W F 40°W G 30°W H

Tropic of Cancer

9

Caribbean Sea

ATLANTIC

OCEAN

8 A B

NORTH

AMERICA

10°N

Barranquilla Maracaibo
Cartagena Cabimas Valencia **Caracas**
San Cristóbal Maracay
Cúcuta Ciudad Ciudad Guayana
Medellín Bucaramanga Bolívar **Georgetown** **Paramaribo**
Manizales **VENEZUELA** **GUYANA** **SURINAME** Cayenne
Buenaventura **Bogotá** **FRENCH**
7 **COLOMBIA** **GUIANA**
Cali

Quito
Equator
0° **ECUADOR**
Guayaquil Manaus Santarém Belém São Luís *Fernando de Noronha (Brazil)*
Islas Iquitos Fortaleza
Galápagos Teresina
(Ecuador) Natal
P 6 Chiclayo Campina João Pessoa
Trujillo Pôrto Velho **B R A Z I L** Grande Recife
E Rio Branco Maceió
10°S **Lima** R Aracaju
Callao Huancayo U Salvador
Cusco Cuiabá **Brasília**
BOLIVIA Goiânia
5 **La Paz**
Arequipa Santa Cruz Corumbá Belo
Cochabamba Horizonte
Arica **Sucre** Campo Ribeirão Vitória *I. da Trindade (Brazil)*
Grande Prêto Nova Campos *Is Martin Vaz (Brazil)*
P A C I F I C Iquique Campinas Iguaçu Tropic of Capricorn
20°S **PARAGUAY** São Paulo Rio de
O C E A N Antofagasta **Asunción** Santos Janeiro
Salta Curitiba
Islas San Miguel Joinville
Desventuradas de Tucumán Corrientes Florianopolis
4 (Chile) Porto Alegre

Córdoba Santa Fé
Archipiélago **Valparaíso** Rosario Paraná Pelotas
Juan Fernández Mendoza **URUGUAY**
30°S (Chile) **Santiago** **Buenos** **Montevideo**
Talcahuano **Aires**
Concepción La
Plata
3 Mar del Plata

Bahía Blanca ATLANTIC

OCEAN

40°S Puerto Montt

Comodoro
Rivadavia
2 *Falkland Islands (UK)*
Stanley
Claimed by
Argentina
Punta Arenas

South Georgia
and South
Sandwich Islands
(UK)
Claimed by
Argentina

Facts about South America

Population *(2019)*
427 199 400

Largest country
Brazil 8 514 879 sq km

Country with most people
Brazil 211 049 500 *(2019)*

Largest city *(2019)*
São Paulo 22 043 000

Key

——— Country boundary

- - - - Disputed boundary

■ Capital city

○ Important city / town

Scale 1 : 35 000 000

0   400   800   1200 km

110°W   100°W A   90°W B   80°W C   70°W D   60°W E   50°W F   40°W G   30°W H   20°W   10°W

Lambert Azimuthal Equal Area projection

Key

over 5000 m
3000 – 5000 m
2000 – 3000 m
1000 – 2000 m
500 – 1000 m
200 – 500 m
0 – 200 m
land below sea level

Ice cap

▲ 6961 Mountain height (in metres)

Scale 1 : 35 000 000

0   400   800   1200 km

Facts about South America

Area
17 815 420 sq km

Highest peak
Cerro Aconcagua 6961 m

Lowest point
Laguna del Carbón -105 m

Longest river
Amazon 6516 km

Largest lake
Lake Titicaca 8340 sq km

Lambert Azimuthal Equal Area projection

Gulf of Mexico
Andros
Bahamas
Yucatan Channel
Yucatán
Cuba
Greater Antilles
Hispaniola
Puerto Rico
Jamaica
Leeward Is
Sierra Madre
G. of Honduras
Lake Nicaragua
Caribbean Sea
Lesser Antilles
Windward Is
Tropic of Cancer
Isthmus of Panama
Golfo del Darién
L. Maracaibo
Trinidad
Orinoco Delta
ATLANTIC OCEAN
I. de Coco
Cordillera Occidental
Cordillera Central
Cordillera Oriental
Llanos
Meta
Orinoco
Mt Roraima 2810 ▲
Essequibo
Guaviare
Guiana Highlands
I. de Malpelo
Volcán Cotopaxi 5896 ▲
Caquetá
Pico da Neblina 2995 ▲
Mouths of the Amazon
▲ 6310 Chimborazo
Japurá
Amazon
Negro
Amazon
Equator
Islas Galapagos
G. de Guayaquil
Marañón
Juruá
Madeira
Tapajós
Xingu
Fernando de Noronha
Pta Negra
Selvas
Purús
C. de São Roque
Nevado de Huascarán ▲ 6768
Cordillera Central
Andes
Cordillera Oriental
Tapajós
Araguaia
Tocantins
Parnaíba
PACIFIC
Cordillera Occidental
L. Titicaca
Mato Grosso Plateau
Brazilian
OCEAN
Altiplano
Lago de Poopó
Atacama Desert
São Francisco
Highlands
Islas Desventuradas (Chile)
Gran Chaco
Paraguay
Paraná
2787 Agulhas Negras ▲
I. da Trindade
Is Martin Vaz
Tropic of Capricorn
6893 Cerro Ojos del Salado ▲
Paraná
Uruguay
Archipiélago Juan Fernández
6961 Cerro Aconcagua ▲
Pampas
Río de la Plata
ATLANTIC
Golfo San Matías
OCEAN
Isla de Chiloé
Patagonia
Laguna del Carbón
Bahía Grande
Str. of Magellan
Falkland Islands
Tierra del Fuego
Cape Horn
South Georgia
South Sandwich Islands

Facts about Africa

Population (2019)
1 308 064 200

Largest country
Algeria 2 381 741 sq km

Country with most people
Nigeria 200 963 600 (2019)

Largest city (2019)
Cairo 20 900 600

EUROPE

Mediterranean Sea

ASIA

Madeira (Portugal)

Canary Is (Spain)

MOROCCO

Rabat
Casablanca

Algiers
Tunis
TUNISIA
Tripoli

Benghazi

Alexandria
Giza
Cairo

Laâyoune

WESTERN SAHARA

ALGERIA

LIBYA

EGYPT

Tropic of Cancer

Lake Nasser

Red Sea

MAURITANIA

Nouakchott

MALI

NIGER

CHAD

SUDAN

ERITREA

Dakar
SENEGAL
Banjul THE GAMBIA
Bissau GUINEA-BISSAU
GUINEA
Conakry
Freetown SIERRA LEONE

Bamako

BURKINA FASO
Ouagadougou

Niamey

Ndjamena

Khartoum

Asmara

DJIBOUTI
Djibouti

Lake Chad

CÔTE D'IVOIRE
Monrovia
Yamoussoukro
LIBERIA
Abidjan
Accra

GHANA
Lake Volta
TOGO
BENIN
Lomé
Porto-Novo

NIGERIA

Abuja

Lagos

CAMEROON

CENTRAL AFRICAN REPUBLIC

SOUTH SUDAN

Juba

Addis Ababa

ETHIOPIA

SOMALIA

Malabo
EQUATORIAL GUINEA
SÃO TOMÉ & PRÍNCIPE
São Tomé

Bangui
Yaoundé

Libreville

GABON

CONGO

Brazzaville

DEMOCRATIC

REPUBLIC

OF THE

CONGO

Kinshasa

UGANDA
Kampala
Kigali
RWANDA
Gitega
BURUNDI

Lake Turkana

KENYA

Nairobi

Mogadishu

Equator

Lake Victoria

Mombasa

INDIAN

OCEAN

SEYCHELLES

Dodoma

TANZANIA

Dar es Salaam

Aldabra Is (Seychelles)

ATLANTIC

OCEAN

Ascension (UK)

St Helena (UK)

Luanda

Lake Tanganyika

ANGOLA

ZAMBIA

Lusaka

MALAWI
Lilongwe

Lake Nyasa

Maroni
COMOROS

Mayotte (France)

MADAGASCAR

Antananarivo

MAUR

Port L

Réunion (France)

Harare
ZIMBABWE

MOZAMBIQUE

Beira

NAMIBIA
Windhoek

Walvis Bay

BOTSWANA

Gaborone

Pretoria

Johannesburg

Mbabane
Maputo
Lobamba
ESWATINI (SWAZILAND)

Tropic of Capricorn

Bloemfontein

Maseru
LESOTHO

SOUTH

AFRICA

Cape Town

Key

— Country boundary
---- Disputed boundary
■ Capital city
○ Important city / town

Scale 1 : 37 000 000
0   500   1000   1500 km

N
W E
S

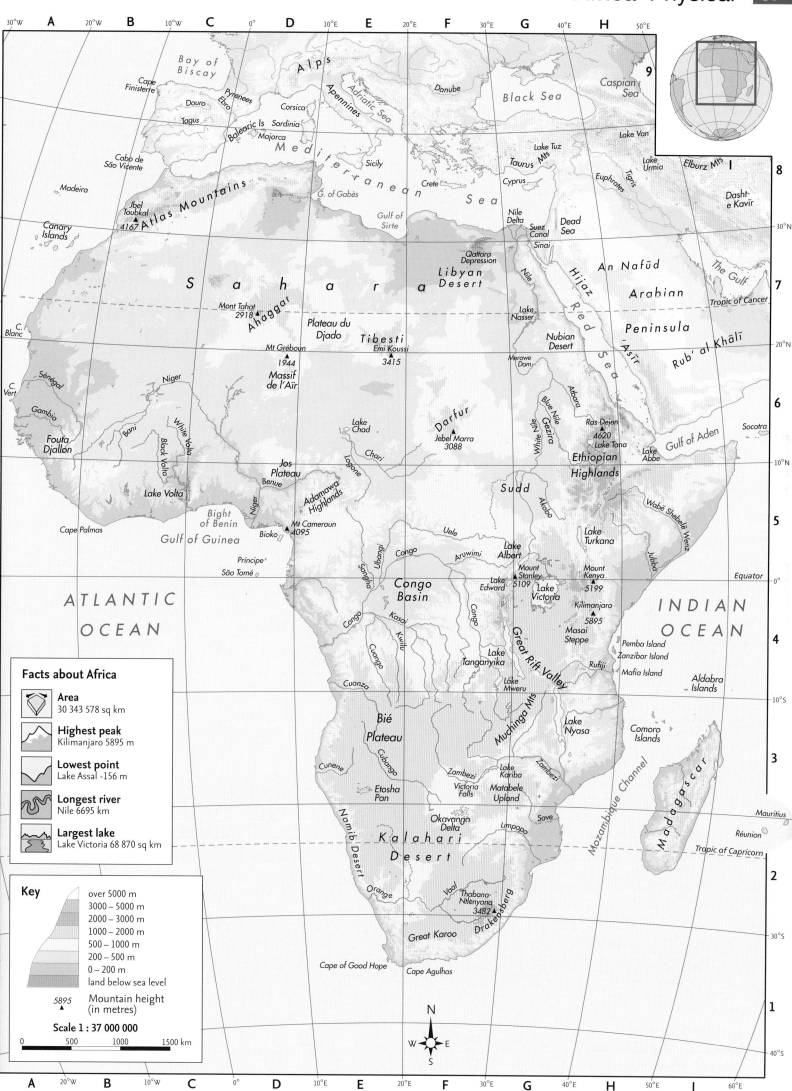

Facts about Africa

Area
30 343 578 sq km

Highest peak
Kilimanjaro 5895 m

Lowest point
Lake Assal -156 m

Longest river
Nile 6695 km

Largest lake
Lake Victoria 68 870 sq km

Key

over 5000 m
3000 – 5000 m
2000 – 3000 m
1000 – 2000 m
500 – 1000 m
200 – 500 m
0 – 200 m
land below sea level

5895 ▲ Mountain height
(in metres)

Scale 1 : 37 000 000

0   500   1000   1500 km

Lambert Azimuthal Equal Area projection

B 20°W C 10°W D 0° E 10°E F 20°E G 30°E H 40°E I 50°E J 60°E K 70°E L 80°E M 70°N

6 A

ATLANTIC OCEAN

Barents Sea

Arctic Circle

ICELAND
Reykjavik

Norwegian Sea

N O R W A Y

S W E D E N

FINLAND

RUSSIA

Faroe Islands (Denmark)

60°N

Oslo

Helsinki

St Petersburg

5

Stockholm

Tallinn

ESTONIA

North Sea

Edinburgh

Belfast

LATVIA Rīga

Moscow

DENMARK

LITHUANIA

IRELAND
Dublin

UNITED KINGDOM

Copenhagen

Vilnius

RUSSIA

Minsk

Volgograd

50°N

Cardiff

London The Hague

NETH.
Amsterdam

Berlin

POLAND
Warsaw

BELARUS

Brussels

GERMANY

BEL.

Luxembourg LUX.

Prague

CZECHIA

Kiev

U K R A I N E

4 40°E

Paris

Munich

Vienna

SLOVAKIA
Bratislava

MOLDOVA

Odesa

Bay of Biscay

F R A N C E

Bern SW.

L.

AUSTRIA

Budapest

Chișinău

Lyon

HUNGARY

ROMANIA

Ljubljana

SL

Zagreb

Caspian Sea

Milan

CROATIA

Belgrade

Bucharest

Crimea: Administered by Russia

MONACO

40°N

SAN MARINO

B.H.

SERBIA

Black Sea

PORTUGAL

Andorra
A. la Vella

ITALY

Sarajevo

MO.

Pristina

BULGARIA

Lisbon

Madrid

Barcelona

V.C.
Rome

Podgorica

K.

Sofia

Istanbul

S P A I N

Tirana

Skopje

N. MAC.

ALBANIA

TURKEY

Mediterranean Sea

ASIA

GREECE

3

Gibraltar (UK)

Athens

Valletta

MALTA

30°N

2

A F R I C A

20°N

Facts about Europe (excluding Russia)

Population (2019)
601 310 600

Largest country
Ukraine 603 700 sq km

Country with most people (2019)
Germany 83 517 000

Largest city (2019)
Istanbul 15 190 300

D 0° E 10°E F 20°E G 30°E H 40°E I

Conic Equidistant projection

Greenland Sea

Spitsbergen

Svalbard

Edgeøya

Barents Sea

Nova Zemlya

7

Jan Mayen

Bjørnøya

North Cape

Ostrov Kolguyev

Mys Kanin

Pechora

Uso

Gora Narodnaya 1895

Ob'

L 6

ATLANTIC OCEAN

Norwegian Sea

Iceland Snæfell 1833

Arctic Circle

60°N

Faroe Islands

Lofoten

Inarijärvi

Lapland

Kola Peninsula

White Sea

Mezen

Northern Dvina

Vychegda

Kama

Gora Narodnaya

Ural Mountains

Irtysh

5

Shetland Islands

Lule

Kemi

Lake Onega

Ben Nevis 1345

Outer Hebrides

Malin Head

Orkney Islands

North Sea

Skagerrak

Ume

Indals

Gulf of Bothnia

Åland Islands

Lake Ladoga

Rybinskoye Vodokhranilishche

Volga

Kuybyshevskoye Vodokhranilishche

Galway Bay

Irish Sea

Shannon

Ireland

Snowdon 1085

British Isles

Great Britain

Vänern

Vättern

Gotland

Öland

Mälaren

Gulf of Finland

Lake Peipus

Gulf of Riga

Valdai Hills

Central Russian Upland

Volga Uplands

50°N

Cape Clear

Land's End

Isles of Scilly

Pennines

Thames

Zealand

Fyn

Bornholm

Baltic Sea

Elbe

Oder

Vistula

Warta

North European Plain

Bug

Pripet Marshes

Dnieper

Kyyivs'ke Vodoskhovyshche

Don

English Channel

Channel Is

Brittany

Maas

Seine

Marne

Rhine

Taunus

Weser

Elbe

Oder

Vistula

Sudety

Dniester

Tsimlyanskoye Vodokhranilishche

Ural

Volga

Strait of Dover

Loire

Moselle

Vosges

Inn

Danube

Danube

Lake Balaton

Carpathian Mts

Dniester

Dnieper

40°N

Bay of Biscay

Gulf of Gascony

Puy de Sancy 1885

Dordogne

L. Geneva

Jura

Rhine

Großglockner 3798

Tisza

Hungarian Plain

Murei

Sava

Sea of Azov

Stavropol'skaya Vozvyshennost

Mt Elbrus 5642

Caspian Sea

Cape Finisterre

Mt Blanc 4810

Alps

Matterhorn 4478

Po

Transylvanian Alps

Crimea

Caucasus

Cantabrian Mts

Massif Central

Rhône

Saône

Gulf of Genoa

Morava

Danube

Black Sea

Douro

Duero

Pyrenees

Aneto 3404

Gulf of Lions

Apennines

Dinaric Alps

Adriatic Sea

Balkan Mts

Mount Ararat

Tagus

Corsica

Rhodope Mts

Sea of Marmara

Kelkit

Ebro

Sierra Morena

Guadalquivir

Balearic Sea

Balearic Is

Minorca

Majorca

Sardinia

Tyrrhenian Sea

Vesuvius 1281

Pindus Mts

Aegean Sea

Sea of Marmara

Kizilirmak

Lake Van

5165

Lake Urmia

Cabo de São Vicente

Sierra Nevada

Strait of Gibraltar

Ibiza

Mediterranean Sea

Sicily

Mt Etna 3323

C. Passero

Ionian Sea

Dodecanese

Crete

Cyprus

Mt Olympus 1951

Lake Tuz

Taurus Mts

Tigris

Lake Urmia

30°N

Atlas Mountains

Atlas Saharien

Chott Melrhir

Gulf of Gabès

Chott el Jerid

Gulf of Sirte

Al Jabal al Akhdar

Libyan Plateau

Nile Delta

Suez Canal

Sinai

Dead Sea

Euphrates

Tigris

An Nafud

The Gulf

Sahara

Qattâra Depression

Gulf of Suez

Eastern Desert

Red Sea

Nile

Libyan Desert

Tropic of Cancer

Lake Nasser

20°N

Plateau du Djado

Tibesti

Emi Koussi 3415

Nile

Jebel Abyad Plateau

Massif Ennedi

Key

over 5000 m
3000 – 5000 m
2000 – 3000 m
1000 – 2000 m
500 – 1000 m
200 – 500 m
0 – 200 m
land below sea level

Ice cap

▲ 5642 Mountain height (in metres)

Scale 1 : 25 000 000

0   250   500   750   1000 km

Facts about Europe

Area
9 908 599 sq km

Highest peak
Mount Elbrus 5642 m

Lowest point
Caspian Sea -28 m

Longest river
Volga 3688 km

Largest lake
Caspian Sea 371 000 sq km

Conic Equidistant projection

Facts about Asia

Population (2019)
4 747 243 500

Largest country (in Asia and Europe)
Russia 17 075 400 sq km

Country with most people (2019)
China 1 441 860 300

Largest city (2019)
Tōkyō 37 393 100

ARCTIC OCEAN

ATLANTIC OCEAN

EUROPE

Aleutian Islands

Bering Sea

Sea of Okhotsk

Sakhalin

Yakutsk

Irkutsk

Harbin

Shenyang

RUSSIA

Novosibirsk

Omsk

Perm

Chelyabinsk

St Petersburg

Moscow

Volgograd

North Sea

Baltic Sea

Barents Sea

Norwegian Sea

Arctic Circle

MONGOLIA

Ulan Bator

KAZAKHSTAN

Nur-Sultan (Astana)

Almaty

Ürümqi

KYRGYZSTAN

TAJIKISTAN

UZBEKISTAN

Tashkent

TURKMENISTAN

Ashgabat

Caspian Sea

IRAN

Tehrān

Baghdād

IRAQ

GEORGIA

ARMENIA

AZERBAIJAN

Black Sea

TURKEY

Ankara

CYPRUS

LEBANON

ISRAEL

JORDAN

SYRIA

Mediterranean Sea

Kuwait

KUWAIT

BAHRAIN

QATAR

UNITED ARAB EMIRATES

The Gulf

Riyadh

SAUDI ARABIA

OMAN

Muscat

YEMEN

Sanaa

Aden

Gulf of Aden

Red Sea

AFRICA

Socotra (Yemen)

Arabian Sea

Karachi

PAKISTAN

Kābul

AFGHANISTAN

Islamabad

Lahore

Delhi

New Delhi

NEPAL

BHUTAN

INDIA

Mumbai

Hyderabad

Chennai

Colombo

SRI LANKA

Sri Jayewardenepura Kotte

MALDIVES

INDIAN OCEAN

Kolkata

BANGLADESH

Dhaka

Bay of Bengal

Andaman Is (India)

Nicobar Is (India)

MYANMAR (BURMA)

Nay Pyi Taw

Yangon

LAOS

Vientiane

THAILAND

Bangkok

Gulf of Thailand

CAMBODIA

Phnom Penh

VIETNAM

Hanoi

Ho Chi Minh City

CHINA

Lanzhou

Xi'an

Chongqing

Wuhan

Nanjing

Shanghai

Tianjin

Beijing

Yellow Sea

East China Sea

Guangzhou

Hong Kong

South China Sea

The People's Republic of China claims Taiwan as its 23rd province

Taipei

TAIWAN

Luzon Strait

Luzon

PHILIPPINES

Manila

Mindanao

Davao

Sulu Sea

Celebes Sea

BRUNEI

MALAYSIA

Kuala Lumpur

Putrajaya

SINGAPORE

Borneo

Sumatra

Java

INDONESIA

Jakarta

Surabaya

Java Sea

Flores Sea

Celebes

Makassar Strait

Banda Sea

Seram

Halmahera

PALAU

Yap

Caroline Islands

Pohnpei

Northern Mariana Islands

Saipan

Guam

PACIFIC OCEAN

Coral Sea

Arafura Sea

EAST TIMOR

Dili

New Guinea

Bismarck Sea

New Ireland

Bougainville

Guadalcanal

Sapporo

JAPAN

Tōkyō

Ōsaka

Kōbe

Fukuoka

Sea of Japan (East Sea)

Korea Strait

NORTH KOREA

Pyongyang

SOUTH KOREA

Seoul

Tropic of Cancer

Equator

Lambert Azimuthal Equal Area projection

Scale 1 : 50 000 000

0 500 1000 1500 2000 km

N
W E
S

Key
— Country boundary
--- Disputed boundary
..... Ceasefire line
■ Capital city
○ Important city / town

Facts about Asia

Area
45 036 492 sq km

Highest peak
Mt Everest 8848 m

Lowest point
Dead Sea –434 m

Longest river
Chang Jiang 6380 km

Largest lake
Caspian Sea 371 000 sq km

ATLANTIC OCEAN

Bay of Biscay

Pyrenees

Alps

Rhine

Carpathian Mts

Danube

Vistula

North Sea

Baltic Sea

Norwegian Sea

North Cape

Kola Peninsula

White Sea

Lake Onega

Lake Ladoga

Northern Dvina

Pechora

Kama

Ural

Volga

Don

Dnieper

Central Russian Upland

North European Plain

Arctic Circle

Barents Sea

Spitsbergen

Franz Josef Land

Severnaya Zemlya

Novaya Zemlya

ARCTIC OCEAN

Taymyr Peninsula

Central Siberian Plateau

West Siberian Plain

Ob'

Yenisey

Nizhnyaya Tunguska

Angara

Lena

SIBERIA

Verkhoyanskiy Khrebet

Khrebet Dzhugdzhur

Yablonovyy Khrebet

Stanovoy Khrebet

Lake Baikal

Selenga

Khrebet Kolymskiy

Mys Lopatka

Kamchatka Peninsula

Bering Sea

Aleutian Islands

Wrangel Island

New Siberian Islands

Laptev Sea

Kara Sea

Ob'

Irtysh

Lake Zaysan

Altai Mountains

Lake Balkhash

Lake

Syr Darya

Aral Sea

Amu Darya

Caspian Sea

Mt Elbrus 5642

Caucasus

Mount Ararat 5165

Gora Narodnaya 1895

Ural Mountains

Black Sea

Mediterranean Sea

Cyprus

Taurus Mts

Tigris

Euphrates

Eastern Desert

Western Desert

Nubian Desert

Red Sea

Hijaz

'Asir

Gulf of Aden

Ethiopian Highlands

An Nafūd

Arabian Peninsula

Rub' al Khālī

Socotra

Arabian Sea

Gulf of Oman

Jazīrat Maşīrah

The Gulf

Zagros Mts

Elburz Mts

Dasht-e Kavir

Iranian Plateau

Makran

Gulf of Oman

Helmand

Hindu Kush

Sulaiman Range

Karakoram Ra.

K2 8611

Taklimakan Desert

Tien Shan

Turpan Pendi

Lop Nur

Kunlun Shan

Plateau of Tibet

HIMALAYA

Dhaulagiri 8167

Annapurna 8091

Mount Everest 8848

Gongga Shan 7514

Gobi Desert

Manchuria

Da Hinggan Ling

Amur

Argun

Amur

Sea of Okhotsk

Sakhalin

Kuril Islands

Hokkaido

Honshu

Sea of Japan (East Sea)

Sikhote-Alin'

Korea Strait

Kyushu

Shikoku

Yellow Sea

Huang He

Hai He

Huang He

North China Plain

Qang Jiang

Xi Jiang

Nan Ling

Hainan

East China Sea

Okinawa

Ryukyu Islands

Taiwan

Luzon Strait

Luzon

Philippines

Samar

Mindanao

PACIFIC OCEAN

Tropic of Cancer

Northern Mariana Islands

Saipan

Guam

Yap

Pohnpei

Caroline Islands

Equator

New Ireland

Bougainville

Bismarck Sea

New Guinea

Puncak Jaya 4884

Cape York

Gulf of Carpentaria

Arafura Sea

Timor

Timor Sea

Flores

Flores Sea

Bali

Lombok

Java Sea

Java

Sumatra

Borneo

Celebes

Celebes Sea

Sulu Sea

South China Sea

Palawan

Buru

Seram

Banda Sea

Talamahera

Palau Islands

Strait of Malacca

Peninsular Malaysia

Gulf of Thailand

Mekong

Kepulauan Mentawai

Irrawaddy

Arakan Yoma

Andaman Sea

Andaman Islands

Nicobar Islands

Bay of Bengal

Mouths of the Ganges

Brahmaputra

Ganges

Yamuna

Sutlej

Indus

Thar Desert

Narmada

Godavari

Deccan

Eastern Ghats

Western Ghats

Cape Comorin

Sri Lanka

Maldives

Laccadive Islands

Chagos Archipelago

INDIAN OCEAN

Lambert Azimuthal Equal Area projection

N
W   E
S

Key

Mountain height (in metres)
over 5000 m
3000 – 5000 m
2000 – 3000 m
1000 – 2000 m
500 – 1000 m
200 – 500 m
0 – 200 m
land below sea level

Ice cap

8848 ▲ Mountain height (in metres)

Scale 1 : 50 000 000

0   500   1000   1500   2000 km

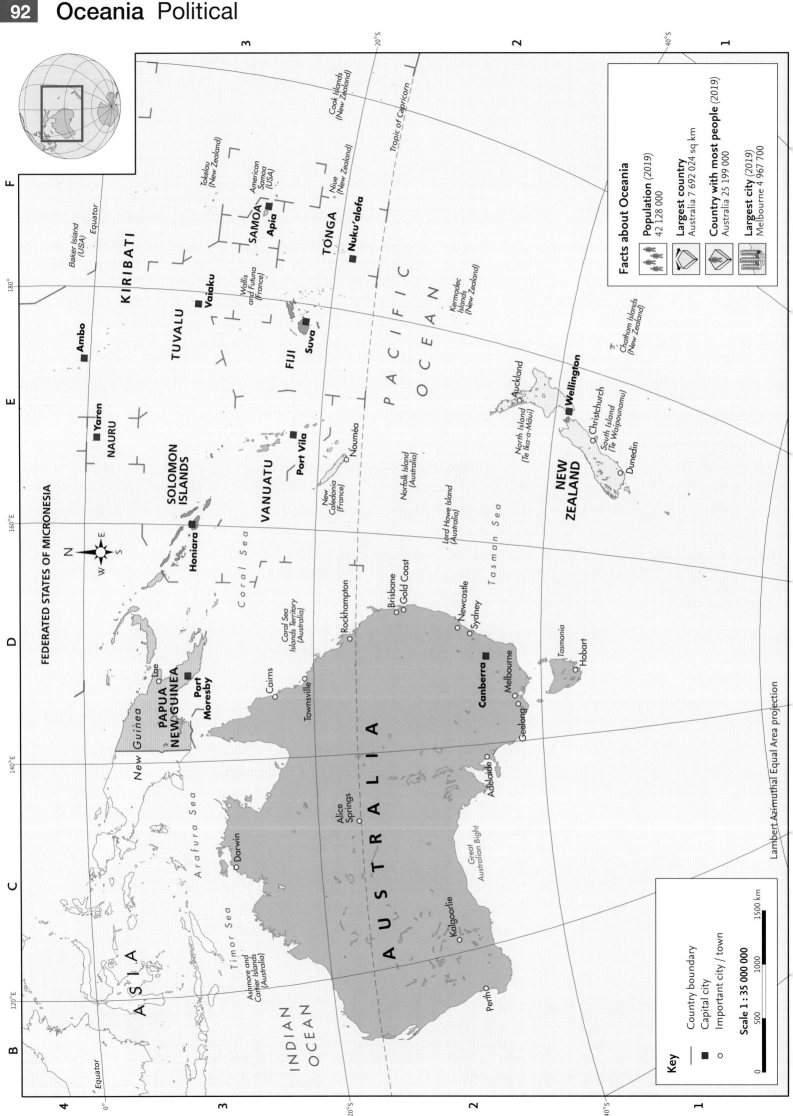

Facts about Oceania

Population (2019)
42 128 000

Largest country
Australia 7 692 024 sq km

Country with most people (2019)
Australia 25 199 000

Largest city (2019)
Melbourne 4 967 700

FEDERATED STATES OF MICRONESIA

KIRIBATI

Ambo

Baker Island
(USA)

Equator

TUVALU

Vaiaku

Tokelau
(New Zealand)

Wallis
and Futuna
(France)

SAMOA Apia

American
Samoa
(USA)

Cook Islands
(New Zealand)

Niue
(New Zealand)

TONGA

Nuku'alofa

Tropic of Capricorn

FIJI

Suva

NAURU

Yaren

SOLOMON
ISLANDS

VANUATU

Port Vila

Honiara

Nouméa

New
Caledonia
(France)

PACIFIC

OCEAN

Kermadec
Islands
(New Zealand)

Norfolk Island
(Australia)

Lord Howe Island
(Australia)

Chatham Islands
(New Zealand)

Auckland

Wellington

Christchurch

North Island
(Te Ika-a-Māui)

South Island
(Te Waipounamu)

Dunedin

NEW
ZEALAND

Tasman Sea

PAPUA
NEW GUINEA

Port
Moresby

Lae

New Guinea

Coral Sea
Islands Territory
(Australia)

Coral Sea

Rockhampton

Brisbane
Gold Coast

Newcastle
Sydney

Cairns

Townsville

Canberra

Melbourne

Geelong

Adelaide

Tasmania

Hobart

AUSTRALIA

Alice
Springs

Darwin

Arafura Sea

Timor Sea

Ashmore and
Cartier Islands
(Australia)

ASIA

INDIAN
OCEAN

Equator

Great
Australian Bight

Kalgoorlie

Perth

N
W — E
S

Key
—— Country boundary
■ Capital city
○ Important city / town

Scale 1 : 35 000 000

0   500   1000   1500 km

Lambert Azimuthal Equal Area projection

Facts about Oceania

Area
8 844 516 sq km

Highest peak
Puncak Jaya 4884 m

Lowest point
Kati Thanda-Lake Eyre -16 m

Longest river
Murray-Darling 3672 km

Largest lake
Kati Thanda-Lake Eyre 0–8900 sq km

Key

over 5000 m
3000 – 5000 m
2000 – 3000 m
1000 – 2000 m
500 – 1000 m
200 – 500 m
0 – 200 m
land below sea level

Mountain height
(in metres)

4884 ▲

Scale 1 : 35 000 000

0   500   1000   1500 km

Lambert Azimuthal Equal Area projection

N
W · E
S

ASIA

INDIAN OCEAN

PACIFIC OCEAN

Equator

Tropic of Capricorn

Timor Sea

Arafura Sea

Coral Sea

Tasman Sea

North West Cape

Cape Leeuwin

Pilbara
Mount Bruce 1235 ▲

Kimberley Plateau

Great Sandy Desert

Lake Disappointment

Gibson Desert

Great Victoria Desert

Nullarbor Plain

Great Australian Bight

Lake Gairdner

Lake Torrens

Kati Thanda-Lake Eyre

Spencer Gulf

Kangaroo Island

Musgrave Ranges

Uluru/ Ayers Rock 863 ▲

Macdonnell Ranges

Lake Mackay

Barkly Tableland

Arnhem Land

Melville Island

Gulf of Carpentaria

Cape York Peninsula

Cape York

Torres Strait

Gulf of Papua

Mount Wilhelm 4509 ▲

Puncak Jaya 4884 ▲

Admiralty Islands

New Ireland

New Britain

Bismarck Sea

Bougainville Island

Solomon Islands

Guadalcanal

Santa Cruz Islands

Espirito Santo

New Caledonia

Loyalty Islands

Nauru

Gilbert Islands

Niue

Samoa

Vanua Levu

Fiji

Viti Levu

Tomanivi 1323 ▲

Tonga

Great Barrier Reef

Great Dividing Range

Grey Range

Darling Downs

Lachlan

Darling

Murray

Mount Kosciuszko 2228 ▲

Blue Mts

Cape Howe

Flinders Island

Bass Str.

Tasmania

Mount Ossa 1617 ▲

South East Cape

North Cape

East Cape

Cook Strait

Aoraki/ Mount Cook 3724 ▲

Southern Alps

Stewart Island

Auckland Islands

Chatham Islands

Equator

20°S

Tropic of Capricorn

40°S

0°   100°E   120°E   140°E   160°E   180°   160°W   140°W

Manned bases in the Antarctic Peninsula

① Comandante Ferraz (Brazil)
② King Sejong (South Korea)
③ Artigas (Uruguay)
④ Eduardo Frei (Chile)
⑤ Bellingshausen (Russia)
⑥ Great Wall (China)
⑦ Carlini (Argentina)
⑧ Henryk Arctowski (Poland)
⑨ Bernardo O'Higgins (Chile)
⑩ San Martin (Argentina)

Ice shelf
Ice cap
Polar pack ice
Drifting ice
Glacier

Scale 1 : 35 000 000
0 500 1000 1500 km

Antarctic Circle

Orcadas (Arg.)
South Orkney Is.
Neumayer III (Germany)
Troll (Norway)
Maitri (India)
Novolazarevskaya (Russia)
SANAE IV (South Africa)
▲ Mt Wideroe 3180
Syowa (Japan)
South Shetland Is.
Esperanza (Arg.)
Marambio (Arg.)
Weddell Sea
Halley VI (UK)
Queen Maud Land
Enderby Land
Arturo Prat (Chile)
Palmer (USA)
Vernadskiy (Ukraine)
Rothera (UK)
Graham Land
Antarctic Peninsula
Belgrano II (Arg.)
3807 ▲
Mawson (Australia)
Mount Jackson ▲ 3184
Palmer Land
Alexander I.
Berkner Subglacial I.
Mount Menzies 3355 ▲ Kemp Land
Prydz Bay
Bharati (India)
Zhongshan (China)
Davis (Australia)
Progress III (Russia)
SOUTHERN OCEAN
Bellingshausen Sea
Transantarctic Mountains
ANTARCTICA
4083 ▲
SOUTHERN OCEAN
Mount Vinson ▲ 4892
South Pole
Amundsen-Scott (USA)
A
Ellsworth Land
Marie Byrd Land
Amundsen Sea
Mirny (Russia)
Queen Mary Land
Mount Amundsen 1445 ▲
C
Vostok (Russia)
3206 ▲
Concordia (France/Italy)
Casey (Australia)
Mount Sidley ▲ 4285
Ross Ice Shelf
B
Mount Siple 3100
Roosevelt I.
80°S
McMurdo (USA)
Mount Erebus 3794
Scott Base (NZ)
Wilkes Land
Ross Sea
Jang Bogo (South Korea)
Oates Land
4165 ▲ Mount Minto
Dumont d'Urville (France)
70°S

Under the Antarctic Treaty of 1959 all territorial claims south of 60° south are held in abeyance in the interest of international cooperation for scientific purposes.

Cross-section

Bellingshausen Sea
metres
4000 3000 2000 1000 sea level 0 1000 2000
A Western ice sheet
B Ross Ice Shelf
Transantarctic Mountains
Eastern ice sheet
C
80°S 80°S 70°S Antarctic Circle

Polar Stereographic projection

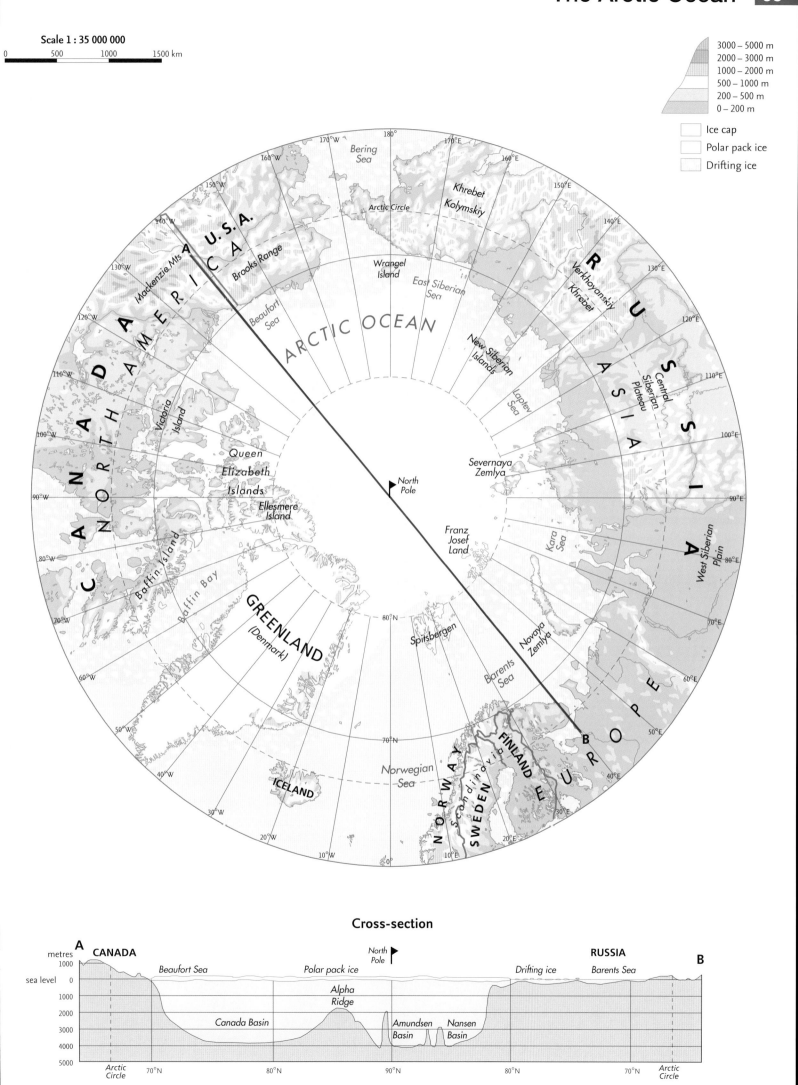

Scale 1 : 35 000 000

0   500   1000   1500 km

3000 – 5000 m
2000 – 3000 m
1000 – 2000 m
500 – 1000 m
200 – 500 m
0 – 200 m

Ice cap
Polar pack ice
Drifting ice

Bering Sea
Khrebet Kolymskiy
Arctic Circle
Wrangel Island
Brooks Range
East Siberian Sea
Verkhoyanskiy Khrebet
Beaufort Sea
ARCTIC OCEAN
New Siberian Islands
R U S S I A
Mackenzie Mts
U.S.A.
A S I A
N O R T H   A M E R I C A
Central Siberian Plateau
Laptev Sea
Victoria Island
Severnaya Zemlya
C A N A D A
Queen Elizabeth Islands
West Siberian Plain
North Pole
Ellesmere Island
Franz Josef Land
Kara Sea
Baffin Island
Baffin Bay
GREENLAND (Denmark)
Spitsbergen
Novaya Zemlya
E U R O P E
Barents Sea
Norwegian Sea
ICELAND
NORWAY
SWEDEN
FINLAND
Scandinavia

170°W 180° 170°E 160°E 150°E 140°E 130°E 120°E 110°E 100°E 90°E 80°E 70°E 60°E 50°E 40°E 30°E 20°E 10°E 0°
160°W 150°W 140°W 130°W 120°W 110°W 100°W 90°W 80°W 70°W 60°W 50°W 40°W 30°W 20°W 10°W
80°N 70°N

Cross-section

metres A CANADA
1000
sea level 0
1000
2000
3000
4000
5000

North Pole

RUSSIA B

Beaufort Sea
Polar pack ice
Drifting ice
Barents Sea

Alpha Ridge
Canada Basin
Amundsen Basin
Nansen Basin

Arctic Circle 70°N 80°N 90°N 80°N 70°N Arctic Circle

Polar Stereographic projection

- ■ Capital city
- ○ Other town/city

GREENLAND (Denmark)

Nuuk (Godthåb)

RUSSIA

U.S.A.

Arctic Circle

Anchorage

C A N A D A

Edmonton

Vancouver

Winnipeg

Ottawa Montreal

Seattle

Toronto

Chicago Detroit Boston

Pittsburgh New York

UNITED STATES OF AMERICA

San Francisco

Washington D.C. Philadelphia

Azores (Port.)

Rabat

Los Angeles

Phoenix

MOROCC

Dallas

Laâyoune

WESTERN SAHARA

Houston

Tropic of Cancer

Monterrey

Miami

THE BAHAMAS

Guadalajara

Havana

Nassau

MAURITANIA

MEXICO

CUBA

Nouakchott

Mexico City

Belmopan

BELIZE

Kingston

DOMINICAN REP.

San Juan

CAPE VERDE

SENEGAL

Dakar

Bamako

GUATEMALA

HONDURAS

JAMAICA

PUERTO RICO (USA)

THE GAMBIA

Bissau

Ouagadou

Guatemala City

Tegucigalpa

HAITI

SEE INSET FOR MORE DETAIL

GUINEA-BISSAU

GUINEA

EL SALVADOR

NICARAGUA

Conakry

SIERRA LEONE

Freetown

C.D

Yamouss

Managua

Panama City

Caracas

TRINIDAD & TOBAGO

Monrovia

LIBERIA

COSTA RICA

San José

PANAMA

Port of Spain

VENEZUELA

Georgetown

Paramaribo

Cayenne

Hawaiian Islands (USA)

Bogotá

GUY.

SUR.

FR.G.

COLOMBIA

PACIFIC

Quito

ECUADOR

Galapagos Is (Ec.)

OCEAN

B R A Z I L

Recife

ATLANTIC

KIRIBATI

PERU

Marquesas Is (Fr.)

Lima

OCEAN

SAMOA

French Polynesia

Society Is (Fr.)

Tuamoto Is

La Paz

Brasília

BOLIVIA

Belo Horizonte

Cook Islands (NZ)

Tahiti

Sucre

PARAGUAY

Rio de Janeiro

TONGA

São Paulo

Tropic of Capricorn

Pitcairn Island (UK)

Easter I. (Chile)

Asunción

Valparaíso

URUGUAY

Santiago

Buenos Aires

Montevideo

ARGENTINA

CHILE

Falkland Islands (UK)

South Georgia and South Sandwich Islands (UK)

Antarctic Circle

Inset map

ATLANTIC OCEAN

Santiago

HAITI

Santo Domingo

Port-au-Prince

DOMINICAN REPUBLIC

Mona Passage

Mayagüez

San Juan

PUERTO RICO (USA)

US Virgin Is (USA)

British Virgin Is (UK)

Anguilla (UK)

Sint Maarten (Neth.)

St-Martin (Fr.)

St-Barthélemy (Fr.)

St Eustatius (Neth.)

Basseterre

ANTIGUA AND BARBUDA

ST KITTS AND NEVIS

St John's

Montserrat (UK)

Guadeloupe (Fr.)

Basse-Terre

C a r i b b e a n

S e a

DOMINICA

Roseau

Martinique (Fr.)

Fort-de-France

ST LUCIA

Castries

Scale 1 : 15 000 000

Aruba (Neth.)

Curaçao (Neth.)

Bonaire (Neth.)

ST VINCENT AND THE GRENADINES

Kingstown

BARBADOS

Bridgetown

Willemstad

GRENADA

St George's

Scarborough

TRINIDAD AND TOBAGO

Port of Spain

SOUTH AMERICA

World facts

Population (2019) 7 713 468 200	
Largest country Russia 17 075 400 sq km	
Country with most people (2019) China 1 441 860 300	
Largest city (2019) Tōkyō 37 393 100	

International boundaries in the sea shown on this map indicate ownership of islands and island groups only. They do not imply the alignment of legal maritime boundaries.
Not all countries are named on the map.

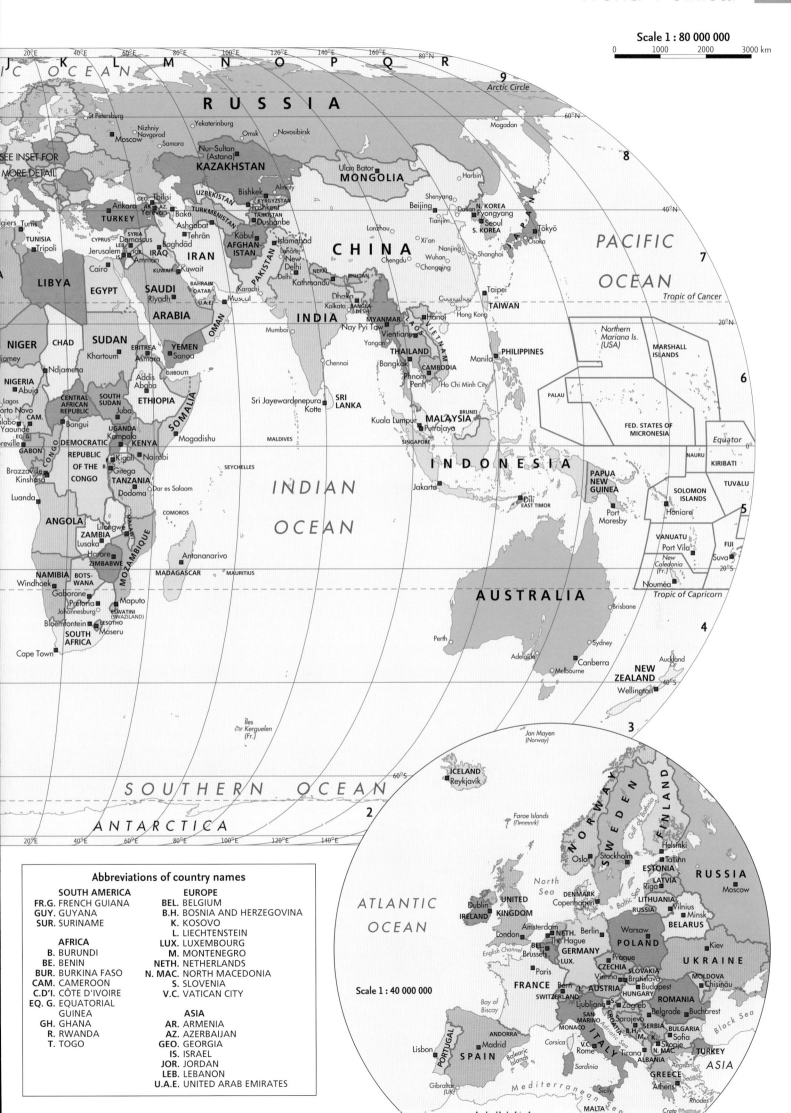

Scale 1 : 80 000 000

0   1000   2000   3000 km

Abbreviations of country names

SOUTH AMERICA		EUROPE	
FR.G.	FRENCH GUIANA	BEL.	BELGIUM
GUY.	GUYANA	B.H.	BOSNIA AND HERZEGOVINA
SUR.	SURINAME	K.	KOSOVO
		L.	LIECHTENSTEIN
AFRICA		LUX.	LUXEMBOURG
B.	BURUNDI	M.	MONTENEGRO
BE.	BENIN	NETH.	NETHERLANDS
BUR.	BURKINA FASO	N. MAC.	NORTH MACEDONIA
CAM.	CAMEROON	S.	SLOVENIA
C.D'I.	CÔTE D'IVOIRE	V.C.	VATICAN CITY
EQ. G.	EQUATORIAL		
	GUINEA	**ASIA**	
GH.	GHANA	AR.	ARMENIA
R.	RWANDA	AZ.	AZERBAIJAN
T.	TOGO	GEO.	GEORGIA
		IS.	ISRAEL
		JOR.	JORDAN
		LEB.	LEBANON
		U.A.E.	UNITED ARAB EMIRATES

Scale 1 : 40 000 000

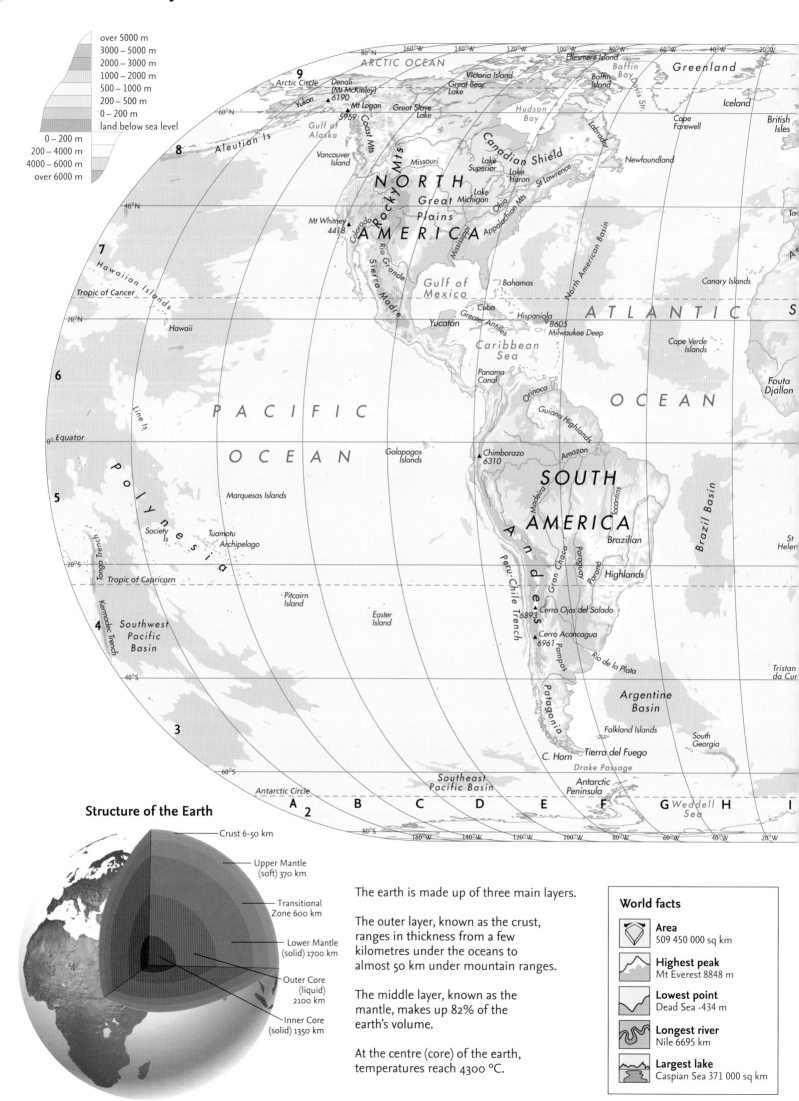

over 5000 m
3000 – 5000 m
2000 – 3000 m
1000 – 2000 m
500 – 1000 m
200 – 500 m
0 – 200 m
land below sea level

0 – 200 m
200 – 4000 m
4000 – 6000 m
over 6000 m

ARCTIC OCEAN

Greenland

9

Arctic Circle

Denali
(Mt McKinley)
▲ 6190

Victoria Island

Great Bear
Lake

Ellesmere Island

Baffin
Bay

Baffin
Island

Davis Str.

60°N

Yukon

Mt Logan
▲ 5959

Coast Mts

Great Slave
Lake

Hudson
Bay

Labrador

Iceland

8

Aleutian Is

Gulf of
Alaska

Great Slave
Lake

Cape
Farewell

British
Isles

Vancouver
Island

Rocky Mts

Missouri

Canadian Shield

Newfoundland

40°N

N O R T H

Lake
Superior

Lake
Huron

St Lawrence

Lake
Michigan

Ohio

Appalachian Mts

7

Mt Whitney ▲
4418

Colorado

Great
Plains

A M E R I C A

Mississippi

Hawaiian Islands

Sierra Madre

Rio Grande

Canary Islands

Tropic of Cancer

Gulf of
Mexico

Bahamas

A T L A N T I C

20°N

Hawaii

Yucatán

Cuba

Greater Antilles

Hispaniola

▽ 8605
Milwaukee Deep

Cape Verde
Islands

Fouta
Djallon

6

Caribbean
Sea

P A C I F I C

Panama
Canal

Orinoco

Guiana Highlands

O C E A N

O C E A N

0° Equator

Galapagos
Islands

▲ Chimborazo
6310

Amazon

Line Is

Marquesas Islands

S O U T H

5

Polynesia

Society
Is

Tuamotu
Archipelago

Madeira

A M E R I C A

Brazilian

Brazil Basin

Tocantins

St
Hele

Tonga Trench

Pitcairn
Island

Easter
Island

A
n
d
e
s

Gran Chaco

Paraguay

Paraná

Highlands

Tropic of Capricorn

20°S

Peru-Chile Trench

▲ Cerro Ojos del Salado
6893

Kermadec Trench

4

Southwest
Pacific
Basin

▲ Cerro Aconcagua
6961

Pampas

Rio de la Plata

Tristan
da Cur

40°S

Patagonia

Argentine
Basin

3

Falkland Islands

South
Georgia

C. Horn

Tierra del Fuego

Drake Passage

60°S

Antarctic Circle

Southeast
Pacific Basin

Antarctic
Peninsula

Weddell
Sea

A

2

B

C

D

E

F

G

H

I

80°S

160°W

140°W

120°W

100°W

80°W

60°W

40°W

20°W

Structure of the Earth

Crust 6–50 km

Upper Mantle
(soft) 370 km

Transitional
Zone 600 km

Lower Mantle
(solid) 1700 km

Outer Core
(liquid)
2100 km

Inner Core
(solid) 1350 km

The earth is made up of three main layers.

The outer layer, known as the crust, ranges in thickness from a few kilometres under the oceans to almost 50 km under mountain ranges.

The middle layer, known as the mantle, makes up 82% of the earth's volume.

At the centre (core) of the earth, temperatures reach 4300 °C.

World facts

Area
509 450 000 sq km

Highest peak
Mt Everest 8848 m

Lowest point
Dead Sea -434 m

Longest river
Nile 6695 km

Largest lake
Caspian Sea 371 000 sq km

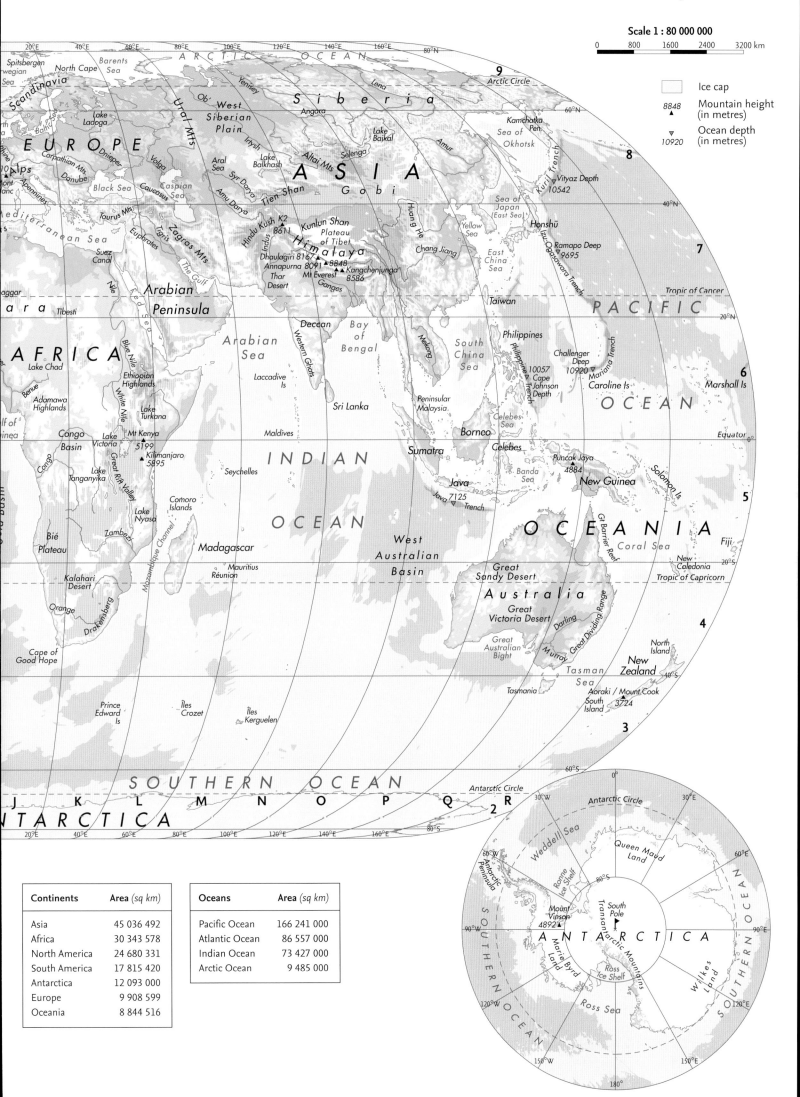

Scale 1 : 80 000 000

| 0 | 800 | 1600 | 2400 | 3200 km |

Ice cap

8848 ▲ Mountain height (in metres)

10920 ▽ Ocean depth (in metres)

Continents	Area (sq km)
Asia	45 036 492
Africa	30 343 578
North America	24 680 331
South America	17 815 420
Antarctica	12 093 000
Europe	9 908 599
Oceania	8 844 516

Oceans	Area (sq km)
Pacific Ocean	166 241 000
Atlantic Ocean	86 557 000
Indian Ocean	73 427 000
Arctic Ocean	9 485 000

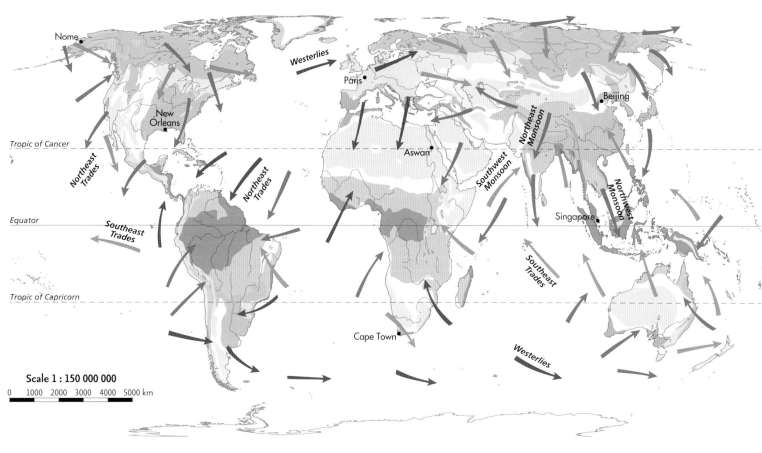

Climate types

Ice cap Very cold and dry	**Continental** Rainy climate, cold winters, mild summers	**Subtropical** Wet warm winters, hot summers	**Desert** Very hot and dry all year
Tundra and mountain Very cold winters, altitude affects climate	**Continental** Rainy climate, cold winters, warm summers	**Mediterranean** Rainy mild winters, dry hot summers	**Tropical** Hot with wet and dry seasons
Subarctic Rainy climate with long cold winters	**Temperate** Rainy climate, mild winters, warm summers	**Semi-arid** Hot and dry with rainy season	**Tropical** Hot and wet all year

- Climate station

→ Wind direction (January)

→ Wind direction (July)

→ Wind direction (all year)

Rainfall

Average annual rainfall

	more than 3000 mm
	2000 – 3000 mm
	1000 – 2000 mm
	500 – 1000 mm
	250 – 500 mm
	less than 250 mm

- Climate station

Scale 1 : 250 000 000

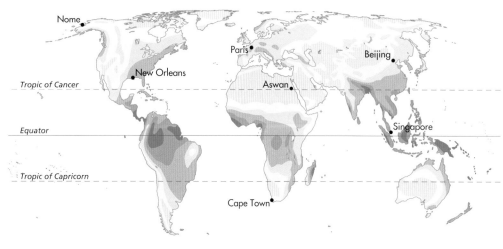

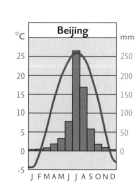

Climate graphs

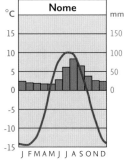

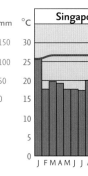

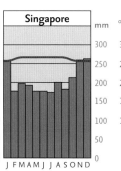

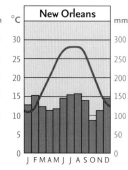

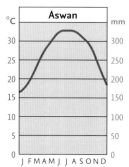

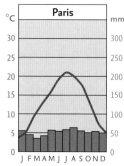

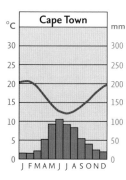

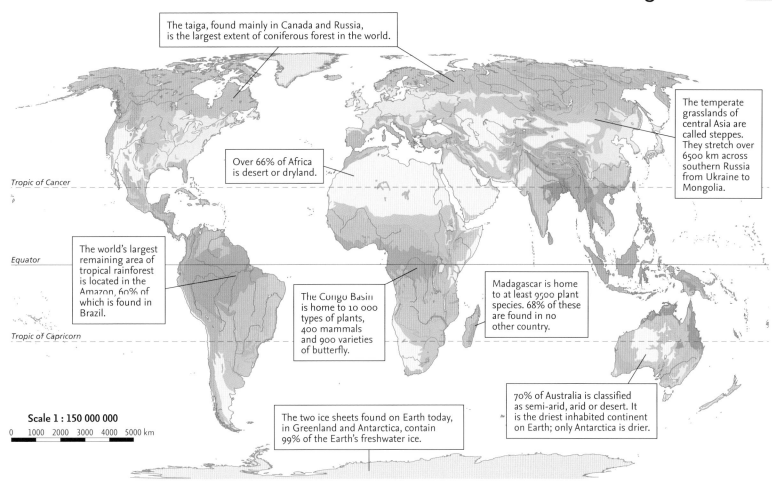

The taiga, found mainly in Canada and Russia, is the largest extent of coniferous forest in the world.

The temperate grasslands of central Asia are called steppes. They stretch over 6500 km across southern Russia from Ukraine to Mongolia.

Over 66% of Africa is desert or dryland.

Tropic of Cancer

Equator

The world's largest remaining area of tropical rainforest is located in the Amazon, 60% of which is found in Brazil.

The Congo Basin is home to 10 000 types of plants, 400 mammals and 900 varieties of butterfly.

Madagascar is home to at least 9500 plant species. 68% of these are found in no other country.

Tropic of Capricorn

70% of Australia is classified as semi-arid, arid or desert. It is the driest inhabited continent on Earth; only Antarctica is drier.

The two ice sheets found on Earth today, in Greenland and Antarctica, contain 99% of the Earth's freshwater ice.

Scale 1 : 150 000 000
0   1000 2000 3000 4000 5000 km

Types of vegetation

Ice cap and ice shelf
Extremely cold. No vegetation.

Arctic tundra
Very cold climate. Simple vegetation such as mosses, lichens, grasses and flowering herbs.

Mountain/Alpine
Very low night-time temperatures. Only a few dwarf trees and small leafed shrubs can grow.

Mediterranean
Mild winters and dry summers. Vegetation is mixed shrubs and herbaceous plants.

Savanna grassland
Warm or hot climate. Tropical grasslands with scattered thorn bushes or trees.

Temperate grassland
Grassland is the main vegetation. Summers are hot and winters cold.

Desert
Hot with little rainfall. Very sparse vegetation except cacti and grasses adapted to the harsh conditions.

Boreal/Taiga forest
Found between 50° and 70°N. Low temperatures. Cold-tolerant evergreen conifers.

Coniferous forest
Dense forests of pine, spruce and larch.

Mixed forest
Broadleaf and coniferous forests.

Tropical forest
Dense rainforest found in areas of high rainfall near the equator.

Dry tropical forest
Semi deciduous trees with low shrubs and bushes.

Sub tropical forest
Rainfall is seasonal. Mainly hard leaf evergreen forest.

Monsoon forest
Areas which experience Monsoon rain. All trees are deciduous.

Arctic tundra in Alaska.

Taiga forest in Siberia, Russia.

Savanna grassland in Tanzania, Africa.

The Sahara desert in Morocco, Africa.

Earthquakes and volcanoes

- ● Earthquake
- ▲ Volcano
- ---- Plate boundary
- ←→ Direction of movement

Floods

- ⌇ Rivers that experience major flooding
- ▦ Country affected annually by severe flooding
- ⬦ Severe floods causing over 1000 deaths in 1 year (1985–2018)
- ⬦ Severe floods causing 500–1000 deaths in 1 year (1985–2018)

Plates

The earth's crust is broken into huge plates which fit together like parts of a giant jigsaw. These float on the semi-molten rock below. The boundaries of the plates are marked by lines of volcanoes and earthquake activity.

Diverging plates

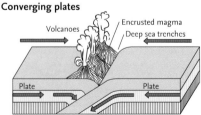

Diverging convection currents

Converging plates

Converging convection currents

Shearing plates

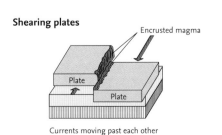

Currents moving past each other

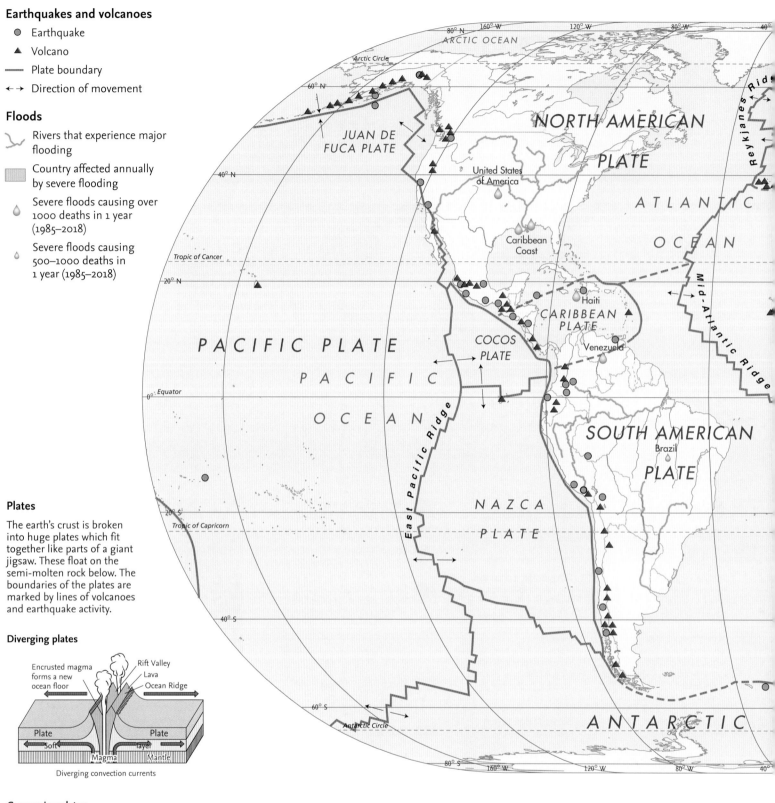

Plate structure: Asia to South America

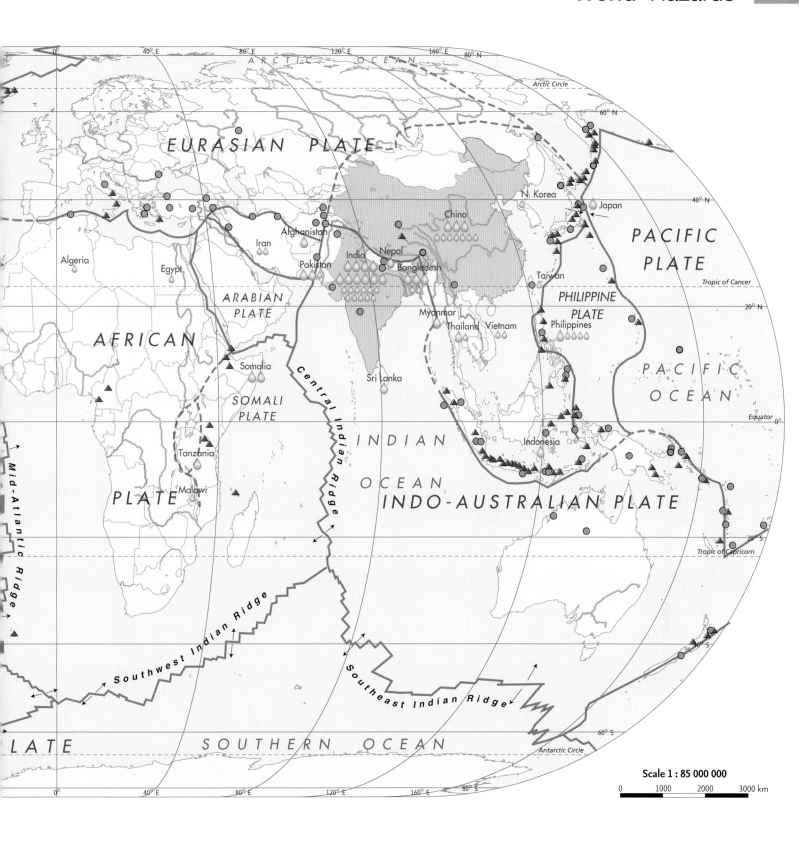

Scale 1 : 85 000 000

0   1000   2000   3000 km

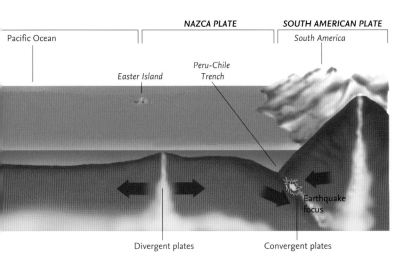

Pacific Ocean

NAZCA PLATE   SOUTH AMERICAN PLATE

South America

Easter Island

Peru-Chile
Trench

Earthquake
focus

Divergent plates   Convergent plates

Earthquakes

Earthquakes occur most frequently along the junction of
plates which make up the earth's crust.
They are caused by the release of stress which builds up at
the plate edges. When shock waves from these movements
reach the surface they are felt as earthquakes which may
result in severe damage to property or loss of lives.

Volcanoes

The greatest number of volcanoes are located in the Pacific
'Ring of Fire'. Violent eruptions often occur when two plates
collide and the heat generated forces molten rock (magma)
upwards through weaknesses in the earth's crust.

See pages 16–17 for more on earthquakes and volcanoes
in the Caribbean.

Desertification

Existing deserts

Areas at risk of desertification

Deforestation

Existing tropical forests

Forests cleared since 1940

Forest fires

Recent major forest fires

Pollution

Coastal pollution

River pollution

Major city with air pollution

The pink-boxed text on the map shows some of the signs of climate change.

Desertification is the transformation of fertile land into an arid or semi-arid region as a result of climatic change and human activities.

Deforestation is the clearance of forests so that the land can be used for other purposes – usually agriculture, but also urban expansion.

Forests are also lost through repeated **forest fires** that occur accidentally. These are also called wildfires or bushfires, and occur most often in forested regions that have a dry season.

Ocean acidification, due to increasing carbon dioxide levels, reduces the ability of marine life, such as coral, to extract calcium carbonate to make their shells and skeletons.

The Greenhouse Effect

Greenhouse gases build up in the Earth's atmosphere, stopping heat bouncing back into space from the Earth's surface. Without these gases temperatures on Earth would be around 15°C lower.

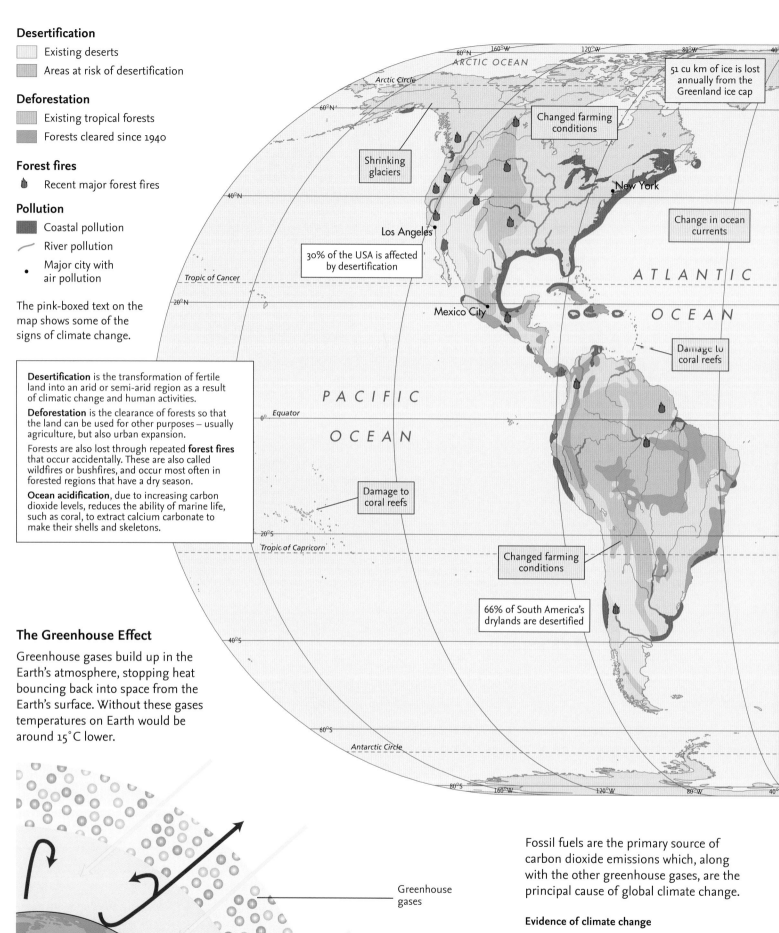

51 cu km of ice is lost annually from the Greenland ice cap

Changed farming conditions

Shrinking glaciers

Change in ocean currents

30% of the USA is affected by desertification

Damage to coral reefs

Damage to coral reefs

Changed farming conditions

66% of South America's drylands are desertified

Greenhouse gases

Heat from the sun

Heat from the Earth

Fossil fuels are the primary source of carbon dioxide emissions which, along with the other greenhouse gases, are the principal cause of global climate change.

Evidence of climate change

- Warming oceans
- Shrinking ice sheets
- Declining Arctic sea ice
- Global surface temperature rise
- Sea level rise
- Retreating glaciers
- Ocean acidification
- Extreme events

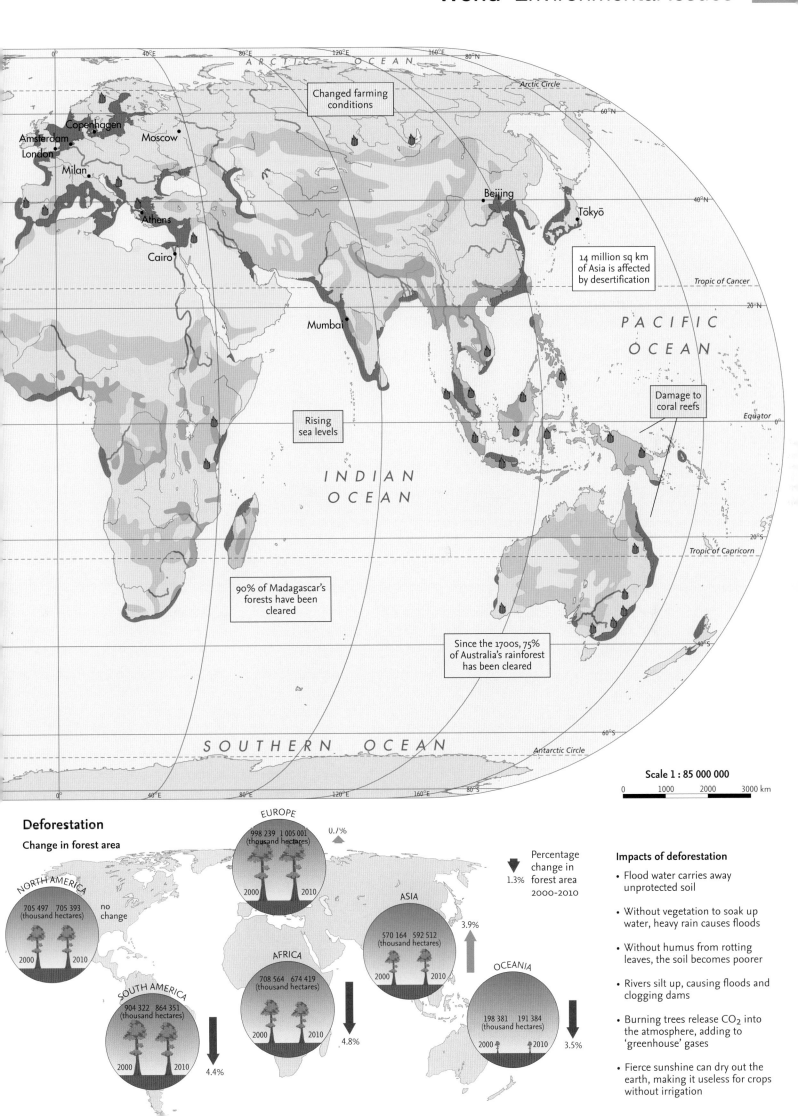

ARCTIC OCEAN

Arctic Circle

Changed farming conditions

Copenhagen
Amsterdam
London
Milan
Moscow

Beijing

Tōkyō

Athens
Cairo

14 million sq km of Asia is affected by desertification

Tropic of Cancer

20°N

PACIFIC OCEAN

Mumbai

Rising sea levels

Damage to coral reefs

Equator 0°

INDIAN OCEAN

90% of Madagascar's forests have been cleared

Since the 1700s, 75% of Australia's rainforest has been cleared

20°S
Tropic of Capricorn

40°S

SOUTHERN OCEAN

Antarctic Circle

60°S

Scale 1 : 85 000 000

0   1000   2000   3000 km

Deforestation

Change in forest area

EUROPE
998 239   1 005 001
(thousand hectares)
2000   2010

0.1%

Percentage change in forest area 2000-2010

1.3%

Impacts of deforestation

NORTH AMERICA
705 497   705 393
(thousand hectares)
2000   2010
no change

ASIA
570 164   592 512
(thousand hectares)
2000   2010

3.9%

AFRICA
708 564   674 419
(thousand hectares)
2000   2010

4.8%

OCEANIA
198 381   191 384
(thousand hectares)
2000   2010

3.5%

SOUTH AMERICA
904 322   864 351
(thousand hectares)
2000   2010

4.4%

• Flood water carries away unprotected soil

• Without vegetation to soak up water, heavy rain causes floods

• Without humus from rotting leaves, the soil becomes poorer

• Rivers silt up, causing floods and clogging dams

• Burning trees release CO_2 into the atmosphere, adding to 'greenhouse' gases

• Fierce sunshine can dry out the earth, making it useless for crops without irrigation

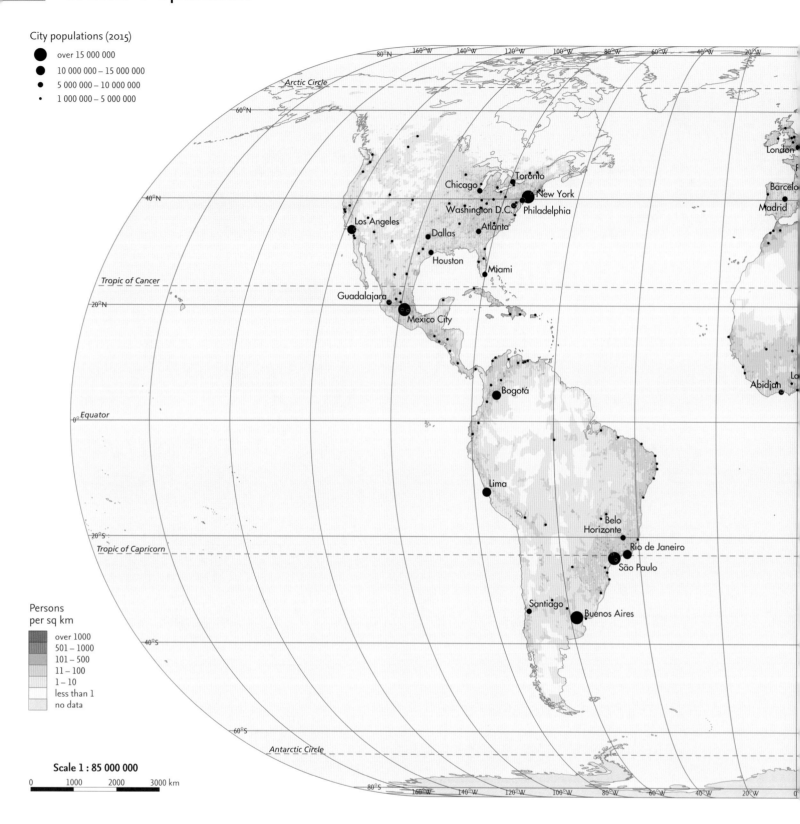

City populations (2015)
- ● over 15 000 000
- ● 10 000 000 – 15 000 000
- ● 5 000 000 – 10 000 000
- · 1 000 000 – 5 000 000

Persons per sq km
- over 1000
- 501 – 1000
- 101 – 500
- 11 – 100
- 1 – 10
- less than 1
- no data

Scale 1 : 85 000 000

0   1000   2000   3000 km

World population distribution by continent

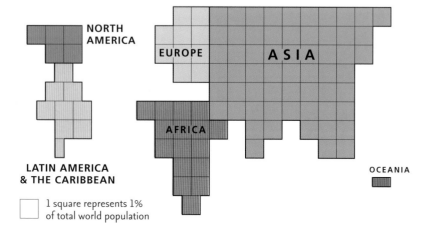

NORTH AMERICA

EUROPE

ASIA

AFRICA

OCEANIA

LATIN AMERICA & THE CARIBBEAN

☐ 1 square represents 1% of total world population

Facts about world population

World population, 2019 . . . . 7 713 468 200

World population, 2050* 9 735 033 900

Population 60 years and over, 2019 . . . . 13.2%

Population 60 years and over, 2050* 21.4%

Population under 15 years, 2019 . . . . 25.6%

Population under 15 years, 2050* 21.1%

Life expectancy, 2015-2020* 72

Male life expectancy, 2015-2020* 70

Female life expectancy, 2015-2020* 75

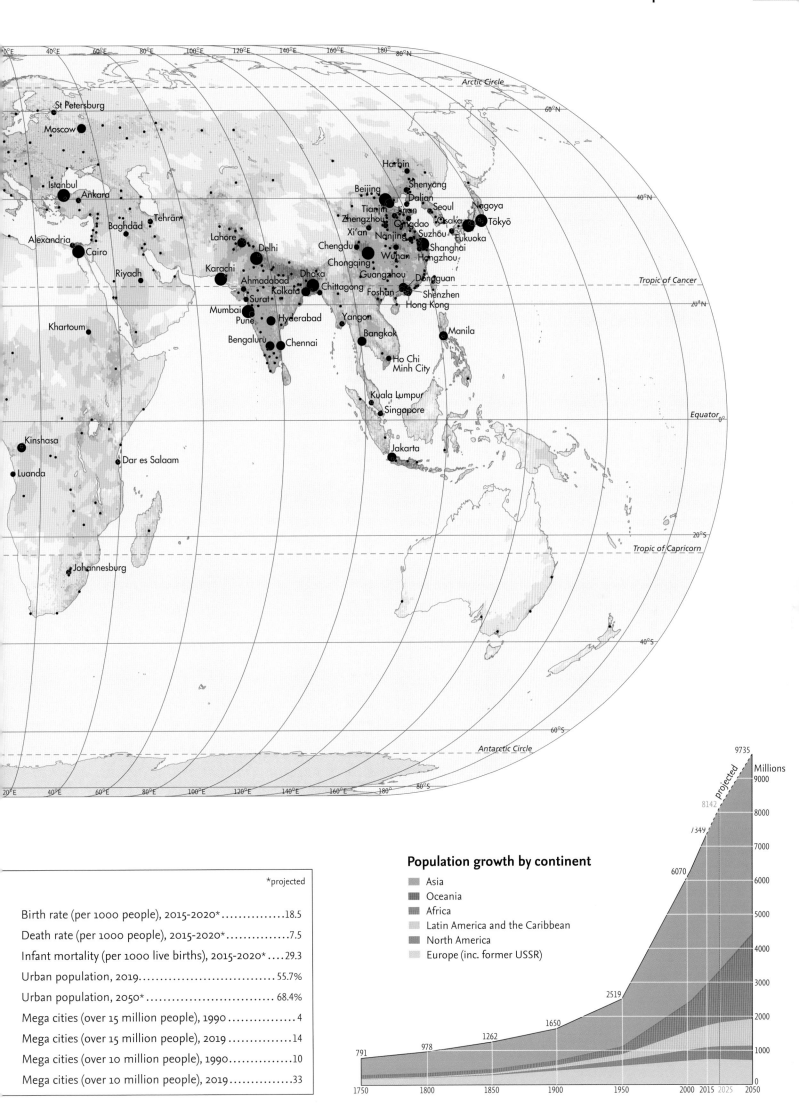

	*projected
Birth rate (per 1000 people), 2015-2020*	18.5
Death rate (per 1000 people), 2015-2020*	7.5
Infant mortality (per 1000 live births), 2015-2020*	29.3
Urban population, 2019	55.7%
Urban population, 2050*	68.4%
Mega cities (over 15 million people), 1990	4
Mega cities (over 15 million people), 2019	14
Mega cities (over 10 million people), 1990	10
Mega cities (over 10 million people), 2019	33

Population growth by continent

- Asia
- Oceania
- Africa
- Latin America and the Caribbean
- North America
- Europe (inc. former USSR)

9735
8142
7349
6070
2519
1650
1262
978
791

Millions

1750 1800 1850 1900 1950 2000 2015 2025 2050

projected

Flag	Country	Capital city	Area sq km	Total population 2019[†]
	Afghanistan	Kābul	652 225	38 041 700
	Albania	Tirana	28 748	2 880 900
	Algeria	Algiers	2 381 741	43 053 000
	Andorra	Andorra la Vella	465	77 100
	Angola	Luanda	1 246 700	31 825 200
	Antigua & Barbuda	St John's	442	81 799
	Argentina	Buenos Aires	2 766 889	44 780 600
	Armenia	Yerevan	29 800	2 957 700
	Australia	Canberra	7 692 024	25 199 000
	Austria	Vienna	83 855	8 955 100
	Azerbaijan	Baku	86 600	10 047 700
	Bahamas, The	Nassau	13 939	353 658
	Bahrain	Manama	691	1 641 100
	Bangladesh	Dhaka	143 998	163 046 100
	Barbados	Bridgetown	430	277 821
	Belarus	Minsk	207 600	9 452 400
	Belgium	Brussels	30 520	11 539 300
	Belize	Belmopan	22 965	312 971
	Benin	Porto-Novo	112 620	11 801 100
	Bhutan	Thimphu	46 620	763 000
	Bolivia	La Paz/Sucre	1 098 581	11 513 100
	Bosnia and Herzegovina	Sarajevo	51 130	3 300 900
	Botswana	Gaborone	581 370	2 303 700
	Brazil	Brasília	8 514 879	211 049 500
	Brunei	Bandar Seri Begawan	5 765	433 200
	Bulgaria	Sofia	110 994	7 000 100
	Burkina Faso	Ouagadougou	274 200	20 321 300
	Burundi	Gitega	27 835	11 530 500
	Cambodia	Phnom Penh	181 035	16 486 500
	Cameroon	Yaoundé	475 442	25 876 300
	Canada	Ottawa	9 984 670	37 411 000
	Cape Verde	Praia	4 033	549 900
	Central African Republic	Bangui	622 436	4 745 100
	Chad	Ndjamena	1 284 000	15 946 800
	Chile	Santiago/Valparaíso	756 945	18 952 000
	China	Beijing	9 606 802	1 441 860 300
	Colombia	Bogotá	1 141 748	50 339 400
	Comoros	Moroni	1 862	850 800
	Congo	Brazzaville	342 000	5 380 500
	Congo, Dem. Rep. of the	Kinshasa	2 345 410	86 790 500
	Costa Rica	San José	51 100	5 047 500
	Côte d'Ivoire	Yamoussoukro	322 463	25 716 500
	Croatia	Zagreb	56 538	4 130 200
	Cuba	Havana	110 860	11 167 325
	Cyprus	Nicosia	9 251	1 198 500
	Czech Republic	Prague	78 864	10 689 200
	Denmark	Copenhagen	43 075	5 771 800
	Djibouti	Djibouti	23 200	973 500
	Dominica	Roseau	750	71 293

Flag	Country	Capital city	Area sq km	Total populatio 2019[†]
	Dominican Republic	Santo Domingo	48 442	9 445 281
	East Timor	Dili	14 874	1 293 100
	Ecuador	Quito	272 045	17 373 600
	Egypt	Cairo	1 001 450	100 388 000
	El Salvador	San Salvador	21 041	6 453 500
	Equatorial Guinea	Malabo	28 051	1 355 900
	Eritrea	Asmara	117 400	3 497 100
	Estonia	Tallinn	45 200	1 325 600
	Eswatini (Swaziland)	Mbabane/Lobamba	17 364	1 148 100
	Ethiopia	Addis Ababa	1 133 880	112 078 700
	Fiji	Suva	18 330	889 900
	Finland	Helsinki	338 145	5 532 100
	France	Paris	543 965	65 129 700
	French Guiana	Cayenne	90 000	290 800
	Gabon	Libreville	267 667	2 172 500
	Gambia, The	Banjul	11 295	2 347 600
	Georgia	Tbilisi	69 700	3 996 700
	Germany	Berlin	357 022	83 517 000
	Ghana	Accra	238 537	30 417 800
	Greece	Athens	131 957	10 473 400
	Grenada	St George's	348	103 328
	Guatemala	Guatemala City	108 890	17 581 500
	Guinea	Conakry	245 857	12 771 200
	Guinea-Bissau	Bissau	36 125	1 920 900
	Guyana	Georgetown	214 969	747 884
	Haiti	Port-au-Prince	27 750	10 320 000
	Honduras	Tegucigalpa	112 088	9 746 100
	Hungary	Budapest	93 030	9 684 600
	Iceland	Reykjavík	102 820	339 000
	India	New Delhi	3 166 620	1 366 417 700
	Indonesia	Jakarta	1 919 445	270 625 500
	Iran	Tehrān	1 648 000	82 913 800
	Iraq	Baghdād	438 317	39 309 700
	Ireland	Dublin	70 282	4 882 400
	Israel	Jerusalem*	22 072	8 519 300
	Italy	Rome	301 245	60 550 000
	Jamaica	Kingston	10 991	2 730 894
	Japan	Tōkyō	377 727	126 860 200
	Jordan	'Ammān	89 206	10 101 600
	Kazakhstan	Nur-Sultan	2 717 300	18 551 400
	Kenya	Nairobi	582 646	52 573 900
	Kiribati	Ambo	717	117 600
	Kosovo	Pristina	10 908	1 798 500
	Kuwait	Kuwait	17 818	4 207 000
	Kyrgyzstan	Bishkek	198 500	6 415 800
	Laos	Vientiane	236 800	7 169 400
	Latvia	Rīga	64 589	1 906 700
	Lebanon	Beirut	10 452	6 855 700
	Lesotho	Maseru	30 355	2 125 200

[†] or latest data available

* internationally disputed

Flag	Country	Capital city	Area sq km	Total population 2019[†]
	Liberia	Monrovia	111 369	4 937 300
	Libya	Tripoli	1 759 540	6 777 400
	Liechtenstein	Vaduz	160	38 000
	Lithuania	Vilnius	65 200	2 759 600
	Luxembourg	Luxembourg	2 586	615 700
	Madagascar	Antananarivo	587 041	26 969 300
	Malawi	Lilongwe	118 484	18 628 700
	Malaysia	Kuala Lumpur/Putrajaya	332 965	31 949 700
	Maldives	Male	298	530 900
	Mali	Bamako	1 240 140	19 658 000
	Malta	Valletta	316	440 300
	Marshall Islands	Dalap-Uliga-Darrit	181	58 700
	Mauritania	Nouakchott	1 030 700	4 525 600
	Mauritius	Port Louis	2 040	1 269 600
	Mexico	Mexico City	1 972 545	127 575 500
	Micronesia, Fed. States of	Palikir	701	113 800
	Moldova	Chişinău	33 700	4 043 200
	Mongolia	Ulan Bator	1 565 000	3 225 100
	Montenegro	Podgorica	13 812	627 900
	Morocco	Rabat	446 550	36 471 700
	Mozambique	Maputo	799 380	30 366 000
	Myanmar	Nay Pyi Taw	676 577	54 045 400
	Namibia	Windhoek	824 292	2 494 500
	Nauru	Yaren	21	10 700
	Nepal	Kathmandu	147 181	28 608 700
	Netherlands	Amsterdam/The Hague	41 526	17 097 100
	New Zealand	Wellington	270 534	4 783 000
	Nicaragua	Managua	130 000	6 545 500
	Niger	Niamey	1 267 000	23 310 700
	Nigeria	Abuja	923 768	200 963 600
	North Korea	Pyongyang	120 538	25 666 100
	North Macedonia	Skopje	25 713	2 083 400
	Norway	Oslo	323 878	5 376 400
	Oman	Muscat	309 500	4 974 900
	Pakistan	Islamabad	881 888	216 565 300
	Palau	Ngerulmud	497	18 000
	Panama	Panama City	77 082	4 246 400
	Papua New Guinea	Port Moresby	462 840	8 776 100
	Paraguay	Asunción	406 752	7 044 600
	Peru	Lima	1 285 216	32 510 400
	Philippines	Manila	300 000	108 116 600
	Poland	Warsaw	312 683	37 887 700
	Portugal	Lisbon	88 940	10 226 100
	Puerto Rico	San Juan	9 104	3 725 789
	Qatar	Doha	11 437	2 832 000
	Romania	Bucharest	237 500	19 364 500
	Russia	Moscow	17 075 400	145 872 200
	Rwanda	Kigali	26 338	12 626 900
	St Kitts & Nevis	Basseterre	261	54 940

Flag	Country	Capital city	Area sq km	Total population 2019[†]
	St Lucia	Castries	617	166 526
	St Vincent & the Grenadines	Kingstown	389	109 991
	Samoa	Apia	2 831	197 000
	San Marino	San Marino	61	33 800
	São Tomé & Príncipe	São Tomé	964	215 000
	Saudi Arabia	Riyadh	2 200 000	34 268 500
	Senegal	Dakar	196 720	16 296 300
	Serbia	Belgrade	77 453	6 973 700
	Seychelles	Victoria	455	97 700
	Sierra Leone	Freetown	71 740	7 813 200
	Singapore	Singapore	639	5 804 300
	Slovakia	Bratislava	49 035	5 457 000
	Slovenia	Ljubljana	20 251	2 078 600
	Solomon Islands	Honiara	28 370	669 800
	Somalia	Mogadishu	637 657	15 442 900
	South Africa	Pretoria/Cape Town/ Bloemfontein	1 219 090	58 558 200
	South Korea	Seoul	99 274	51 225 300
	South Sudan	Juba	644 329	11 062 100
	Spain	Madrid	504 782	44 437 800
	Sri Lanka	Sri Jayewardenepura Kotte	65 610	21 323 700
	Sudan	Khartoum	1 861 484	42 813 200
	Suriname	Paramaribo	163 820	581 300
	Sweden	Stockholm	449 964	10 036 300
	Switzerland	Bern	41 293	8 591 300
	Syria	Damascus	184 026	17 070 100
	Taiwan	Taipei	36 179	23 773 800
	Tajikistan	Dushanbe	143 100	9 321 000
	Tanzania	Dodoma	945 087	58 005 400
	Thailand	Bangkok	513 115	69 625 500
	Togo	Lomé	56 785	8 082 300
	Tonga	Nuku'alofa	748	104 400
	Trinidad & Tobago	Port of Spain	5 127	1 328 019
	Tunisia	Tunis	164 150	11 694 700
	Turkey	Ankara	779 452	83 429 600
	Turkmenistan	Ashgabat	488 100	5 942 000
	Tuvalu	Vaiaku	25	11 600
	Uganda	Kampala	241 038	44 269 500
	Ukraine	Kiev	603 700	43 993 600
	United Arab Emirates	Abu Dhabi	77 700	9 770 500
	United Kingdom	London	243 609	67 530 100
	United States of America	Washington, D.C.	9 826 635	329 064 900
	Uruguay	Montevideo	176 215	3 461 700
	Uzbekistan	Tashkent	447 400	32 981 700
	Vanuatu	Port Vila	12 190	299 800
	Venezuela	Caracas	912 050	28 515 800
	Vietnam	Hanoi	329 565	96 462 100
	Yemen	Sanaa	527 968	29 161 900
	Zambia	Lusaka	752 614	17 861 000
	Zimbabwe	Harare	390 759	14 645 400

The important names on the maps in the atlas are found in the index. The names are listed in alphabetical order. Each entry gives the country or region of the world in which the name is located followed by the page number, its grid reference and then its co-ordinates of latitude and longitude.

Some abbreviations have been used in the index; these are listed on the right.

A&B	Antigua and Barbuda	mts.	mountains
Austa.	Australasia	N. America	North America
b.	bay	Oc.	Ocean
C. America	Central America	p.	parish
Cr.	Creek	r.	river
d.	administrative division	S. Africa	South Africa
des.	desert	S. America	South America
Dom. Rep.	Dominican Republic	StK&N	St Kitts and Nevis
f.	physical feature e.g. valley, plain	StV&G	St Vincent and the Grenadines
g.	gulf	str.	strait
i.	island	T&C Is.	Turks and Caicos Islands
Is.	Islands	T&T	Trinidad and Tobago
l.	lake	U.K.	United Kingdom
mtn.	mountain	U.S.A.	United States of America

Photo credits

front cover Richard Semik/SS (photo), Ondrej Prosicky/SS (bird), PURIPAT PENPUN/SS (flowers); **back cover** NASA Earth Observatory (satellite image); **p3** NASA Earth Observatory (satellite image); **p5** glenda/SS (Haiti), Martin Mecnarowski/SS (scarlet ibis); **p8-9** Antony McAulay/SS; **p9** xfox01/SS (sun); **p12** Vilainecrevette/SS; **p13** Vyshnivskyy/SS; **p15** NASA Earth Observatory (satellite image), THONY BELIZAIRE/AFP/Getty Images (Red Cross); **p16** Jonathan Torgovnik/Getty Images; **p17** Christopher Pillitz/Getty Images; **p20** bayazed/SS (Taino village), Christopher Garrick/SS (Caguana Indigenous Ceremonial Park), Lorna Roberts/SS (basket weaving), Yatra/SS (cassava), Jeremy Beeler/SS (El Castillo), Design Pics Inc/Alamy Stock Photo (artefacts); **p21** Everett Historical/SS (Columbus), British Library (Ptolemy map); **p22** Everett Historical/SS (sugar plantation & cotton plantation), BOULENGER Xavier/SS (Goree); **p23** Trinimummy/SS (temple), Homo Cosmicos/SS (mosque), pansticks/SS (doubles), NICOLAS DERNE/AFP/Getty Images (shopkeeper), SEAN DRAKES/Alamy Stock Photo (Diwali), sal73it/SS (sea sponges); **p24** Contraband Collection/Alamy Stock Photo (Empire Windrush), ALBERTO PIZZOLI/AFP/Getty Images (Baroness Scotland), Hulton Archive/Getty Images (Miami), Ms Jane Campbell/SS (carnival), Crush Rush/SS (Marco Rubio); **p25** Grey Villet/The LIFE Picture Collection/Getty Images (Adams), Popperfoto/Getty Images (Williams), Keystone Pictures USA/Alamy Stock Photo (Gairy), Allstar Picture Library/Alamy Stock Photo (Price) **p26-27** Planet Observer/Getty Images; **p26** Broadbelt/SS (Climate change), Ethan Daniels/SS (Waste); **p** Sven Creutzmann/Mambo photo/Getty Images (Mining damage), National Geographic Image Collection/Alamy Stock Photo (Deforestation); **p27** Gillian Holliday/SS (cane toad), Pierre-Yves Babelon/SS (cassava), Frolova_Elena/SS (lionfish), Ethan Daniels/SS (Endangered species), Steve Photography/SS (Wind power), Wild Horizon/Getty Images (Coral reef damage), Altin Osmanaj/SS (Carbon dioxide emissions); **p28** Universal Images Group North America LLC/Alamy Stock Photo; **p30** Gail Johnson/SS (Port of Spain), ICW/SS (Maracas Bay); **p32** Patrick Meissier/SS (San Fernando); LatitudeStock/Alamy Stock Photo (methanol plant); **p35** Avalon/Photoshot License/Alamy Stock Photo; **p36** Styve Reineck/SS (Fort St George), Richard Semik/SS (Parlatuvier Bay); **p37** Sodacan (CC BY-SA 3.0) (coat of arms), Jaboticaba Fotos/SS (Scarlet Ibis), Martin Mecnarowski/SS (Cocrico), Sophie Leguil/SS (Chaconia), K Tabaka/SS (steelpan); **p38** Universal History Archive/Getty Images (canoe), Print Collector/Getty Images (Columbus); **p39** Heritage Image Partnership Ltd/Alamy Stock Photo (cane cutting), Niday Picture Library/Alamy Stock Photo (Columbus); **p40** Keystone Press/Alamy Stock Photo (Clarke), BasPhoto/SS (building), Laaven Dasrep/SS (flag), Bettmann/Getty Images (Williams); **p43** Val Wilmer/Getty Images (Williams), Keystone Press/Alamy Stock Photo (Lewis), AFP/Getty Images (Crawford), Mark Leech/Offside/Getty Images (Keshorn Walcott), Allstar Picture Library/Alamy Stock Photo (Lara), Stacy Walsh Rosenstock/Alamy Stock Photo (Derek Walcott), Ebet Roberts/Getty Images (Francisco); **p44** LatitudeStock/Alamy Stock Photo (Port of Spain), John de la Bastide/SS (Stollmeyers Castle), LatitudeStock/Alamy Stock Photo (barracks), Anna Krasnopeeva/SS (temple),

Anna Krasnopeeva/SS (Red House), Homo Cosmicos/SS (Academy), Patrick Messier/SS (gardens) **p45** Everett Historical/SS (dancing), John de la Bastide/SS (Exodus), Joel Trick/SS (jungle), Jonathan ORourke/Alamy Stock Photo (Asa Wright), pansticks/SS (doubles), Amlan Mathur/SS (dholak), Anna Krasnopeeva/SS (coconuts); **p46** Tomas Kotouc/SS (manatee), Darryl Hernandez/SS (Pawi), ACEgan/SS (turtle), WalterJF/SS (orchid), Darryl Hernandez/SS (hummingbird), Dr Morley Read/Science Photo Library (frog), EyeEm/Alamy Stock Photo (blackbird), Nature Photographers Ltd/Alamy Stock Photo (bat); **p47** Divine Artisan Studios/SS (mangroves), Nicolas RINALDO/SS (waterfall), bcampbell65/SS (reef), Anton_Ivanov/SS (Pitch Lake); **p48** Laaven Dasrep/SS (fire), Danicek/SS (power plant), Avalon/Photoshot License/Alamy Stock Photo (water pollution), Francois LOCHON/Getty Images (tanker); **p49** gustavomellossa/SS (cacao), kev6677/SS (Valencia); **p50** Richard Semik/SS (beach), Laaven Dasrep/SS (waterfall), Papilio/Alamy Stock Photo (orchid); **p51** Henner Damke/SS (storm), Johner Images/Alamy Stock Photo (rainforest), Art Directors & TRIP/Alamy Stock Photo (weather station); **p52** Janusz Pienkowski/SS (money), levgenii Bakhvalov/SS (container ship); **p53** Laaven Dasrep/SS (both); **p54** Tami Freed/SS; **p55** NASA Earth Observatory; **p56** Nazar Skladanyi/SS (cruise ships), Maddie Benavent/SS (blue hole); **p57** Ramunas Bruzas/SS (Duke Street), jpbarcelos/SS (Grace Bay); **p58** Wikimedia Commons; **p59** Frontpage/SS; **p60** twiggyjamaica/SS, Paul_Brighton/SS; **p61** UniversalImagesGroup// Getty Images; **p62** Universal Images Group North America LLC/DeAgostini/Alamy Stock Photo (Cockpit Country), Ruth Peterkin/SS (Ocho Rios); **p63** delaflow/SS; **p64** Ian Cumming/Getty Images (coffee), Education Images/Getty Images (Port Kaiser); **p65** jiawangkun/SS (Falmouth Courthouse), Joseph Okpako/Getty Images (Chronixx), Aspen Photo/SS (Fraser-Pryce); **p66** glenda/SS (Haiti), hessbeck/SS (Santo Domingo); **p67** Sean Pavone/SS; **p68** R.A.R. de Bruijn Holding BV/SS; **p70** PlusONE/SS; **p71** OkFoto/SS; **p72** T photography/SS; **p73** Paul Wishart/SS; **p74** LatitudeStock/Alamy Stock Photo; **p75** Qin Xie/SS; **p77** CJG - Caribbean/Alamy Stock Photo (Oistins), LOOK Die Bildagentur der Fotografen GmbH/ Alamy Stock Photo (festival); **p79** ZUMA Press, Inc/Alamy Stock Photo (carnival), Nature Picture Library/Alamy Stock Photo (mining); **p80** Danicek/SS (power plant); **p101** George Burba/SS (tundra), Serg Zastavkin/SS (taiga), Oleg Znamenskiy/SS (savanna), oleandra/SS (Sahara). [SS = Shutterstock]

Acknowledgements

p19 Center for International Earth Science Information Network - CIESIN - Columbia University, International Food Policy Research Institute - IFPRI, The World Bank, and Centro Internacional de Agricultura Tropical - CIAT. 2011. Global Rural-Urban Mapping Project, Version 1 (GRUMPv1): Population Density Grid. Palisades, NY: NASA Socioeconomic Data and Applications Center (SEDAC). http://dx.doi.org/10.7927/H4R20Z93. Accessed 18 11 2013 (population data).